Waterloo Commanders

French infantry in action against guerrillas during the Peninsular War.

Waterloo Commanders

Napoleon, Wellington and Blücher

Andrew Uffindell

Pen & Sword
MILITARY

First published in Great Britain in 2007 by
Pen & Sword Military
an imprint of
Pen & Sword Books Ltd
47 Church Street
Barnsley
South Yorkshire
S70 2AS

ISBN 978-1-84415-249-0

A CIP catalogue record for this book is available from the British Library.

Typeset in 10/12 Ehrhardt by Concept, Huddersfield, West Yorkshire
Printed and bound in England by Biddles Ltd

Pen & Sword Books Ltd incorporates the imprints of Pen & Sword Aviation, Pen & Sword Maritime, Pen & Sword Military, Wharncliffe Local History, Pen & Sword Select, Pen & Sword Military Classics and Leo Cooper.

For a complete list of Pen & Sword titles please contact
Pen & Sword Books Limited
47 Church Street, Barnsley, South Yorkshire, S70 2AS, England
E-mail: enquiries@pen-and-sword.co.uk
Website: www.pen-and-sword.co.uk

Contents

Maps, Illustrations and Key to Maps vi
Acknowledgements viii
Introduction ix

Part One: Napoleon
1 Formative Years 3
2 Forging a Reputation 11
3 Head of State 19
4 The Years of Victory, 1805–9 23
5 Decline and Fall, 1810–14 32

Part Two: Wellington
6 Formative Years 51
7 India, 1797–1805 55
8 Interlude, 1805–8 64
9 The Peninsular War, 1808–11 67
10 The Peninsular War, 1812–14 76

Part Three: Blücher
11 Formative Years 87
12 The Downfall of Prussia, 1806–12 94
13 The Army of Silesia, 1813–14 101

Part Four: The Waterloo Campaign, 1815
14 The First Battles 115
15 The Battle of Waterloo 127

Part Five: Aftermath, 1815–52
16 Aftermath 143

Part Six: Assessment
17 Personalities 151
18 Styles of Leadership 158
19 Methods of Command and Control 170
20 Strategy and Tactics 183

Conclusion 197
Notes 201
Further Reading 202
General Index 206
Index of Armies and Formations 221

Maps, Illustrations and Key to Maps

Maps

Napoleon's Italian campaign, 1796–7 12
Napoleon's expedition to Egypt, 1798–9 17
The Marengo campaign, May–June 1800 21
Napoleon's campaigns in central Europe, 1805–9 24
Napoleon's Empire, 1812 33
Napoleon's invasion of Russia, 1812 35
Napoleon's 1813 campaign 40
Napoleon's 1814 campaign 44
Wellington in India, 1797–1805 57
Wellington in the Peninsula, 1808–14 68–9
Wellington invades France, October–December 1813 81
The 1806 campaign 95
The Battle of Auerstädt, 14 October 1806 97
The Leipzig campaign, Autumn 1813 105
Blücher in 1814 109
The Battles of Quatre Bras and Ligny, 16 June 1815 119
The Battle of Waterloo, 18 June 1815 128–9
The *bataillon carré*: Napoleon's 1806 campaign against Prussia 188
Wellington's Vitoria campaign, May–June 1813 190

Plates

Between pages 118 and 119
Napoleon: detail from his statue at Montereau.
Wellington at Waterloo, after Sir Thomas Lawrence.
Blücher, sketched during his visit to England in June 1814.
Napoleon on the bridge at Arcole, 15 November 1796.
The Battle of Rivoli, 14 January 1797.
Austerlitz, 2 December 1805.
Napoleon and his staff.
Napoleon at Wagram, 6 July 1809.
The rout of Napoleon's army after Waterloo, 18 June 1815.
Napoleon on HMS *Bellerophon* in July 1815.
Colonel the Hon. Arthur Wellesley in India, September 1800.
Wellington at Waterloo.
Major-General the Hon. Sir Arthur Wellesley in 1804.
Field Marshal the Duke of Wellington.
Blücher.
Gneisenau.
The Battle of Leipzig, 19 October 1813.

Illustrations

Frontispiece: French infantry in action against guerrillas during the
Peninsular War ii
The end at Waterloo: Napoleon and his army flee the battlefield 137
Napoleon on the morning of Wagram, 6 July 1809 153
Wellington at Waterloo 162
Waterloo: Napoleon at his command post 171
Marshal Davout at Auerstädt, 1806 195

Key to Maps

Infantry

Cavalry

Artillery

Division

Corps

Army

Acknowledgements

I wish to thank all my family and friends for their support with this project, especially Rupert Harding of Pen and Sword Books for his advice and guidance; John Richards, who drew the excellent maps; Martin Rodgers; and the ever-helpful staff of the British Library, the Bibliothèque Nationale de France and the German Historical Institute.

Introduction

Waterloo is one of the most important battles in history. It opened a new era, for it ended Napoleon's extraordinary career and the two decades of conflict that had blighted Europe since the outbreak of war with Revolutionary France in 1792.

But the decisiveness of Waterloo has distorted the popular view of the three army commanders who fought there. Of all Napoleon's battles, it is his defeat at Waterloo that is the most famous, rather than such victories as Marengo, Austerlitz, Jena or Friedland. Similarly, the commanders who beat him were remarkable men in their own right and had made a name for themselves even before the battle. The Duke of Wellington helped to establish British imperial power in India and then made his reputation defeating a series of French marshals in the Peninsular War (1808–14). Indeed, some of his Indian and Peninsular achievements required more skill and imagination than his straightforward, attritional defence at Waterloo, as he himself pointed out: 'It is generally thought that the Battle of Waterloo was one of the greatest battles ever fought; such is not my opinion, but I say nothing upon that point.'

Wellington's ally, the Prussian commander-in-chief, Prince Gebhard Leberecht von Blücher, was a seventy-two-year-old who had first seen service in the Seven Years' War (1756–63) and since acquired a wealth of experience fighting the French during the Revolutionary Wars and in the campaign of 1806, before winning fame at the head of the Army of Silesia in the campaigns of 1813–14, which ended with Napoleon's first abdication. Yet his career has also been overshadowed, at least outside Germany, by his final battle at Waterloo.

It would be difficult to find a more extraordinary combination of commanders than these three men, or more intriguing contrasts in personalities and styles of leadership. This book has been written to explore these contrasts and the lessons to be learned from them. It concentrates on their military careers and offers an analysis of their strengths and weaknesses as soldiers. Their political and private lives have been covered as far as is necessary to understand them as military commanders, and more information on these aspects can be found in the suggestions for further reading at the end of this book. Similarly, the composition, tactics and weapons of their armies will be covered in detail in a companion title, *Waterloo Armies*, by Philip Haythornthwaite.

These books are intended to supplement Pen and Sword's Battleground Europe volume, *Waterloo: The Battlefield Guide*, and to provide both the battlefield visitor and the armchair reader with a fuller understanding of how and why Waterloo was fought and won.

Part One

Napoleon

Chapter 1

Formative Years

Despite his status as a great French national hero, Napoleon was actually the son of Corsican freedom fighters who opposed the French annexation of the island. For the first twenty-three years of his life, he identified with Corsica as his homeland and saw France as an oppressor, even after spending over seven years at schools in France and being commissioned a French officer. He owed much of his character to his childhood on Corsica, including his proudly independent spirit, superstition and a strong sense of clan loyalty.

Youth and Education

Napoleon was born on 15 August 1769 at Ajaccio, the Corsican capital. Although originally from Tuscany, his family, the Buonapartes, had lived on the island for three centuries. His father, Carlo-Maria Buonaparte, had married Maria-Letizia Ramolino, the daughter of an inspector of roads and bridges, in 1764, when he was eighteen and she just fourteen. When King Louis XVI of France annexed Corsica in May 1768, Carlo joined the patriot Pasquale Paoli in resisting the occupation and was seen as a possible successor to him. Letizia was actually pregnant with Napoleon when she and Carlo fled through the mountains following Paoli's decisive defeat at Ponte Nuovo on 9 May 1769. Paoli went into exile in June, his men were allowed to return home, and Letizia reached Ajaccio in time to give birth. Napoleon was given his unusual name because Carlo followed the example of his grandfather, who had called his sons Joseph, Napoleon and Lucien.

Letizia was a formidable and spirited woman who lived to be eighty-seven and she imbued her family with a strict code of honour and the importance of courage. She bore twelve children, eight of whom survived to adulthood: Joseph (born in 1768); Napoleon (1769); Lucien (1775); Elisa (1777); Louis (1778); Pauline (1780); Caroline (1782); and Jérôme (1784). Some, especially Elisa and Caroline, shared Napoleon's calculating and egotistical traits, while others, including Joseph, Louis and Jérôme, were more laid-back. Letizia later claimed that while her other children jumped around and scribbled on the walls of the family playroom, Napoleon used to beat a drum, play with a wooden sword and draw soldiers.

Napoleon was bold as well as precociously focused and inquisitive. When he was seven, he mounted a lively horse, to the alarm of his relatives, and rode off to the family farm, where he inspected the mill, found out how much corn it could grind every hour and calculated the daily and weekly output. He was also aggressive and did not hesitate to fight his older brother Joseph.

After Paoli's defeat, Carlo Buonaparte pragmatically came to terms with the French occupation and enjoyed the rewards of collaboration. Count Louis de Marbeuf, the French Governor of Corsica between 1772 and 1786, became a close family friend and admirer of Napoleon's mother. The French were keen to establish their rule by developing a Corsican nobility that was attached to the government by self-interest and Carlo was a prime candidate as he both claimed noble descent and was one of Paoli's former lieutenants. Carlo had intended Napoleon and his eldest son, Joseph, to follow in his footsteps and study law in Pisa, but Marbeuf ensured that Napoleon and other members of the family received a good education on the French mainland.

Napoleon first had to learn French and on Marbeuf's advice was sent with Joseph to the College of Autun, where he arrived on 1 January 1779. After four months, Napoleon was transferred to the royal military school at Brienne-le-Château, while Joseph, who seemed more suited for a career in the Church, remained at Autun. Carlo's status as an impoverished noble, and a recommendation from Marbeuf, ensured that Napoleon was educated on a scholarship paid for by the King.

Brienne, and eleven other royal military schools, had been founded by Louis XVI only three years earlier as part of the military reforms of the Minister of War, Count Claude-Louis de Saint-Germain. The intention was to form the character of the cadets by isolating them at school for six years from the age of eight or nine, without leave even during the long autumn vacation. Thus life at Brienne was monastic rather than military and the school was in fact run by a religious order. The cadets wore a uniform, but received a general education, to fit them for further study as priests or lawyers and not necessarily soldiers.

The five and a half years that Napoleon spent at Brienne were crucial to his development. His accent, foreign name and pride in his Corsican heritage resulted in some teasing and isolation from his fellow cadets and he was serious, reserved and self-controlled. The emphasis at Brienne was on physical education, spartan conditions and practical subjects such as geography, drawing, mathematics and the history of France and Ancient Greece and Rome. The quality of the teaching varied and Brienne was criticized by an inspector, but Napoleon benefited in particular from good instruction in mathematics. He also acquired a sound knowledge of geography and liked reading history, although he did not excel at languages, music or fencing. He was grateful for the education he received at the school and later provided pensions, promotions and employment for the staff.

At first, Napoleon seemed destined for the navy, but was selected by an inspector to enter the *Ecole militaire*, the military school in Paris for gentlemen cadets, and left Brienne in October 1784. In any case, his mother had feared to see him exposed to the dangers of both enemy fire and the sea and he himself came to favour a military career.

At the *Ecole militaire*, he was once again educated as a scholar at royal expense. Although it was designed to produce gentlemen rather than professional soldiers, the curriculum included fortification, drawing and some military drill. Napoleon successfully passed an examination in September 1785 to become an artillery officer. It was based primarily on knowledge of mathematics and Napoleon studied so hard that he qualified directly as a second lieutenant, without having to pass through the intermediate stage of *élève*, or cadet, which would have necessitated a second exam. He therefore left the *Ecole militaire* on 28 October after just one year and was the first Corsican to graduate. He was particularly fortunate to benefit from this education, since the *Ecole militaire* was suppressed in 1787, soon after he left, as the government had to economize.

Napoleon was now sixteen. He was assigned to the Regiment of Artillery of La Fère and joined it at Valence in the Rhône valley to begin his professional training as a gunner. It was an excellent regiment, but Napoleon had wanted to join it more because of its location: it was based in the south of France, near Corsica, and supplied the artillery for the island's garrison.

In August 1786, Napoleon helped quell a riot in Lyons by workers seeking an increase in their wages. The following month, after a year's service, he qualified for six months' leave and returned to Corsica, which he had not seen for almost eight years. Such long periods of leave were an accepted practice at the time and were hardly unreasonable given that Napoleon had spent over five years of uninterrupted seclusion at Brienne and then a year in the *Ecole militaire* without being able to roam the city of Paris outside.

Napoleon's father, Carlo, had died from stomach cancer on 24 February 1785, leaving the family in debt. Napoleon increasingly took the lead in managing its affairs, displacing his sixty-eight-year-old great uncle, Lucien, the Archdeacon of the Cathedral of Ajaccio, who had been acting as head of the family. Napoleon extended his absence from his regiment, partly by claiming sick leave, and went to Paris in September 1787 to press, unsuccessfully, his family's claims for a government subsidy relating to a nursery of mulberry trees that Carlo had undertaken to plant. From Paris, he returned to Corsica in January 1788 and only in June, after nearly two years of absence, did he rejoin his regiment, which was now at Auxonne.

Napoleon found a mentor in the Commandant of the Auxonne Artillery School, General Baron Jean-Pierre du Teil, one of the foremost gunners of the time, who recognized his potential and lent him books. Napoleon worked hard and wrote in July 1789: 'I have nothing to do here except work; I only put on my uniform once a week. I sleep very little since my illness; I go to bed at ten and get up at four, and have only one meal a day.'

At Auxonne, and previously at Valence, Napoleon primarily acquired a gunner's technical education. He studied the theory and practice of artillery, learnt military drill and also gained experience in leadership, for he was attached to a company of bombardiers and helped look after the men. But at the same time, he read avidly on a broad range of topics, including military history, classical authors such as Plutarch, Livy and Tacitus, politics, philosophy and histories of Corsica and he digested what he learnt by writing many papers and essays. He effectively gave himself a university education. At the time, it was not obvious that he would be a commander in war, for his future seemed to lie in Corsica and in a political rather than military role. He therefore studied widely and, although he became familiar with the principles of the art of war, he seems to have fully developed his higher military studies only later, in the early 1790s, particularly after the outbreak of war between Revolutionary France and the European powers.

Napoleon himself was responsible for one of the myths about his education. He later urged would-be commanders to study again and again the campaigns of Alexander, Hannibal, Caesar, Gustavus Adolphus, Turenne, Eugène and Frederick the Great and to take these great captains as models. But in fact he drew his key concepts less from former commanders and more from the military theorists of the late eighteenth century, especially Generals Pierre de Bourcet and Count Jacques de Guibert. For example, it was the theorists who advocated what became one of Napoleon's most characteristic methods, the concentration of forces and massed artillery fire against a single point to make a breach in the enemy's battle line. Napoleon is known to have read a life of Frederick the Great, but it was a superficial account of his campaigns and gave little detail of his tactics. In any case, it was the theorists, rather than the past commanders, who offered the most useful lessons on how future wars should be fought.

Corsican Adventures

The summer of 1789 was a momentous one. Following the Revolutionary upheavals in Paris, the people of Auxonne rioted on 19 July. A month later, Napoleon's regiment mutinied and was therefore dispersed in different quarters along the Saône river. It was the French Revolution that provided Napoleon with the opportunities to advance himself both in politics and the army and to emerge a decade later as the ruler of France. But in 1789, he still saw Corsica as his country and revealed the depth of his feeling in a letter of 12 June to his childhood hero, the patriot Paoli:

> Thirty thousand Frenchmen vomited out on our coast, flooding the throne of freedom with rivers of blood – that was the hateful scene first given to my eyes. ... Slavery followed upon our submission: subjected to the threefold tyranny of the mercenary, the magistrate, and the tax collector, our country-men live on despised – despised by those who have the reins of government in their hands. Is that not the most hideous of all the tortures that a man can be put to?

Napoleon saw the Revolution as a chance to reduce the power of the French monarchy over Corsica and supported the Jacobins, the most radical and anti-monarchical political faction. Unlike most of his former comrades at the *Ecole militaire*, who emigrated rather than break their oath of allegiance, he showed no loyalty to Louis XVI and even advocated his execution.

Napoleon became eligible for another period of absence from his regiment and left Auxonne in September. Along with his brother Joseph, he now pursued an active political career in Corsica and spent almost half the time between September 1789 and June 1793 in three periods of leave on the island.

Napoleon's methods of obtaining these long absences included mendacious claims of sickness, overstaying his leave and using connections to bypass a refusal by his colonel. He was fortunate that the shortage of officers as the result of large-scale emigration reduced the likelihood of dismissal. In January 1792, he was appointed adjutant-major of one of the four battalions of volunteers formed in Corsica. But all French officers were then ordered to rejoin their regular regiments or be struck off, with exceptions being made only for the first and second-in-command of volunteer battalions. Napoleon therefore secured his election on 1 April 1792 as second-in-command of Ajaccio's volunteer battalion, partly by forcibly taking one of the election commis-sioners from the house of an opponent and into his own protective custody.

Ajaccio had been occupied in March by four companies of volunteers as a result of unrest following the suppression of the Capuchin convent. On 8 April, a detachment of the volunteers was attacked and disarmed by a mob and Napoleon, who took some of his officers to the scene, had to retreat after a lieutenant was shot and mortally wounded. Next day, his volunteers opened fire indiscriminately on civilians. The colonel commanding the regular garrison of the citadel at Ajaccio had to intervene to try and restore order, but Napoleon and his battalion commander refused to withdraw and even occupied more buildings. Their men looted, killed livestock, destroyed crops and vineyards outside the city and prevented supplies from entering it. During this stand-off, Napoleon apparently tried to undermine the loyalty of the regular garrison to its commander, but without success. The confrontation was finally ended by a convention on the 12th and subsequently by the arrival of commissioners from the Corsican Directory, or executive committee, who ordered thirty-five of the inhabitants to be arrested and the volunteer battalion to leave Ajaccio. It was an unsavoury episode in Napoleon's career and indicated at best a loss of control of his men and at worst complicity in the murder of civilians.

Napoleon returned to Paris in May 1792 and had himself reinstated as a captain in the regular army. He was in the city on 20 June, when a mob broke into the Tuileries palace and forced Louis XVI to wear a tricolour cockade. He was also there on 10 August, when the Tuileries was again attacked and the King's Swiss Guards massacred in its defence. The incident contributed to his fear and loathing of mobs and reinforced his conviction of the need for swift and decisive action in a crisis: he remarked that if the King had appeared on horseback and provided some leadership, he would have repulsed the mob. As it was, France became a republic on 25 September following the overthrow of the monarchy.

During his final period in Corsica (October 1792–June 1793), Napoleon saw action for the first time in February, when he took part in an expedition under Colonel Colonna Cesari Rocca to the small but strategically located island of La Maddalena off the northern coast of Sardinia. But the expedition's sailors panicked and forced the troops to re-embark without having a chance to attain their objectives. Napoleon, who had set up a battery and fired on the island's fortifications, had to abandon three guns. It was a disappointing end to a venture intended to help liberate Sardinia from its King and secure it as a valuable source of grain for France.

Political enmities, and a growing rift between Paoli and the French Revolutionary government, forced Napoleon and his family to flee Ajaccio in May and leave Corsica altogether the following month. Thus, his career began with a series of failures. After four years, he had little to show for his Corsican ambitions except valuable experience in leadership and politics. Henceforth, he sought opportunities in France and abandoned his once-fervent Corsican patriotism. From 1796, he would spell his name in the French manner, Napoleon Bonaparte, rather than the Italian, Napoleone Buonaparte.

Toulon, 1793

On 13 June, the Buonapartes landed as refugees at the southern naval base of Toulon. They found France not only at war with most of the European powers and threatened by foreign invasion following the execution of Louis XVI on 21 January 1793, but riven with civil conflict. Royalist sympathies were strong in the southern provinces and the Revolutionary government needed to restore its authority.

At first, Napoleon helped prepare the Mediterranean coastal defences to resist British naval attacks. In July, he was sent to Avignon to collect a convoy of material for these defences, but was diverted and joined a force commanded by General Jean-François Carteaux to suppress an insurrection at Marseilles. At this time, Napoleon wrote *Le Souper de Beaucaire* ('The Supper at Beaucaire'), a political tract that supported the Jacobins and an end to France's internal strife and that was intended to raise his profile and win favour with the authorities.

By 25 August, Carteaux had occupied Marseilles. But two days later, Toulon declared itself for Louis XVII, the imprisoned eight-year-old son of the late Louis XVI. Next day, a British fleet under Vice-Admiral Lord Hood entered the harbour and British, Spanish, Sardinian and Neapolitan troops began to occupy the city.

Toulon's loss was a potential disaster to France's position as a naval power and her presence in the Mediterranean. Carteaux was sent to recapture it, but his chief artillery officer, Major Dommartin, was wounded in a skirmish on 7 September. Napoleon had returned to his former role with the coastal defences and happened to be passing by on his way back to Nice. He was appointed as Dommartin's replacement by Antonio Cristoforo Saliceti, who was an influential Representative of the People, or political commissar, as well a fellow Corsican and a family friend.

Napoleon played an important role at the siege of Toulon and energetically organized the artillery and sited batteries. Although General Jean du Teil, the brother of the Commandant of the Auxonne Artillery School, arrived to take charge of the artillery, he was old and sick and assumed only nominal command over Napoleon. But Napoleon did not personally produce the plan that recaptured Toulon, despite later claims to the contrary. It was obvious to both the local commanders and the authorities in Paris that the most effective way of forcing Lord Hood to evacuate the port was by capturing a fortified headland that commanded the inner harbour from the south-west.

Nor was it likely that the defenders of Toulon, outnumbered, overstretched and of mixed quality, would be able to prevent its fall for long, especially after the capable General Jacques Dugommier took command of the besiegers on 16 November.

Napoleon played a subordinate role during the final assault early on 17 December and was dismounted and wounded in the leg by a British soldier with a bayonet or pike. The French Revolutionary forces took the forts on the crucial headland and forced Lord Hood to sail after he had destroyed the arsenal and several of the French ships in the harbour.

Toulon was Napoleon's first experience of military success. He had demonstrated his bravery, leadership and expertise as a gunner and was promoted to general of brigade on 22 December at the age of twenty-four. Accounts of his life often imply that he was singled out for promotion and that his role at Toulon was pre-eminent. In fact, he was just one of a group of officers who had distinguished themselves and who were promoted one rank. For example, André Massena, who later became one of Napoleon's most famous marshals, was promoted to general of division. Nonetheless, Napoleon did impress his superiors and influential political figures and General Jean du Teil wrote to the Minister of War: 'We are at a loss for words to describe adequately to you Buonaparte's conspicuous services; to say that he showed the greatest insight and knowledge and extraordinary bravery is to give a very inadequate account of the merits of this exceptionally good officer.'

One of the Representatives of the People at Toulon was Augustin Robespierre, whose brother Maximilien was the head of the Committee of Public Safety and virtually dictator of France. Such connections enabled Napoleon to secure an appointment as the artillery commander in the French Army of Italy, which was based at Nice. He spent six weeks in February and March 1794 organizing coastal defences, which were essential to secure the army's communications and supply routes by sea. He then planned an offensive campaign that captured the port of Oneglia, the inland fortress of Saorgio and the strategic pass of Tende in April and early May.

But political events in Paris now interrupted Napoleon's career. On 27 July 1794, a coup d'état toppled Maximilien Robespierre and the Jacobins. Napoleon's connections now became a source of danger: he was accused of treason and placed under arrest on 9 August, but was cleared of the charges and released within a fortnight.

An Austrian opponent, Archduke Ferdinand, noted on 3 September that Napoleon had returned to the Army of Italy after his imprisonment: 'He is a bold and enterprising Corsican, who will certainly want to try some attack.'

Another offensive by the Army of Italy, again planned by Napoleon, pushed the Austrians back into the plains of Piedmont and won a victory at Dego on 21 September. These operations helped secure the French position in the Alps and made it possible to try and recover Corsica. First, the French navy had to destroy the British fleet in the Mediterranean and Napoleon apparently took part in this naval expedition in March 1795. But after capturing a British ship, the French fleet was defeated and forced to return to France.

Napoleon then went to Paris, where he would have more opportunities to obtain posts. He was ordered to join the Army of the West, which was fighting a royalist insurrection in La Vendée, but claimed sick leave to avoid having to take part in an inglorious civil war. While in the capital, he strengthened his ties to an influential political patron, Paul Barras, whom he had known at Toulon, and in August was appointed to a position at the *Bureau topographique*, a strategic planning office.

Napoleon considered going on a mission to Constantinople, the capital of the Ottoman Empire, to reorganize the artillery of the Sultan, but was detained in Paris. In response to an insurrection against the government at the start of October, Barras was given command of the Army of the Interior and ordered to defend the Tuileries palace against the revolt. Napoleon did not immediately rush to help defend the government and had to be summoned by Barras, who gave him three minutes to decide whether to join him. Napoleon agreed and placed guns to cover the approaches to the Tuileries. When the insurgents advanced on the afternoon of the 5th, they were repulsed by artillery fire. Napoleon himself was with a battery near the Church of St Roch and used it to clear the street of insurgents, who fled when given 'a whiff of grapeshot'.

Barras claimed that Napoleon had been largely responsible for the success and, despite some opposition, he had his protégé appointed to succeed him as commander of the Army of the Interior in order to strengthen his own position. Napoleon was also promoted to general of division.

It was about this time that Napoleon fell passionately in love with Josephine de Beauharnais, a thirty-two-year-old beauty whose aristocratic husband had been guillotined in June 1794 during the Terror, the most extreme phase of the Revolution. She was uneducated and six years older than Napoleon, but had the social graces that he lacked and also important connections, including Barras, of whom she had previously been a mistress. Napoleon married Josephine in Paris on 9 March 1796. It was one of the most famous love affairs in history, but was marked by infidelities on both sides and nearly ended in divorce in 1799 after Napoleon learnt of Josephine's affair with Captain Hippolyte Charles. He himself had a string of mistresses, including two who allegedly became mistresses of Wellington in later years: the opera singer Josephina Grassini and the actress Josephine Weimar ('Mademoiselle Georges'), who in comparing her two famous lovers claimed that Wellington was much the stronger.

Chapter 2

Forging a Reputation

Italy, 1796–7

By now, Prussia had made peace, leaving only two major powers, Britain and Austria, still at war with France. Napoleon was appointed commander of the Army of Italy on 2 March 1796 and left Paris to join his headquarters at Nice just two days after his marriage. Italy was a secondary theatre, but Napoleon could support the main effort in Germany by driving the Austrians from northern Italy and threatening to cross the Alps and attack Vienna from the south.

Some of his veteran subordinates, including Generals Massena and Pierre Augereau, initially felt some resentment at being placed under his command. Napoleon was indeed a political general who had obtained his post through influential connections and he had no prior experience of commanding an army. But he had played a key role in planning the offensives of the Army of Italy in 1794 and knew the army, its generals and the terrain. In addition, he had more experience of the higher art of war than either Massena or Augereau, who were poorly educated and, despite being ten years older than him, had held only subordinate and usually small commands. Massena was naturally intelligent and had a broader outlook than Augereau, but neglected both administration and discipline. In any case, both men congratulated their new commander. Massena wrote on 29 March: 'I compliment you most warmly on your having been made commander-in-chief of the Army of Italy. For a long time, you have known how I recognize your military talents. I will act so as to earn your confidence, just as I have obtained that of all the generals who had commanded up to now.'

Napoleon supposedly exhorted his men in a now-famous proclamation, but it actually seems to have been written years later as an inspiring address to add to his legend:

> Soldiers! you are naked and starving; the Government owes you much and can give you nothing. Among these rocks, your patience, your courage, are admirable; but not one ray of glory can shine down on you. . . . I will lead you into the most fertile plain of the earth. Wealthy cities, great provinces, will be in your power; and there await you honour, glory and riches. Soldiers of Italy, will your courage, will your constancy fail?

In fact, by the time he took the offensive, he had alleviated the worst of his army's deficiencies and his regiments were well organized, as is shown by his correspondence at the time.

Nor was Napoleon significantly outnumbered. At the start of the campaign, he faced two enemy armies in Piedmont (in the north-western corner of the Italian peninsula): about 25,000 Austrians and 20,000 Piedmontese under Generals Baron Johann Beaulieu and Baron Michael von Colli. He himself had 38,000 available for an offensive.

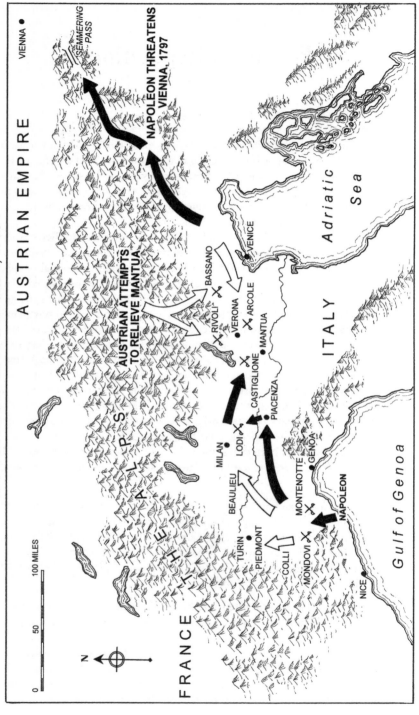

NAPOLEON'S ITALIAN CAMPAIGN, 1796-7

Seizing the initiative, Napoleon advanced northwards from the Mediterranean coast on 11 April and thrust between his two opponents to defeat them piecemeal. He beat part of Beaulieu's army at Montenotte (12 April) and again at Dego two days later, before driving Colli back and defeating him at Mondovi on the 21st. Napoleon then pursued Colli into the plains north of the Apennine mountains and caused the Piedmontese King, Victor Amadeus III, to sign an armistice at Cherasco on the 28th.

Napoleon turned his attention to Beaulieu, who had withdrawn eastwards to defensive positions behind the Po river. Instead of making a direct attack, which would merely have driven Beaulieu back, Napoleon outflanked him by pushing along the south bank of the Po and then crossing at Piacenza in his rear, violating the neutrality of the Duchy of Parma in the process. This bold manoeuvre was only partly successful: it forced Beaulieu to abandon Milan, but failed to intercept him as he escaped eastwards across the Adda river. On 10 May, Napoleon stormed the bridge over the Adda at Lodi, but was too late to do anything except maul the Austrian rearguard.

Napoleon entered Milan on the 15th, but any illusions that he came as a liberator were short-lived. He had been instructed by the Directory to exploit the resources of Italy to help fund the war effort and he extorted money, supplies and art treasures, partly to pay his troops. Not surprisingly, he had to suppress revolts and detach some of his forces to protect his rear.

During this time, Napoleon acted with increasing independence from his political masters and rejected the Directory's plans to send another general to command in northern Italy and to detach him on secondary operations further south. He forced the Directory to back down by insisting that he retain full command and threatening to resign: 'I believe that one bad general is better than two good ones. The art of war, like the art of government itself, is a matter of careful handling. . . . I cannot allow myself to have my feet entangled. I have begun with some success, and I wish to continue to show myself worthy of your esteem.'

Napoleon's military success caused King Ferdinand IV of Naples to conclude an armistice. Then, in June and July, Napoleon led an expedition southwards into central Italy to force Pope Pius VI to come to terms and to occupy Leghorn, an important British naval base. Napoleon thus consolidated his position in the Italian peninsula and extracted valuable tributes of treasure and art works.

By now, Beaulieu had withdrawn his army northwards into the Alps, after leaving a garrison of 12,000 men to hold the formidable fortress of Mantua. Napoleon laid siege to it in June, but would be unable to take it for eight months and during that time had to fight four Austrian relief attempts.

The first of these counter-offensives was commanded by Beaulieu's replacement, General Count Sigismond von Wurmser, who advanced southwards in four converging columns on 29 July. Napoleon was outnumbered and belatedly realized that he would have to raise the siege of Mantua to concentrate enough troops to check the offensive. In the process, he had to abandon 179 guns and would have been defeated had Wurmser been less hesitant. As it was, Napoleon managed to check an Austrian column at Lonato (3 August) and then rout Wurmser himself two days later at Castiglione.

Despite their defeat, the Austrians had been able to replenish Mantua. Napoleon resumed the siege and on 2 September led his field army northwards on Trento, intending to invade Austria before the winter. But Wurmser now made a second advance. This time, he moved down the Brenta valley and thus outflanked Napoleon to the east. Napoleon pursued and defeated him at Bassano (8 September), but was unable to prevent Wurmser and part of his defeated army from retreating to Mantua and reinforcing the garrison.

A third relief attempt was commanded by General Baron Joseph Alvintzy von Berberek, who advanced westwards from the Piave valley. But he was checked as he approached Verona when Napoleon turned his southern flank and crossed the Adige river to threaten his rear. A battle ensued around the village of Arcole (15–17 November), during which Napoleon led an attack on the bridge over the Alpone river. Paintings later depicted him dramatically leading a charge, but the incident was actually a less heroic one and led to him being pushed into the water. The battle ended when Alvintzy decided to retreat.

Napoleon defeated the fourth and final Austrian offensive at Rivoli, to the east of Lake Garda, on 14 January 1797, after Alvintzy advanced down the Adige valley from the north. He skilfully manoeuvred to defeat Alvintzy's columns separately and then launched a vigorous pursuit and captured nearly half of his army.

On 2 February, the garrison of Mantua finally capitulated after a vain attempt to break out, leaving Napoleon with another 16,000 prisoners and 1,500 guns. Napoleon was now reinforced to over 40,000 men and on 11 March began an advance north-eastwards against Vienna. He was opposed by another Austrian commander, Archduke Charles, who was organizing an army in the Frioul, north-east of Venice. Napoleon combined a frontal offensive with outflanking threats to drive Archduke Charles north-eastwards, through the Alps to Leoben.

By 7 April, Napoleon was at the Semmering Pass, just 75 miles from Vienna, and had inflicted heavy losses on the Austrians in a series of engagements. But he had advanced 400 miles and outrun his supplies, was faced with insurrections to his rear and would be vulnerable if Archduke Charles received reinforcements and launched a counter-offensive. He agreed a preliminary convention near Leoben on 18 April and, after subsequent negotiations, a definitive peace, the Treaty of Campo Formio, on 17 October. Austria surrendered Belgium, Lombardy and the west bank of the Rhine. Napoleon compensated her with Venice, which he had occupied and plundered, even though it was an independent republic.

Napoleon negotiated the treaty himself and with little reference to the Directory and emerged as a popular figure in France by securing peace. This made him a potential threat to the government should he try to translate his influence into political power. He had already shown his willingness to become politically involved when he sent one of his generals, Augereau, to Paris to command the troops in a coup d'état planned by his patron, Barras, against moderates in the Directory and royalist-sympathizing deputies in the legislative bodies. The coup, on the night of 3–4 September 1797, undermined the Directory's legitimacy and increased the likelihood of further military interventions.

The Expedition to Egypt, 1798–9

Britain was isolated now that peace had been restored on the Continent. Napoleon, who returned to Paris in December 1797, considered the feasibility of attempting a cross-Channel invasion, but recognized that the French navy was unable at that time to secure the crossing. He instead advocated an expedition to Egypt to secure French strategic and commercial control of the Mediterranean and threaten British trade and possessions further east, especially in India. The idea of conquering Egypt was not a new one, for it had been seriously considered after the Seven Years' War (1756–63), to compensate for France's lost colonies in America and the Indies. But Napoleon was keen to win further military glory and the Directory approved his plan: despite being reluctant to reduce the number of its troops in Europe, it was doubtless keen to see him at a safe distance from France.

On 10 May 1798, Napoleon informed the men of his expedition:

> Soldiers! You are one of the wings of the Army of England. You have waged mountain, plain and siege warfare, but you have yet to wage maritime warfare.
>
> The Roman legions, whom you have sometimes imitated, but still not equalled, fought Carthage both on this same sea and on the plains of Zama. Victory never abandoned them, because they were always brave, patient in bearing fatigue, disciplined and united.
>
> Soldiers, the eyes of Europe are on you.
>
> You have great destinies to fulfil, battles to fight, dangers and fatigues to overcome. You will do more than you have ever done for the prosperity of the fatherland, the happiness of mankind and your own glory.

He sailed from Toulon on 19 May and on his way captured the island of Malta from the Knights of St John on 9 June. (He left a French garrison on the island, but it would be forced to surrender in September 1800 after being besieged by the British.)

Napoleon landed on the Egyptian coast on 1 July and seized the city of Alexandria the next day. Although nominally part of the Ottoman Empire, Egypt was really controlled by the local Mameluke rulers. Napoleon exploited this fact to try and win the hearts and minds of the inhabitants and issued a proclamation on 2 July:

> Peoples of Egypt, you will be told that I come to destroy your religion. Do not believe it! Reply that I come to restore your rights, to punish the usurpers and that I respect God, his prophet and the Koran more than the Mamelukes do.
>
> Qadis, sheiks, imams, *tchorbadjis*, tell the people that we are friends of true Muslims.
>
> Was it not us who destroyed the Pope, who was saying that war had to be waged on the Muslims? Was it not us who destroyed the Knights of Malta, because the madmen believed that God wanted them to wage war on the Muslims? Was it not us who have been in every century the friends of the [Ottoman] Grand Vizier (may God grant his wishes!) and the enemy of his enemies? In contrast, are not the Mamelukes still in revolt against the authority of the Grand Vizier, whom they still do not recognize? ...
>
> The sheiks, qadis and imams will continue to carry out their duties. All inhabitants will remain at their homes and the prayers will continue as usual. Everyone will thank God for the destruction of the Mamelukes and will

exclaim: 'Glory to the Sultan! Glory to the French army, his friend! Curses to the Mamelukes and happiness to the peoples of Egypt!'

Napoleon marched on Cairo and on 21 July defeated the Mamelukes 2 miles outside the city at the Battle of the Pyramids. Before the battle, he famously exhorted his men by pointing at the Ancient Egyptian pyramids: 'Soldiers, forty centuries of history look down on you.' But it was actually an undemanding victory, for the brave and richly dressed Mameluke horsemen and their Egyptian footsoldiers were outclassed by the discipline and firepower of the French army. The French had 25,000 troops against only 6,000 Mamelukes supported by about 20–30,000 men of dubious military worth.

Napoleon occupied Cairo three days later and began to consolidate his occupation of Egypt. But despite its initial success, his expedition ended in disaster. In crossing the Mediterranean to Egypt, he had narrowly evaded a British fleet under Rear-Admiral Horatio Nelson. But on 1 August, after locating the French fleet in Aboukir Bay, Nelson boldly attacked and destroyed the bulk of it in the so-called Battle of the Nile. Nelson's victory left the Royal Navy in control of the Mediterranean and Napoleon isolated in Egypt. It also encouraged the Ottoman Sultan, Selim III, to declare war on France on 2 September and attempt the reconquest of Egypt. An Ottoman army assembled in Rhodes for a descent by sea with British help, while a second concentrated at Damascus for an overland advance. Napoleon was also faced with a holy war, which undermined his claims that he had come to fight only the Mamelukes and not the Egyptian people. When a revolt broke out at Cairo on 21 October, he crushed it mercilessly.

Napoleon could have defended Egypt by awaiting the Ottoman armies and forcing the land-based one to cross the desert from the east. But he took the more hazardous option of seizing the initiative and in February 1799 advanced along the Mediterranean coast into Syria, which included what is now Palestine. He took with him 13,000 troops and left another 10,000 men in the main cities of Egypt and 5,000 more south of Cairo under General Louis Desaix to pacify upper Egypt.

Beyond the immediate aim of forcing Selim III to make peace, Napoleon apparently sought to follow in Alexander the Great's footsteps and found an empire stretching from Egypt to India with the support of friendly minorities in Palestine and Lebanon. But he lacked the resources to fulfil his ambitions and soon encountered delays. He took El Arish on 20 February only after a twelve-day siege. He then continued his advance, took Gaza on the 24th and Jaffa on 7 March. In one of his most controversial actions, he had 2,400 of Jaffa's captured defenders massacred, allegedly as some of them had previously been captured at El Arish and had broken their word not to fight again. If Napoleon also intended the bloodshed at Jaffa to terrorize the defenders of his next objective, the port of St-Jean-d'Acre, he miscalculated, for the slaughter left them in no doubt of their likely fate if they fell into his hands.

At this time, Napoleon also faced an outbreak of bubonic plague in his army and courageously visited his sick at Jaffa to set an example of coolness and avert a panic. On 19 March, he laid siege to St-Jean-d'Acre, but underestimated his opponent, Ahmed Djezzar, the ruthless governor of the province of Saida. Djezzar was a skilled tactician and, since he paid well, had more formidable troops than those Napoleon had previously fought in Egypt. He was supported in his defence of the city by a squadron of

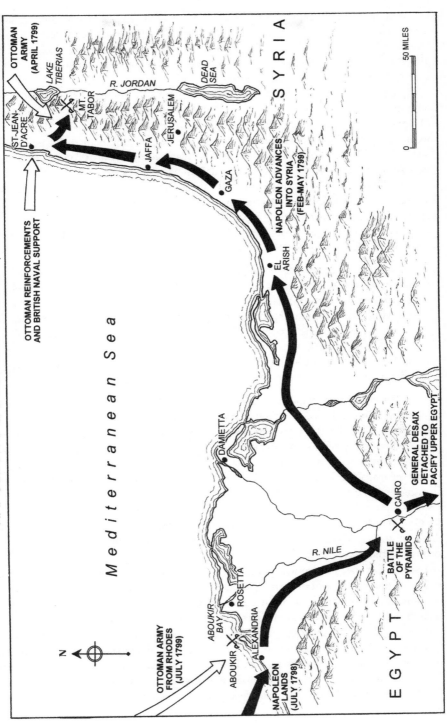

NAPOLEON'S EXPEDITION TO EGYPT, 1798-9

the Royal Navy under Captain Sir Sidney Smith, which provided naval gunfire, landed Royal Marines to serve the city's guns and brought Ottoman reinforcements from Rhodes. He was also advised by a French royalist artillery expert, Colonel Louis Edmond de Picard de Phélipeaux, who had been one of Napoleon's fellow cadets at the *Ecole militaire*, where they had detested each other.

Napoleon's attempts to storm St-Jean-d'Acre, made using insufficient troops, guns and ammunition, were hasty, piecemeal and unimaginative. When the Ottoman army at Damascus tried to relieve the city, Napoleon crushed it at the Battle of Mount Tabor on 16 April. But the other Ottoman army now posed an imminent seaborne threat to Egypt from Rhodes and Napoleon had to retreat from St-Jean-d'Acre after a sixty-two-day siege. He shamelessly hid the defeat when he wrote to the Directory on 27 May: 'I have already informed you . . . of the glorious events for the Republic, which have occurred in the last three months in Syria and of my decision promptly to recross the desert in order to return to Egypt before June.' He even claimed that only the plague had prevented him from entering St-Jean-d'Acre after the repulse of an enemy sortie on 16 May:

> It seemed a favourable moment for taking the city, but our spies, the deserters and the prisoners all agreed that the plague was causing dreadful ravages in the city of Acre, that over sixty people were dying from it every day, that the symptoms were terrible and that victims expired in thirty-six hours, in convulsions like those of rabies. The soldiers, once dispersed in the city, could not have been prevented from looting it and in the evening they would have brought back into the camp the germs of this terrible calamity, which is more fearsome than all the armies in the world.

The truth was that Napoleon had been outwitted and out-fought by Djezzar. He had lost 1,200 men killed in action in Syria and another 2,300 sick and wounded. He had little to show for these casualties and was openly criticized by his troops. He was alleged during the retreat to Egypt to have poisoned those of his men who were sick with the plague so as not to slow his march. In fact, the incident was exaggerated by hostile propaganda: he had poison left with up to sixty dying men, so they could use it if necessary to avoid being captured alive.

Napoleon had new uniforms issued to his men before they re-entered Cairo on 14 June in order to disguise his failure. Then the Ottoman army from Rhodes landed at Aboukir and on 25 July Napoleon counter-attacked and literally drove it into the sea, drowning thousands of its men.

Back in Europe, France was again fighting a major war on the Continent, against a new coalition led by Britain, Austria and Russia. Napoleon's expedition to Egypt had overstretched French resources at a critical time, but this, and his defeat at St-Jean-d'Acre, were less obvious than the setbacks and political instability at home. Despite its failure to achieve its strategic goals, his expedition captured popular imagination in France, for it had been accompanied by a team of civilian experts who made important discoveries about Egyptian history and culture. Napoleon's battlefield victories at the Pyramids, Mount Tabor and Aboukir had created an illusion of success and his intervention opened Egypt to western ideas, administration and technology.

Chapter 3

Head of State

As an army commander, Napoleon had also developed political and administrative skills as he organized and governed his conquests. This proved an invaluable preparation for his seizure of power in France itself. Sensing his opportunity, he secretly sailed from Egypt on 23 August with a few trusted companions. He left behind a letter entrusting General Jean-Baptiste Kléber with command of his abandoned army, which would remain in Egypt until defeated by a British expedition in 1801 and repatriated under the surrender terms.

After slipping past the Royal Navy in a frigate, Napoleon landed at St Raphaël on 9 October. A week later, he was back in Paris, where plotters, including Emmanuel Sieyès and Charles-Maurice de Talleyrand-Périgord, were planning a coup d'état against the corrupt and unpopular Directory and wanted to use a military hero as a figurehead. Several generals could have filled this role, but none equalled Napoleon's combination of fame, ambition, experience and political influence.

At first, the coup went favourably. On 9 November 1799, three of the five members of the Directory resigned and the other two were arrested. The two legislative councils were transferred to Saint-Cloud, outside Paris, supposedly for their own security in case of a Jacobin threat, but in reality to isolate them from any support by a mob. Napoleon was entrusted with the command of the troops in and around Paris.

But by the second day, 10 November, the plotters no longer enjoyed the advantage of surprise. Napoleon lost his nerve when he addressed the legislative councils and so antagonized the Council of the Five Hundred with a clumsy, threatening speech that he had to be protected by grenadiers as he left the hall. The situation was saved not by Napoleon, but by his brother Lucien, the President of the Five Hundred, who persuaded the legislature's own guards to clear the council chamber. The remnants of the deputies were then convened to abolish the Directory and approve a new government, a triumvirate of three consuls. Thus, the coup succeeded by military force rather than by political means alone, which would at least have preserved the impression of legality.

Despite the coup's flawed execution, Napoleon quickly consolidated his position once it had succeeded. He was initially one of the three consuls, but by the end of the year had established himself as First Consul and replaced his two colleagues with more pliant men. The results of a plebiscite held in April 1800 were fiddled by Lucien, the Minister of the Interior, to give an illusion of overwhelming support for the new constitution.

To win real approval from the French people, Napoleon needed to secure a victorious peace. Russia had withdrawn from the Allied coalition, leaving Austria and Britain to continue the war. The Austrians had two armies in the field. One, under General Baron Paul Kray von Krajova, stood on the defensive in Germany while the other under General Baron Michael von Melas took the offensive in northern Italy, where the French had lost nearly all Napoleon's gains of 1796–7.

In May 1800, as General Jean-Victor Moreau's Army of the Rhine contained Kray in southern Germany, Napoleon led a newly formed Army of the Reserve through the snow-covered passes of the Alps, despite the cold, avalanches and poor quality roads. By the 24th, he had emerged into the plains of the Po valley in Melas's rear. 'We have fallen here like a thunderbolt,' he boasted in a letter to his brother Joseph: 'The enemy did not expect it at all and seem hardly able to believe it. Very big events are going to happen. Their results will be great – I hope so, for the happiness and glory of the Republic.'

Napoleon thus severed Melas's communications and occupied Milan on 2 June, but he then miscalculated and nearly suffered a disaster. As he advanced westwards to bring Melas to battle, he detached two divisions, to prevent him from withdrawing southwards to Genoa or escaping northwards across the Po. To his surprise, Melas instead attacked and forced him to fight the Battle of Marengo (14 June) at a numerical disadvantage. Napoleon was driven back and soon exhausted his reserves. By 3 p.m., Melas considered the battle won and left his subordinates to complete the victory while he returned to the nearby city of Alessandria to rest, since he was seventy-one years old, had been slightly wounded and had twice had a horse shot beneath him.

Napoleon avoided defeat only because the commander of one of his detached divisions, General Desaix, had halted on hearing the sound of the guns, marched back after receiving a recall and arrived in time to help check a final Austrian attack. Desaix was shot dead, but well-timed artillery fire and a charge by General François Kellermann with a cavalry brigade broke the Austrians and clinched the victory. Next day, Melas signed a convention, which established an armistice, and then withdrew east of the Mincio river and north of the Po.

Despite his mistakes, Napoleon later portrayed Marengo as one of his most outstanding battles. He had the official accounts of the battle rewritten to make the victory seem the result more of superior planning and generalship than luck and to minimize the roles played by Desaix and Kellermann.

But Marengo did not end the war. Hostilities resumed in November, and the Austrians signed the Peace of Lunéville on 9 February 1801 only after being decisively beaten by Moreau at Hohenlinden (3 December 1800) in southern Germany and then pursued to within 50 miles of Vienna.

Peace negotiations followed with Britain and led to the Treaty of Amiens on 25 March 1802. Now, Napoleon was able to rebuild France after a decade of war, repair the divisions caused by the Revolution and unite the nation behind him. In fact, it was the civil achievements of his early years in power that constituted Napoleon's most lasting legacy, for his military conquests did not survive his fall. He restored the economy, rationalized and codified French Law, increased the efficiency of the government and administration and reformed and centralized the secondary education system. He also built new roads and canals, improved the ports of Brest, Cherbourg and Antwerp and carried out public works in Paris, including triumphal arches, the addition of a wing to the Louvre and the building of quays along the Seine.

In August 1801, Napoleon signed a Concordat with the Pope, which reopened French churches and thus helped reconcile Catholics and weaken resistance to his

THE MARENGO CAMPAIGN, MAY-JUNE 1800

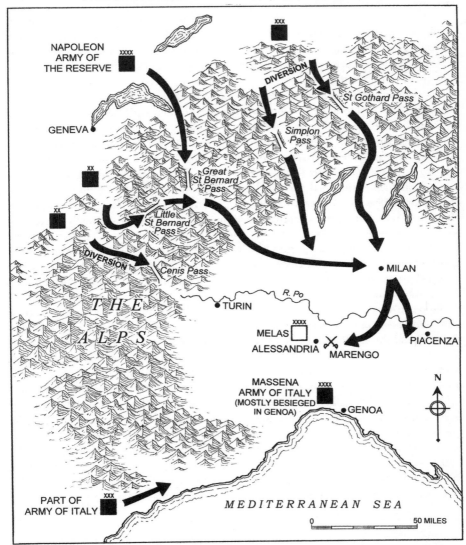

Note: Melas' army was initially dispersed in detachments, besieging Genoa, guarding the exits from the Alps and occupying garrisons across Northern Italy.

regime. In addition, he encouraged the return of royalists who had emigrated during the Revolution, so he could use their skills and prestige to strengthen his regime and drain support from the exiled Bourbons.

Napoleon also made a major contribution to the expansion of the United States when, on 3 May 1803, he sold the French possession of Louisiana in North America. The Louisiana Purchase provided France with valuable financial resources and more than doubled the area of the United States through the addition of New Orleans and a swathe of land along the Mississippi river, which would in any case have been difficult for Napoleon to defend.

Constructive achievements such as these cannot hide the authoritarian nature of Napoleon's regime. He relied on censorship, propaganda and police spies, although to a lesser extent than the more extreme Revolutionary governments. Increasingly, he bypassed the legislature by having decrees issued by the Senate, whose members were appointed, not elected.

Not surprisingly, Napoleon faced a spate of assassination plots and narrowly escaped being killed on 24 December 1800 when a waggon loaded with barrels of powder was blown up in the rue St Nicaise in Paris, causing thirty-five casualties. Napoleon used the plots as an excuse to arrest his foremost rival, General Moreau, and crush the Jacobins, the radical left of French politics, to whom he had previously attached himself as a politically ambitious young officer. He also had a French Bourbon prince, the Duke d'Enghien, kidnapped from Baden on the east bank of the Rhine and executed on 21 March 1804 to discourage further royalist attempts to kill him or foster an insurrection. At the same time, he strengthened his grip on power by gradually adopting a more monarchical character. He became Consul for Life on 2 August 1802 and, at the age of thirty-five, Emperor of the French on 18 May 1804. Both of these steps were approved in plebiscites, which conferred a degree of legitimacy. Napoleon had Pope Pius VII attend his coronation as Emperor on 2 December, but, significantly, placed the crown on his own head.

Napoleon's rise to power had been closely linked with his military success and he now found his twin roles as head of state and military commander of mixed benefit. On the one hand, he could coordinate the full weight of political and diplomatic measures to isolate enemies before the outbreak of a war. But on the other, he would find it politically dangerous to be away from Paris for long on campaign and his military decisions would sometimes be flawed by the weight he gave to political considerations.

War with Britain resumed after fourteen months on 16 May 1803, for the Peace of Amiens had been an unsatisfactory compromise and it proved impossible to reconcile the conflicting strategic needs and ambitions of the two sides. France remained at peace with the Continental powers for another two years. Napoleon reorganized the French army and assembled 200,000 men in camps along the English Channel, where they trained intensively in drill, tactics and large-scale manoeuvres, in preparation for an invasion of England. Napoleon wrote on 16 November 1803:

> I have spent these last three days amidst the camps and the port. Everything here begins to move with the speed and direction that it ought to have. I have seen the English coast from the heights of Ambleteuse, as clearly as the Calvaire from the Tuileries. You could make out the houses and people moving about. It is a ditch that will be leaped once we have the boldness to attempt it.

But he never launched the invasion, for he was diverted by a new war on the Continent, even before Vice-Admiral Horatio Nelson destroyed the main Franco-Spanish fleet at the Battle of Trafalgar (21 October 1805).

Chapter 4

The Years of Victory, 1805–9

Master of Europe: 1805–7

In the eyes of the established monarchies of Europe, Napoleon was a mere usurper. Antagonized by his assumption of the title of Emperor and by the ruthless execution of the Duke d'Enghien, they also became alarmed by his territorial ambitions, especially in the key strategic areas of Italy, the Mediterranean and Germany. In May 1805, for example, Napoleon strengthened his position in the north of the Italian peninsula by crowning himself King of Italy and thus challenging traditional Austrian interests in the region.

Britain and Russia formed a coalition in April 1805 and were joined by Austria four months later. Even though Prussia remained neutral, the Allies could field an array of armies. Covered by diversions against Hanover and Naples in northern and southern Europe, the Allies intended to attack Napoleon's ally, Bavaria, and his satellite Kingdom of Italy and then invade France itself.

Yet Napoleon's confidence was unshaken and he wrote on 13 August:

> The fact is that this power [Austria] is arming. I want it to disarm and if it does not do so, I will go with 200,000 men and pay it a good visit that it will remember for a long time. . . . One would have to be really mad to make war on me. There is certainly not a finer army in Europe than the one that I have today.

At the end of August, having been forced to postpone his planned invasion of England, Napoleon began to move his army from the Channel coast to positions along the Rhine river. On 25 September, his forces, now called the Grand Army, started to cross the Rhine and then, advancing in several converging columns, wheeled southwards through Germany to the Danube. Since the Allies had failed to coordinate their offensive, Napoleon was able to surprise the main Austrian army under General Baron Karl Mack von Leiberich with the speed and direction of his descent and encircle it at Ulm in Bavaria before it could be joined by the Russians. After vain attempts to break out, Mack surrendered on 20 October and Napoleon wrote exuberantly to his wife, Josephine:

> I have worn myself out more than I should have done. I have suffered a bit from cold feet and being drenched in the rain every day for a week, but I have stayed inside today and am restored.
>
> I have fulfilled my objective. I have destroyed the Austrian army simply by marching. I have taken 60,000 prisoners, seized 120 guns, more than ninety flags and over thirty generals.
>
> I am going to advance against the Russians – they are done for. I am pleased with my army. I have lost only 1,500 men.

NAPOLEON'S CAMPAIGNS IN CENTRAL EUROPE, 1805-9

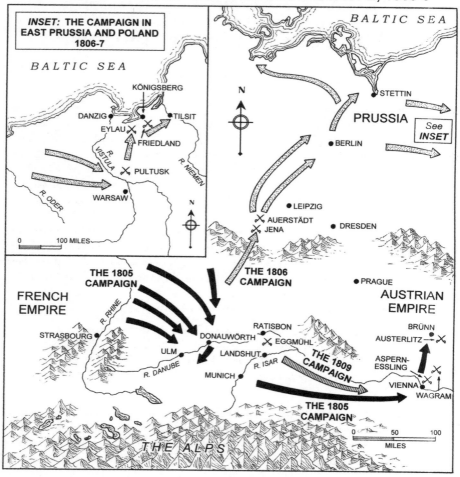

These impressive claims hid an often inglorious experience for his troops. One of his officers, Raymond de Montesquiou, the Duke de Fezensac, later revealed:

> For me, this short campaign was like a summary of those that followed. It had it all: the over-exhaustion, the lack of supplies, the coldness of the season and the disorders committed by the marauders. In a month, I underwent for the first time what I was destined to suffer in the whole course of my career.

Napoleon pushed eastwards down the Danube and occupied Vienna, but failed to prevent the leading Russian army under General Mikhail Kutusov from escaping and uniting with the main Russian force. Napoleon advanced northwards into Bohemia and reached Brünn on 20 November, but was now confronted by a powerful Allied army that had assembled at Olmütz under the Russian and Austrian Emperors.

Napoleon needed a decisive victory, for he had overstretched his lines of communication, faced a financial crisis in Paris and knew that Prussia might join the Allies in the field. He therefore encouraged the Allies to take the offensive against him, so he could counter-attack once they made a false move. He gave an impression of weakness by pretending to be anxious for an armistice. The Allies duly advanced and tried to turn his southern flank, intending to cut him from Vienna, in ignorance of the fact that he had re-routed his lines of communication to the west for added security.

Napoleon lured the Allies further forward by deliberately abandoning the high ground of the Pratzen plateau in his centre and by keeping his southern wing weak. But at the same time, he secretly ordered two detached corps of his army to rejoin him in order to restore the balance of numbers. The stage was set for the Battle of Austerlitz on 2 December. As the Allied columns advanced from the Pratzen to attack him in the south, Napoleon unleashed a powerful counter-attack in the centre. Initially hidden by fog in the valley floor, his troops stormed the Pratzen, pierced the weak Allied centre and repelled Russian attempts to throw them back. After four hours of fierce fighting, Napoleon had split the Allied army into two. He then wheeled his centre to the south and routed the Allied left wing. He killed, wounded or captured 26,000 men and 180 guns. Austria immediately sought an armistice and the Russians withdrew to Poland. Napoleon had smashed the Allied coalition.

'The Battle of Austerlitz is the finest of all that I have fought,' he wrote to Josephine on 5 December. It had been won by boldness, deception, surprise and manoeuvre. He regarded it as a personal triumph: he would reward distinguished generals with dukedoms and the names of other battles as titles, but he never created a Duke of Austerlitz. Yet the battle's decisiveness made Napoleon overconfident and too inclined to see the solution to international problems in war rather than diplomacy. The superior quality and organization of his army would not last, for within four years of Austerlitz, his opponents would be learning from their defeats, reforming their armies and adopting improved strategies and tactics with which to meet him on a more equal footing. Napoleon's own army would suffer from the cumulative effect of heavy casualties in successive campaigns and the replacement of dead or wounded veterans with conscripts. This would make it more difficult to win quick and decisive victories.

As a result of the Peace of Pressburg (27 December), Austria lost large tracts of territory, including her remaining lands in northern Italy, and also her influence in central Europe. In July 1806, Napoleon formed his satellite states in Germany into a Confederation of the Rhine to act as a buffer on the eastern frontiers of France, increase his manpower and replace the Austrian-led Holy Roman Empire.

Prussia had been about to join Austria and Russia when Napoleon crushed them at Austerlitz. She grew increasingly alarmed at the growth in French power and influence and the threat to her position. The Prussian war party, led by Queen Louise, gathered strength, especially after it was rumoured that Napoleon had offered to return Hanover to Britain during abortive peace negotiations following Austerlitz: he had previously agreed to cede it to Prussia in exchange for her neutrality. On 9 August 1806, King Frederick William III ordered the mobilization of the Prussian army and by the end of September had assembled two field armies and a detached corps, a total of 130,000 men.

Napoleon had not sought war with Prussia, but once it became unavoidable, he prepared to seize the initiative with a powerful offensive. By 6 October, he had 208,000 men of the Grand Army available in southern Germany and had arrived from Paris to take personal command. He planned to turn the left flank of the Prussian armies and cut them off from Berlin. He would advance behind a cavalry screen, with his corps moving along three parallel routes on a front of 40 miles so they could rapidly concentrate and support each other as soon as they encountered the enemy.

Prussia could count on little immediate assistance. She had formed a coalition with Britain, Russia and Sweden, but none of these powers was immediately in a position to lend direct military support. Austria, defeated the year before, now remained neutral.

Despite Prussia's isolation, Frederick William III issued an ultimatum on 1 October for the immediate withdrawal of all French troops from the east bank of the Rhine. Napoleon received this ultimatum on the 7th and immediately ordered his army to advance into Saxony, Prussia's smaller neighbour and ally. The Prussian army commanders were indecisive and could not agree on a strategy. Initial clashes with Napoleon's advancing army occurred at Hof on 8 October and again at Saalfeld on the 10th, where Prince Louis Ferdinand of Prussia, the nephew of Frederick the Great, was defeated and killed while commanding an advanced guard.

On the 13th, Napoleon wrote to Josephine:

> I am marvellously well. I have already put on weight since I started and yet I cover over twenty to twenty-five leagues [about 50 to 60 miles] each day, on horseback, in carriages, in every sort of a way. I go to bed at eight, I am up again at midnight; sometimes it occurs to me that you have not yet gone to bed!

Napoleon now wheeled to the west to fall on the Prussians and sever their line of retreat. On 14 October, he crushed one Prussian army at Jena, while in a simultaneous action, a detached corps under Marshal Louis Davout defeated the other army 12 miles to the north at Auerstädt, despite being heavily outnumbered. The Prussians fought bravely, but were handicapped by their more inflexible tactics and by the mistakes and indecision of their commanders. Among those who fought at Auerstädt was Blücher, who commanded several Prussian cavalry squadrons.

Napoleon exploited the victories of Jena-Auerstädt with a relentless pursuit and triumphantly entered Berlin on 27 October. In the wake of the disaster, most of the surviving remnants of the Prussian army surrendered, along with the country's key fortresses, and Napoleon was able to re-equip and remount his army at Prussian expense.

He then advanced eastwards to confront Russian forces who had taken the field in East Prussia and Poland. He had to fight a demoralizing winter campaign between Warsaw and the Baltic coast, in barren and sparsely populated terrain devoid of good roads. He forced the Russians to retreat after the Battles of Pultusk and Golymin (26 December), but was unable to obtain a decisive victory, largely as the weather limited his army's mobility and made it impossible to pursue. 'I write just a quick word,' he informed Josephine three days later: 'I am in a wretched barn. I have beaten the Russians. I have taken from them thirty guns and their baggage and made 6,000 prisoners, but the weather is dreadful; it is raining and we have mud up to our knees.' As usual, he exaggerated his enemy's losses.

The opposing armies occupied winter quarters, but resumed the campaign in January 1807. Napoleon seized an opportunity to try and cut off the Russian commander, General Levin von Bennigsen, who had advanced to attack some of his outlying units. Alerted to his danger by an intercepted order, Bennigsen quickly retreated. Napoleon pursued up to the town of Preussich-Eylau and fought a notoriously bloody battle in the snow (7–8 February). His initial attack strayed into murderous artillery fire in the midst of a snowstorm, was shot to pieces and then overrun by Russian cavalry. He nearly lost the battle and had to throw in his Reserve Cavalry to contain the Russians and win time for Marshal Davout's III Corps to arrive and attack their southern wing. The battle swung in Napoleon's favour, but then a Prussian detachment arrived and checked Davout. Both sides suffered heavy casualties from the intense artillery fire. Chasseur François Billon of the Imperial Guard infantry wrote:

> After riding through our lines, Napoleon came and took position in the middle of the Guard to boost our morale. For the rest of the day, he shared with us all the dangers that threatened the least of his soldiers. During the action, an ADC of [Marshal] Soult was carried off by a cannonball, so close to the Emperor that it made the whole Guard shake. ... But let's be clear: the Guard is never shaken! I mean that it trembled when it saw the danger from which its idol had just escaped.

The battle ended after both sides fought each other to a standstill. Bennigsen retreated in the night, but Napoleon himself withdrew to winter quarters less than two weeks later and his letters to Josephine lack their usual triumphant tone. In the early hours of the morning after Eylau, he wrote: 'Yesterday there was a big battle here. The victory was mine, but I have lost many men. The enemy's losses, which are even greater, do not console me.' Five days later, he added: 'I am still at Eylau. The country here is covered with dead and wounded. This is not the nicest aspect of war. Men are suffering and it is depressing to see so many victims. I am well. I have done what I wanted and I pushed back the enemy, foiling his plans.'

It was difficult to keep troops adequately supplied in such harsh winter conditions, let alone win a decisive battle, and it was only in the summer that Napoleon secured a victorious peace. The besieged city of Danzig in his left rear fell on 24 May, enabling him to use it as an advanced base, and on 8 June, after checking an advance by Bennigsen, he took the offensive. He suffered heavy casualties at the Battle of Heilsberg (10 June), but four days later caught Bennigsen's army with its back to the Alle river at the town of Friedland, fell on its left wing and rolled up its line. Next day, he hurriedly informed Josephine:

> I write just a quick word, for I am very tired. I have been bivouacking for many days. My children have celebrated the anniversary of the Battle of Marengo [on 14 June] in a worthy way.
>
> The Battle of Friedland will be just as famous and is as glorious for my people. The whole Russian army routed; eighty guns; 30,000 men taken or killed; twenty-five Russian generals killed, wounded or captured; the

Russian Guard crushed. It is a worthy sister of Marengo, Austerlitz and Jena.

Napoleon then pursued the Russians to the Niemen river, which marked the western frontier of their territory, and captured their main supply base, the Prussian city of Königsberg on the Baltic. 'The Battle of Friedland has decided everything,' he wrote on 19 June. 'The enemy is confused, demoralized and extremely weakened. My health is good and my army superb.'

Bennigsen sought an armistice that day. Napoleon was keen to end the war, for he had occupied almost the whole of Prussia and was now operating at the end of long and vulnerable lines of communication. On the 25th, he met the young Tsar Alexander I on a raft on the middle of the Niemen river at Tilsit and on 7 and 9 July signed treaties of peace with Russia and Prussia.

Napoleon thus consolidated his mastery of western and central Europe and emerged as its most powerful ruler since Charlemagne. He drastically reduced the size and status of Prussia and contained her between two newly created satellites, Westphalia in northern Germany and a revived Polish state, the Grand Duchy of Warsaw. By securing an alliance with Tsar Alexander, he also isolated Britain, his most persistent foe.

The Peninsular War

Napoleon sought to undermine Britain through economic warfare and tried to impose a trade embargo on her goods throughout Continental Europe. He also wanted to secure the fleets of neutral Sweden, Denmark and Portugal in the hope of acquiring enough ships to overwhelm the Royal Navy. Britain responded with a naval blockade and with an audacious pre-emptive strike on Copenhagen in September 1807, which seized the Danish fleet before Napoleon could do so.

Napoleon found that the Continental System was difficult to enforce, harmed his own economic interests and caused resentment among his allies. His attempts to increase its effectiveness also embroiled him in one of his most disastrous ventures, the occupation of the Iberian Peninsula. First, in November 1807, he had Portugal invaded by 25,000 French troops under General Andoche Junot and thus closed her ports to British trade, although he failed to secure the Portuguese fleet. Next, Napoleon turned on his ally Spain: she had supported the attack on Portugal, but was inefficient and unreliable. Napoleon ruthlessly seized control of Spain, first by stationing units in it and taking over key fortresses and then by exploiting quarrels within the Spanish royal family. He had Madrid occupied, forced King Carlos IV and his son, Ferdinand, to renounce the throne and replaced them with his own brother, Joseph Bonaparte, as King of Spain.

Yet Napoleon had underestimated the complexity and difficulty of his venture and was taken aback by revolts that spread across the country, starting with a bloodily repressed uprising in Madrid on 2 May. In his efforts to pacify Spain, he dispersed his forces, leaving a corps under General Count Pierre Dupont de l'Etang exposed in the southern province of Andalusia. Dupont was trapped by a Spanish army under General Francisco Castaños and capitulated on 20 July. It was a humiliating defeat, which encouraged Napoleon's enemies across Europe and caused King Joseph to abandon Madrid less than a fortnight after his arrival and withdraw to the Ebro river in the north-east. Napoleon was furious:

> Dupont has completely disgraced himself and disgraced my arms. Ineptitude, cowardice and lack of direction have governed my operations of the end of July and disrupted my affairs in Spain. The harm that he does me is insignificant compared to the dishonour. The details of all this, which I want to keep as secret as possible, cause the fiercest indignation. But it is necessary that it comes into the open some day and that the honour of our arms is avenged.

In fact, the fiasco was largely Napoleon's own responsibility and it had serious repercussions. The revolts turned Spain into a British ally and thus relieved the pressure on the Royal Navy, which no longer had to blockade the Spanish ports. They also boosted the British economy by opening important new markets, for the Spanish had large colonies in Central and South America. Furthermore, General Junot's French occupation forces were now isolated in Portugal. On 1 August, a British army, commanded initially by Lieutenant-General Sir Arthur Wellesley, the future Duke of Wellington, landed north of Lisbon and by the end of the month Junot had suffered two defeats and had signed a convention under which his troops were repatriated to France.

As a result of these setbacks, Napoleon personally intervened in the Peninsula in November 1808, using reinforcements, including some veterans from central Europe, to form a reorganized army of 230,000 men. He quickly smashed the under-equipped and poorly led Spanish regular armies in the north-east and reoccupied Madrid on 4 December. But he was then diverted from invading Portugal by the British army, now commanded by Lieutenant-General Sir John Moore, which had advanced to threaten his communications north-west of Madrid. Napoleon pursued, famously leading his men over the Guadarrama mountains in the middle of a blizzard in his determination to destroy the British army. But he failed to trap it in the plains of Leon and Old Castille and left Marshal Jean-de-Dieu Soult to pursue it to Coruña on the north-western coast, from where it was evacuated by sea after a battle in which Moore was mortally wounded.

Napoleon returned to Paris on 24 January 1809, leaving his subordinates to complete the conquest of the Peninsula. He wrote: 'The Spanish business is finished. Italy not only is tranquil, but supplies us with 80,000 men and as for the Emperor of Austria, if he makes the slightest hostile move, he will soon cease to reign. That is very clear. As for Russia, we have never been on better terms.'

In fact, Napoleon's problems in the Peninsula had only just begun. Wellesley returned to Lisbon with reinforcements and built a small but increasingly effective Anglo-Portuguese army with which he inflicted repeated defeats on Napoleon's marshals. The French could counter the Spanish guerrilla insurgents only by dispersing their units, but they repeatedly had to concentrate against offensives by both Wellesley and Spain's revived regular armies.

Napoleon failed to impose a unified command structure over the marshals he left behind, ostensibly because he could not find a subordinate with the skills and authority to serve as a commander-in-chief, but also because he was reluctant to give any one man too much power in case he emerged as a political threat. Napoleon's own attempts to direct the war by remote control from Paris merely made matters worse, for he undermined the authority of King Joseph and often ignored the realities of the situation on the ground, particularly the difficulties of logistics and communications.

The War with Austria: 1809

Napoleon had returned to Paris in January 1809 partly out of concern that Austria was preparing for a war to avenge her defeat of 1805. This confronted Napoleon with the prospect of a conflict on two fronts and he had difficulty mobilizing enough resources to meet the challenge, even though Austria would be without direct military assistance from Britain, her only ally among the great powers. He began to strengthen his forces in central Europe, but knew that he could not yet remove many troops or commanders from Spain. He therefore had to rely more heavily on conscripts and on 70,000 men of mixed quality extracted from his satellite states of the Confederation of the Rhine.

Austria mobilized an army under her foremost general, Archduke Charles, in the Danube valley and on 9 April invaded Bavaria, Napoleon's ally in southern Germany, without previously declaring war. Napoleon was still in Paris and had yet to complete and concentrate his army in Germany. But Archduke Charles advanced too slowly and missed his opportunity to defeat Napoleon's forces piecemeal in the first days of the campaign. Napoleon personally reached Donauwörth on 17 April, assumed command and rapidly regained the initiative.

On 19–22 April, Napoleon counter-attacked and inflicted successive defeats at Abensberg, Landshut and Eggmühl. In the course of these battles, he pierced Archduke Charles's centre, drove his left wing across the Isar river and forced the rest of his army to retreat eastwards after escaping to the north bank of the Danube. On the 23rd, Napoleon stormed the city of Ratisbon, which was held by an Austrian rear-guard. During this action, he was bruised in the foot by a spent ball, one that had neared the end of its flight, and was obliged to ride through his army to dispel concerns that he had been wounded.

Although he failed to destroy the Austrian army in these battles, Napoleon had dramatically reversed the tide of the campaign. It was one of his finest performances, especially as he had been obliged to improvize his manoeuvres, rather than being able to plan them carefully beforehand, as he had done at Austerlitz.

Napoleon now thrust eastwards along the south bank of the Danube and occupied Vienna on 13 May. To end the war, he needed to inflict a decisive defeat on the Austrian army to induce Emperor Francis I to negotiate for peace. On the 20th, he therefore began to cross the Danube 4 miles east of Vienna to the Marchfeld, a vast plain on the north bank. He did not expect to meet Archduke Charles's army until after he had advanced well to the north, but, to his surprise, he found himself counter-attacked on the afternoon of the 21st, before he had been able to deploy beyond a constricted bridgehead or bring all his troops across.

The battle that ensued centred on the villages of Aspern and Essling. Napoleon blunted Archduke Charles's disjointed attacks on the 21st and then, on the morning of the 22nd, tried to break out with a powerful attack between the two villages. But his army was checked and forced back by counter-attacks, before being pounded by massed artillery. At the same time, he risked being trapped on the north bank, for the Austrians repeatedly broke the pontoon bridge behind him by floating objects down the Danube, which was already swollen with the spring meltwaters. Napoleon evacuated the bridgehead that night, after suffering his first personal defeat as a commander since his failure to take the fortress of Saint-Jean-d'Acre ten years earlier.

Napoleon learnt from his mistakes and over the next six weeks made thorough preparations for a renewed attempt. By 4 July, when he again crossed the Danube to attack Archduke Charles, he had assembled an army of 175,000 men. Over the next two days, he fought one of his biggest and bloodiest battles around the village of Wagram. He skilfully checked a dangerous Austrian offensive on his left, drove a powerful thrust into the Austrian centre and began rolling up their line with his right wing. Archduke Charles broke off the battle and retreated, but with his army intact. Napoleon's troops were too exhausted to pursue until the next day.

Despite its incompleteness, Wagram was enough to result in an armistice on 11 July. Peace was signed at Schönbrunn on 14 October but this was the last time that Napoleon would end a campaign victoriously.

Chapter 5

Decline and Fall, 1810–14

The events of 1808–9 dispelled the impression of Napoleonic dominance that had been projected by the Peace of Tilsit. His Empire was strategically overextended and inherently unstable, for as a result of his ruthless centralization of power it depended on him alone and was unlikely to survive should he be killed on campaign. By intervening in the Iberian Peninsula, he had saddled himself with an ongoing attritional conflict that would become known as his 'Spanish ulcer' and yet he could not cut his losses and evacuate Spain without dangerously undermining his prestige.

After defeating Austria, Napoleon prepared to return to the Peninsula with 100,000 reinforcements and even boasted to the Legislative Assembly: 'When I show myself beyond the Pyrenees, the terrified Leopard [the British] will seek to escape by sea from shame, defeat and death.'

Had he carried through this plan and remained long enough, he would almost certainly have crushed Spanish resistance and forced Wellington to evacuate his army from Portugal by weight of numbers. But he allowed other projects to detain him in Paris. He wanted to secure the future of his Empire by producing a son and heir and in December 1809 he divorced his wife, the Empress Josephine, with whom he had been unable to produce a child. The following year, he married Marie-Louise, the nineteen-year-old daughter of the Austrian Emperor, in a dynastic alliance intended to consolidate his position in Europe. She gave birth to a son on 20 March 1811, who was given the title of the King of Rome but was destined never to reign.

Napoleon faced an economic crisis in 1811, just as his problems with enforcing the Continental System threw more of the costs of maintaining the Empire on to the French people. He had also lost much Catholic support as a result of quarrels with the Pope and the annexation of the Papal States in June 1809. Even more seriously, his alliance with Tsar Alexander I had broken down.

The Invasion of Russia: 1812
Napoleon's alliance with Russia was essentially an unstable compromise rather than a lasting meeting of interests, and relations deteriorated dramatically in the four years after Tilsit. In particular, Russia suffered commercially by enforcing Napoleon's economic measures against Britain and withdrew from his Continental System at the end of 1810. She also felt threatened by Napoleon's enlargement of his satellite state, the Grand Duchy of Warsaw, with the incorporation of territory taken from Austria in 1809 and was further antagonized by Napoleon's annexation in January 1811 of the Grand Duchy of Oldenburg, a German state with which she had close dynastic links.

Temperamentally unable to accept anything less than subservience from his allies, Napoleon resorted to a military solution. Despite the ongoing war in the Peninsula, he began towards the end of 1811 to prepare an army of over half a million men for an

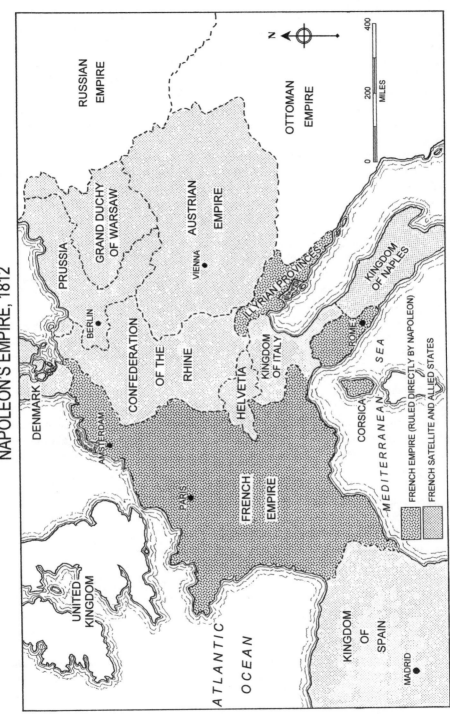

NAPOLEON'S EMPIRE, 1812

N

400

200

MILES

0

RUSSIAN EMPIRE

OTTOMAN EMPIRE

PRUSSIA

GRAND DUCHY OF WARSAW

AUSTRIAN EMPIRE

VIENNA

BERLIN

CONFEDERATION OF THE RHINE

ILLYRIAN PROVINCES

DENMARK

HELVETIA

KINGDOM OF ITALY

KINGDOM OF NAPLES

AMSTERDAM

ROME

CORSICA

MEDITERRANEAN SEA

PARIS

FRENCH EMPIRE

FRENCH EMPIRE (RULED DIRECTLY BY NAPOLEON)

FRENCH SATELLITE AND ALLIED STATES

UNITED KINGDOM

ATLANTIC OCEAN

KINGDOM OF SPAIN

MADRID

invasion of Russia. Over half of these troops were foreign-born, being drawn from throughout his Empire, from satellites and from defeated states like Austria and Prussia that had been forced into an alliance. Napoleon disregarded warnings of the inadvisability and difficulties of such a vast undertaking and, although he read widely on the history and topography of Russia, he ignored the lessons of the disastrous invasion of 1708–9 by King Charles XII of Sweden. Napoleon made careful logistic preparations, but could not adequately support such a vast venture using the horse-drawn transport of the time; nor did he calculate on the campaign lasting into the winter.

At first, Russia could oppose Napoleon with two main armies, a total of only 200,000 men, but would be able to bring up reinforcements later in the campaign, especially as she ended her war with the Ottoman Turks on 28 May 1812.

On 22 June, with his Grand Army poised on the Niemen river, Napoleon issued a proclamation:

> Soldiers! The second Polish war has begun; the first ended at Friedland and Tilsit. At Tilsit Russia pledged an eternal alliance with France, and war on England! Today her oath is broken. She refuses all explanations of her strange conduct unless the French eagles recross the Rhine. Fate draws Russia on; her destiny must be accomplished! Does she then think us degenerate? Are we no longer the soldiers of Austerlitz? She places us between dishonour and war; can our choice be in doubt? Forward, then, across the Niemen, and let us carry the war on to her own soil.

Two days later, Napoleon crossed the river into the Russian territory of Lithuania. He planned on crushing the Russians without having to advance deep into old Russia and certainly not as far as Moscow. Yet he failed to trap and force them to fight a decisive battle, despite the antagonism and poor cooperation between the commanders of their two armies, Prince Mikhail Barclay de Tolly and Prince Peter Bagration. After retreating 300 miles, the outnumbered Russians united at the city of Smolensk on 3 August.

Napoleon had already encountered serious problems. He was unable to maintain a relentless advance and had to spend over a fortnight regrouping at Vilna. He lost many horses and men through sickness caused by alternating summer heat and torrential rain and by a shortage of proper forage. But the need for a decisive victory drew him on and for a moment it seemed he might win one at Smolensk. For the Russians halted their demoralizing retreat and launched a counter-offensive westwards from the city. But they hurriedly abandoned their advance when they learnt that Napoleon was sweeping round their flank south of the Dnieper river in order to reach Smolensk and cut their line of retreat. Napoleon attacked the city on 17 August, but was too late to catch the Russians: he merely forced their rearguard to evacuate it and continue the retreat.

Napoleon considered whether to halt at Smolensk for the winter, but knew that this would have been seen as an admission of failure and he could not have sustained his army there indefinitely, so he advanced deeper into Russia. A new commander, General Mikhail Kutusov, took command of the united Russian army and offered battle at a fortified position at Borodino, 65 miles west of Moscow.

NAPOLEON'S INVASION OF RUSSIA, 1812

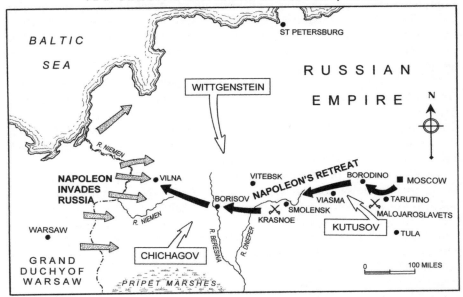

By now, Napoleon had suffered heavy losses during the advance and had been obliged to detach many of his forces to guard his overstretched communications. He had only 130,000 men and 587 guns at Borodino, too few to ensure a decisive victory over Kutusov's 120,000 men and 640 guns. He could not attempt to outflank the Russians without running the risk of them either resuming their retreat or attacking his own communications. He therefore made a frontal attack, intending to pound Kutusov into submission, and informed his army:

> Soldiers! Here at last is the battle that you have so long expected! Victory now depends on your efforts, and is essential. It will give us abundance, good winter quarters, and a speedy return to our country. Do what you did at Austerlitz, at Friedland, at Vitebsk, at Smolensk, and let prosperity point with pride to your conduct on this day: let people say of you: 'He was at that great battle fought under the walls of Moscow!'

The Battle of Borodino began at 6 a.m. on 7 September. Napoleon had a heavy cold and commanded for most of the day from the rear, but rode forward later on to assess the situation. By the middle of the afternoon, he had driven the Russians back and captured their fortifications, but he declined to commit his reserve, the Imperial Guard infantry. The decision was one of his most controversial as a commander, but was in fact justified. Although hard-hit, the Russians still had fresh units and could probably have checked another frontal attack. Napoleon expected to have to fight again before he could enter Moscow and needed to keep his Imperial Guard intact as the nucleus of his army. As it was, he lost about 30,000 men and the Russians over 40,000.

Kutusov pondered whether to offer another battle on the hills outside Moscow, the religious capital of Russia, but realized that it was likely to destroy his already battered army and he therefore abandoned the city without a fight. Napoleon entered on 15 September, but found that it was a hollow triumph. Amid the looting and disorder, fires broke out and destroyed large parts of the city; many were started deliberately by Russian arsonists. Napoleon waited five weeks in the hope of securing peace, but Tsar Alexander I, who was at St Petersburg, his political capital, refused to negotiate while foreign troops remained on Russian soil.

After evacuating Moscow, Kutusov had circled round and established his army at a camp at Tarutino, 46 miles south-west of Moscow, where he reorganized and rein-forced it to over 100,000 men, so that he was now numerically superior to the forces that Napoleon had with him around Moscow. Kutusov's position covered the impor-tant Russian arsenal at Tula, 100 miles to the south of Moscow, and also threatened Viasma, an important depot in Napoleon's rear.

Napoleon had lost the initiative and almost exhausted his options. Cossack raids were constantly threatening his lines of communication. On 18 October, his cavalry under Marshal Joachim Murat was surprised by a sudden Russian attack and driven back. Next day, Napoleon left Moscow. He intended to break through to the more fertile provinces of southern Russia, but clashed indecisively with part of Kutusov's army at Malojaroslavets, 80 miles south-west of the city, on the 24th. He lost his nerve, decided not to fight his way through and instead retreated along his line of advance, shadowed and harassed by Kutusov.

On 3 November, the Russians attacked at Viasma. They were repulsed, but heavy snow began to fall two days later and Napoleon's troops continually had to repel Cossack raids and attempts to cut off stragglers or isolated detachments. The physical strain of the relentless retreat, the winter weather and the collapse of much of his logistics demoralized and all but destroyed his army.

When Napoleon reached Smolensk on 9 November, he had only 50,000 men left with him and was unable to halt there as he had planned. Its stores were insufficient to supply his army and he knew that additional Russian forces were advancing in a pincer move from the north and south to threaten his escape, while Kutusov pursued from the east.

Napoleon's army left Smolensk from the 12th onwards, but became strung out and this allowed the Russians to isolate the three rearmost corps. Napoleon halted tem-porarily at Krasnoë, 30 miles south-west of Smolensk, and used his Imperial Guard, which was still largely intact, to counter-attack the Russians, make them more cautious and enable two of his missing corps to rejoin him. The approximately 800 survivors of the final corps later fought and evaded their way to safety under Marshal Michel Ney, whom Napoleon dubbed 'the bravest of the brave'.

Even in the middle of the unfolding disaster, Napoleon remained unsubdued. One of his Imperial Guardsmen, Henri Ducor, described how Napoleon occasionally left his carriage and walked with his troops to encourage them:

> He walked on the ice between two files of grenadiers and sailors of the Guard, while leaning on a branch from a fir tree, with his greatcoat as grey as the Russian sky, his big gloves and his fur hat of green velvet, trimmed with astrakhan. His imperial face bore so much serenity and steadfastness that he made us doubt his and our misfortune. At Krasnoë, when he personally went

forward to meet the Russians, he noticed a grenadier who was stamping heavily on the ground nearby.

'Are you very cold, then?' he said to him.

'Sire, since you mention it, I'm not bad.'

'Yet you still have a way to go: you must go to St Petersburg.'

'Well then, Sire, we'll become warmer again by marching forward.'

An even greater threat confronted Napoleon at the Beresina river, 120 miles to the west. An untimely thaw meant that the river was no longer frozen, but the bridge at Borisov had been broken and 34,000 Russian troops of Admiral Paul Chichagov's Army of the Danube had arrived from the south and were on the far bank. Another 30,000 Russians under General Ludwig von Wittgenstein were descending from the north, while Kutusov had a further 65,000 men.

By this stage, Napoleon had no more than 25,000 troops fit to fight, along with thousands more stragglers. Yet he managed to escape the trap. First, he skilfully diverted Chichagov's attention and then secured a bridgehead 8 miles to the north-west of Borisov, at the village of Studianka. Here, his pontoniers under General Baron Jean-Baptiste Eblé sacrificed their lives working in the icy river to build two trestle bridges, which enabled the army to begin crossing on 26 November. Napoleon's forces repulsed Russian attacks on both banks of the Beresina on the 28th, but many men died in a stampede when artillery fire struck a mob of stragglers and caused hordes of men to be pushed into the river by the panic-stricken crowd after a bridge broke. Thousands more stragglers had to be abandoned on the east bank when the bridges were burned on the morning of the 29th to deny them to the Russians.

Napoleon had escaped capture and the total destruction of his forces, but saw his army completely fall apart in the following weeks as the cold intensified again. One of his officers described how:

> In this last phase of our retreat, the Old Guard was worthy of itself until the end, although death did not spare its old soldiers. The rest of the army was no more than a confused mass whose disarmed individuals left, marched and stopped when they felt like it. The indiscipline had passed all limits. No more leaders, no more subordinates: everything was levelled. Our excessive miseries had made men forget not only the military laws that had been so respected before, but also those of civilization.

On 5 December, Napoleon left his army and returned to Paris on the 18th. He needed to reassert his authority and calm nerves in the city, where in his absence a political opponent, General Claude François de Malet, had attempted a coup d'état on 23 October. Claiming that Napoleon had died in Russia and brandishing forged authorization from the Senate, Malet was able to obtain troops and arrest the Minister of Police before being apprehended and shot. The incident revealed the shallow foundations of the Empire, for the authorities had blindly obeyed Malet instead of rallying to Napoleon's son and heir, the King of Rome. Napoleon had demanded passive obedience rather than initiative from his servants and, since he had relied largely on the cynical use of bribery and intimidation, he had secured little genuine loyalty for his dynasty.

On 14 December, Marshal Ney, the hero of the retreat, crossed the Niemen river into East Prussia with the rearguard.

Central Europe: 1813

The retreat from Moscow is remembered today as the most famous military disaster in history. But it did not inevitably lead to Napoleon's downfall, even though it shook his hold on occupied Europe and, in particular, crippled his cavalry for a year because of the difficulty in replacing so many horses and trained riders. He was able to raise a fresh army by the middle of April 1813, using conscripts, veterans withdrawn from Spain and men from depots, naval formations and units from the interior of France such as the National Guard. King Frederick William III of Prussia only hesitantly defected to join the Russians and declare war on Napoleon on 12 March. Austria withdrew from her alliance with Napoleon, but for the moment remained neutral. The Russians themselves had suffered severe losses in 1812, not least during their pursuit of Napoleon's army from Moscow, and some of their commanders, including Kutusov, were reluctant to continue the war and suffer further casualties, as Napoleon's fall was likely to be of less benefit to Russia than to other powers, particularly Britain.

Thus, in the spring of 1813, Napoleon had to face armies from only Prussia, Russia and Sweden in central Europe and actually enjoyed an advantage of numbers over them. General Wittgenstein became the Allied commander-in-chief after the death of the sixty-seven-year-old Kutusov on 28 April, but was a mediocre general and found himself hindered by the presence and interference of the Allied monarchs, especially Tsar Alexander I.

Napoleon returned to central Europe from Paris and reached Erfurt on 25 April. He united his new army with the survivors of the Russian campaign and advanced eastwards on Leipzig, hoping to outflank the Allied armies and pin them against the neutral Austrian frontier. But on 2 May, Wittgenstein attacked the southern flank of his advance near the town of Lützen. Napoleon hurriedly concentrated his army to meet the attack, and calculated on having superior numbers descending on the Allies from three sides by the end of the day. But until then, he had to fight hard to contain their assaults. Napoleon rarely exposed himself more to danger than on this day and personally rallied many of his conscripts who were falling back in confusion. Major Ernst von Odeleben, a Saxon officer serving as a topographical adviser on his staff, wrote:

> His presence filled the troops with enthusiasm, although the majority of Ney's corps consisted only of young conscripts who were perhaps going into action for the first time. Almost every wounded man who passed before Napoleon greeted him with the customary cheer. Even those who had lost a limb and who would die in a few hours, paid him this homage.

Lieutenant Pierre Robinaux of the 139th Regiment of Line Infantry recalled how:

> Napoleon and his entire suite appeared among our masses. Despite the shots that were falling on us, he nonetheless stopped in the centre, where he asked our colonel: 'Which regiment is this?'
>   'Sire, it is the 139th Line.'
>   'What have you done with your eagle [standard]?'

'Sire, it is in a safe place.'

The Emperor immediately said: 'Rally your regiment – the battle is ours.'

At the same time, one of his guards was struck by a cannonball and fell dead beside him. I do not know if the Emperor even noticed it, for he was in conversation, while taking from time to time a pinch of snuff.

By the end of the Battle of Lützen, Napoleon had driven the Allies back, but without inflicting a decisive defeat. He followed them as they retreated 100 miles eastwards to a new position at Bautzen. Here, he fought a second battle on 20–1 May, but his plan to smash the Allies miscarried when Marshal Ney, ordered to descend on their right wing, failed to press forward and cut their line of retreat. The Allies again withdrew, but Napoleon lacked the cavalry to pursue effectively.

By 1 June, Napoleon had reached Breslau, but was short of food and ammunition and had too many of his men sick to risk another major battle. He was also concerned by the possibility that Austria would abandon her neutrality and attack his lines of communication, which were dangerously over-extended and within striking distance north of her frontier. In fact, both sides had become too exhausted to continue the campaign and on 4 June they signed an armistice at Pleischwitz, as a result of which, and a subsequent extension, hostilities were not to resume until 17 August.

Napoleon used the summer to reorganize and expand his army, but its quality was reduced as his cadres of experienced men had been sapped by casualties and swamped by an influx of young, weak and poorly trained conscripts. He rejected peace terms offered by Russia, Prussia and Austria at a conference at Prague, as they would have entailed surrendering his control of central Europe. Yet within four months, he would be forced to retreat from Germany anyway after suffering another disaster and by then he could not expect such favourable terms.

The Allies benefited more than Napoleon from the two-month truce and were now joined by Austria, which declared war on 12 August. When hostilities resumed a few days later, Napoleon had 375,000 men available for active operations. In contrast, the Allies had 435,000 troops, with reinforcements arriving later. Never before had Napoleon been pitted simultaneously against Austria, Prussia, Russia and Sweden. Despite their disagreements and often-conflicting war aims, the Allied monarchs and commanders now knew how to counter Napoleon's art of war. They fielded three armies, arranged around him in a semi-circle: the Army of the North (110,000 men) under the Crown Prince of Sweden; the Army of Silesia (95,000) under Blücher to the east; and the main Allied force, the Army of Bohemia (240,000) under Prince Karl von Schwarzenberg to the south. Under a plan agreed at the Trachenburg conference, the Allies would avoid battle with Napoleon in person unless they enjoyed an overwhelming numerical superiority. If he advanced against one of their armies, it would withdraw, while the others attacked the secondary, detached forces that covered his flanks and rear.

This strategy forced Napoleon to react to developments, thereby depriving him of the strategic initiative and wearing down his army in constant marching to meet a succession of threats. He could not be everywhere in person and lacked enough subordinates sufficiently capable of commanding detached armies beyond his immediate supervision. 'The worst feature of the situation is the lack of confidence of the

NAPOLEON'S 1813 CAMPAIGN

Situation in mid-August 1813

generals,' he complained on 22 August. 'Whenever I am absent they imagine the enemy are in large numbers.'

Napoleon initially based his operations on the city of Dresden, the capital of his ally, the King of Saxony. There, he occupied a central position between his opponents and hoped to manoeuvre and defeat each of them in turn. First, he thrust eastwards against Blücher, his most energetic opponent, who had advanced from Silesia. Napoleon forced him to retreat, but was unable to bring him to battle and had to break off the pursuit and return to save Dresden from the advance of Schwarzenberg's Army of Bohemia.

As Napoleon approached Dresden, he planned to cross the Elbe river 10 miles south-east of the city and cut Schwarzenberg's line of retreat. This encircling man-oeuvre would probably have won a crushing victory, but Napoleon had to abandon the scheme on the evening of 25 August, after learning that the garrison of Dresden could not hold out for more than another twenty-four hours and needed direct support. He therefore diverted his army to the city on the 26th and personally arrived in the morning, to be greeted by the relieved inhabitants, who were terrified by the prospect of the Allied troops storming it. 'Napoleon is here!' they exclaimed. 'Things will soon change now!'

Late that afternoon, as the Army of Bohemia attacked the city's suburbs, Napoleon ordered his army to break out of Dresden. The attacks from the city gates were spearheaded by units of the Imperial Guard and drove the Allies back to the heights 1 mile to the south.

Napoleon resumed the battle in pouring rain on the 27th. By mid-afternoon, he had used his cavalry to destroy the Allied left wing, which was isolated on the west bank of the Weisseritz river. Schwarzenberg ordered a retreat and fell back to Bohemia, but suffered further losses during this demoralizing withdrawal along poor quality roads and with inadequate supplies.

Napoleon had won a major victory at Dresden and captured at least 13,000 men, but its impact was reduced by three successive defeats suffered by his subordinates. On 23 August, Marshal Nicolas Oudinot, who had been sent against the Prussian capital, Berlin, 100 miles north of Dresden, was drubbed by the Army of the North at Grossbeeren. Three days later, Marshal Jacques Macdonald's army containing Blücher was routed at the Katzbach river. The losses suffered by these two marshals amounted to 23,000 men and 126 guns. Then, during the pursuit of Schwarzenberg, General Dominique Vandamme's corps had the misfortune to become trapped in the mountains at Kulm and lost its commander, half its men and all its artillery in fighting its way out.

In response to these setbacks, Napoleon tried to regain the initiative by ordering Marshal Ney to try again to take Berlin. The result was a further defeat on 6 September, with Ney losing 24,000 men and eighty guns at Dennewitz. Napoleon repeatedly found himself unable to inflict a decisive defeat on the Allied armies and could not devise an effective strategy to resolve this problem. Early in September, he moved against the Army of Silesia once more, only to see it avoid battle as before. He then advanced southwards from Dresden against the Army of Bohemia, again fruitlessly. After that, he pulled all his forces back to the west bank of the Elbe and waited for the Allies to make the next move.

Napoleon's position at Dresden was becoming untenable. The city lay only 20 miles north of the Austrian frontier and too far to the east. He knew that his supplies were running low and that the Allies would become stronger as they received reinforcements, whereas he himself could not easily replace his steadily mounting losses. Cossacks and irregular troops were raiding his rear areas and even caused his brother Jérôme, the King of Westphalia in northern Germany, to evacuate his capital.

On 26 September, the Allies began a coordinated offensive designed to bypass Napoleon's army and converge on the city of Leipzig to the west in order to unite their forces, cut him off from France and use their combined weight of numbers to inflict a crushing defeat. Napoleon belatedly left Dresden on 7 October in response to this developing threat, but left 30,000 men to garrison the city. He was reluctant to cut his losses or abandon politically important cities or territories for fear of damaging his prestige, yet by refusing to do so he weakened his army at a time when he needed every man.

The Allies were able to close in on Napoleon, with the Army of Bohemia advancing against Leipzig from the south, while their other two armies concentrated to the north of the city. Napoleon now had little chance of manoeuvring and defeating them piecemeal. The four-day battle that ensued around Leipzig (16–19 October) was an attritional struggle decided by weight of numbers. Napoleon with his army of 190,000 men vainly defied a total Allied force that eventually numbered 300,000 men and 1,500 guns. The outcome was decided on the first day, when Napoleon attacked the Army of

Bohemia to the south, but failed to defeat it before the Allies could deploy the full weight of all their armies. Already, Blücher's Army of Silesia had begun driving back the forces that Napoleon had deployed north of the city.

Both sides regrouped on the 17th. Napoleon wasted the day, failing either to retreat while he could or to renew the attack on Schwarzenberg. Then, on the 18th, the Allies mounted attacks around Napoleon's perimeter, with the Army of the North joining the offensive in the afternoon. Although they failed to break through, they forced Napoleon to realize that he could not postpone retreat in the face of such unfavourable odds. On the next day, the 19th, his defeat turned into a disaster when some drunken engineers blew up the single bridge over the Elster river too early, leaving his rearguard trapped on the east bank.

Napoleon had lost 68,000 men killed, wounded or captured, besides 260 guns. The Allies had also suffered heavily, taking over 54,000 casualties, but could absorb these losses more readily given their numerical superiority. Strategically, the catastrophe cost Napoleon central Europe and forced him to withdraw to the frontiers of France. His German satellite states, including the largest, Bavaria, had begun to desert him even before the battle and some Saxon and Württemberg units had gone over to the Allies while it was being fought. The Kingdom of Westphalia, which had been created from an amalgamation of territories, now collapsed and Holland, which had been incorporated into France, would rise in revolt in November. The cycle of imperial expansion, in which Napoleon had made conquered territories pay for further wars, had gone into reverse, for as his Empire disintegrated, so too did his sources of man-power, finance and supplies.

The Allies failed to harry Napoleon with an effective pursuit as he retreated south-westwards from Leipzig. But on 30 October, as he neared the town of Hanau 20 miles east of the Rhine, he was confronted by an Austro-Bavarian army under General Count Karl von Wrede that had advanced from the south and barred the road. Napoleon ordered forward his Guard artillery, formed a massed battery of fifty guns and hurled Wrede aside.

Napoleon's surviving men crossed the Rhine at Mainz on 2 November. They were back in France, but were further reduced in number by an outbreak of typhus.

The Defence of France: 1814

For the second time within a year, Napoleon had to raise a new army after suffering a disaster. He had brought only 56,000 men back across the Rhine after Leipzig, as a result of both the losses he had suffered in the 1813 campaign and the large numbers of men he had left tied up in besieged garrisons in central Europe, such as Hamburg where Marshal Davout was isolated with 30,000 troops. Napoleon was now reduced to defending France itself, for apart from Belgium, northern Italy and pockets of territory, he had lost his Empire.

By the start of January 1814, Napoleon's enemies had already penetrated on to French soil. In the south, Wellington had crossed the Pyrenees and reached the city of Bayonne on the Atlantic coast, while east of Paris the two main Allied armies under Blücher and Schwarzenberg had passed the Rhine.

Napoleon had secondary, detached, armies defending the south-west of France, Lyons, northern Italy and the Low Countries. He himself concentrated his main field army of over 85,000 at Châlons-sur-Marne, 90 miles east of Paris, but many of his troops were raw, teenage conscripts who barely knew how to use a musket and they would be outnumbered by Blücher and Schwarzenberg, who had over 160,000 men immediately available. Many of Napoleon's senior subordinates were tired of war and ready for a negotiated peace and their war weariness was reflected by that of the French people. His own brother-in-law, King Joachim Murat of Naples, abandoned him and signed a treaty with Austria on 11 January in order to safeguard his throne.

Napoleon had again ignored moderate peace terms when they were offered to him in November 1813. He believed that he could gain more after inflicting military defeats on Blücher and Schwarzenberg and was confident of being able to do so, provided he attacked them separately so that he did not have to face the overwhelming numerical superiority of their combined armies. On 29 January, he attacked Blücher at Brienne-le-Château, where he had attended the military school thirty years earlier. He won a tactical victory, but merely drove Blücher back to unite with Schwarzenberg. Blücher counter-attacked on 1 February at La Rothière, 4 miles south-east of Brienne. Napoleon contained him and then broke contact and withdrew, but lost fifty guns.

The Battle of La Rothière made the Allies, especially Blücher, overconfident. They separated again and advanced on Paris along different routes, which made it easier to feed their armies, but more difficult to support each other. Napoleon concentrated his army in a central position and then counter-attacked into the southern flank of Blücher's advance. In five days, he inflicted four defeats on Russian and Prussian elements of his Army of Silesia, at Champaubert (10 February), Montmirail (11th), Château-Thierry (12th) and Vauchamps (14th).

Exuberant at his string of victories, Napoleon wrote to his Minister of Police on the 12th:

> You will have learnt the results of the Battle of Montmirail and of the action of Château-Thierry. Russia's best army has been destroyed. My Old Guard infantry and my Guard cavalry have performed miracles; the [Guard] dragoons have distinguished themselves. I had engaged little more than 2,000 men of my Old Guard. What they have done can be compared only with the novels of chivalry and with the warriors of those times in which, by the impact of their armour and the deftness of their horses, one of them was able to fight 300 or 400. The enemy must have been remarkably terrified.

After detaching a covering force to watch Blücher, Napoleon then moved south-westwards against Schwarzenberg's army, which had advanced down the Seine valley to within 30 miles of Paris. His forces encountered Schwarzenberg's right wing at Nangis (17 February) and drove it back over the Seine river. To complete his counter-stroke, Napoleon attacked one of Schwarzenberg's subordinates, the Crown Prince of Württemberg, at Montereau on the 18th and seized intact the town's important bridges over the Seine and Yonne rivers with a cavalry charge led by General Count Claude Pajol. These victories averted a panic in the capital and forced Schwarzenberg to withdraw 50 miles eastwards to Troyes.

Napoleon again refused to consider a negotiated peace following these successes. By nature, he found it difficult to treat with equals instead of dominating everyone. He also doubted that all the Allies, especially Britain, genuinely wanted peace with him

NAPOLEON'S 1814 CAMPAIGN

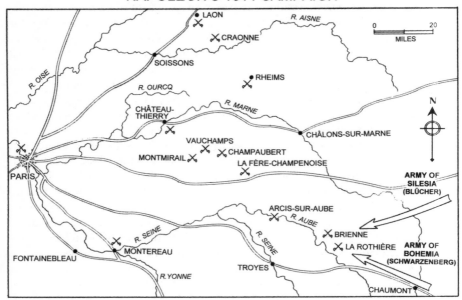

still on the throne and he wanted to secure a stronger bargaining position. He made this clear in a sarcastic letter to his brother Joseph on the 18th:

> Prince Schwarzenberg has just shown signs of life. He has just sent a negotiator to request an armistice. It is difficult to be so cowardly. . . . At the first check, these wretches fall to their knees! Luckily, Prince Schwarzenberg's ADC was not let in, so I have received only his letter and I will take my time in replying to it. I will grant no armistice until they have been flushed out from my land. According to my information, everything has changed in the Allied camp.

But Napoleon would be unable to defy the superior numbers of the Allies indefinitely. He had won his recent battles at an unsustainable cost in casualties and was wearing down his army with relentless marching. He could only hope that the continued campaign would cause at least one of the Allied powers to become exhausted and withdraw from the war, just as the death of Tsarina Elizabeth had caused Russia to leave the coalition against Frederick the Great of Prussia during the Seven Years' War (1756–63). But this became unlikely on 9 March, when the Allies consolidated their coalition by signing the Treaty of Chaumont, by which they agreed their war aims and undertook not to make peace separately with Napoleon.

On 27 February, Napoleon moved to counter a renewed advance by Blücher's Army of Silesia, but was unable to inflict a decisive defeat as he chased him 40 miles northwards across the Marne and Aisne rivers. When Blücher occupied a strong position across the top of the Chemin des Dames ridge north of the Aisne, Napoleon attacked and drove him from it, but lost at least 5,400 men in doing so.

Blücher had now collected two corps of reinforcements and gave battle again 9 miles further north, at the hilltop city of Laon, where he deployed his 90,000 men and checked Napoleon's army of 36,500 in a two–day battle on 9–10 March. At the end of the first day, Napoleon's detached right wing under Marshal Auguste Marmont, which was operating on the eastern side of Laon, was surprised and smashed in a night attack. Napoleon stood his ground on the 10th, but then broke contact and withdrew. Napoleon blatantly played down the defeat in a letter to his brother Joseph on 11 March, but could not ignore the way the constant marching and fighting were draining his troops:

> I have reconnoitred the enemy's position at Laon. It was too strong to be attacked without heavy losses, so I decided to return to Soissons. The enemy would probably have evacuated Laon out of fear of being attacked there, if the Duke of Ragusa [Marmont] had not had a little action and behaved like a second lieutenant. The enemy has suffered enormous losses; yesterday he made five attacks on the village of Clacy and was repulsed each time. The Young Guard is melting away like snow. The Old Guard bears up. Much of my Guard cavalry also melts away ...

On 13 March, Napoleon attacked a Russian corps and recaptured the city of Rheims, but it proved to be his last victory of the campaign. He then moved south to counter a renewed advance by Schwarzenberg, but was checked by superior numbers at the Battle of Arcis-sur-Aube on 20–1 March and disengaged after losing 4,000 men.

After falling back, Napoleon boldly decided to strike eastwards with his army of 40,000 into the Allied rear to threaten Schwarzenberg's communications. He calculated on being able to increase his strength by collecting garrisons from fortresses left isolated by the Allied invasion and also on intimidating the usually cautious Schwarzenberg into retreating.

But the Allied high command discovered Napoleon's plan when Cossacks intercepted a letter from him to the Empress Marie-Louise. They decided to ignore the threat to their rear, unite their armies and advance on Paris. Only 26,000 French troops under Marshals Marmont and Mortier were available to defend the city, supported by second-line troops such as National Guardsmen. The two marshals vigorously defended the hills overlooking Paris on 30 March in the bloodiest battle of the entire campaign. But once driven from the heights, they had no choice but to seek an armistice and evacuate the capital. It was the first time that Paris had fallen to a foreign army since the fifteenth century.

Meanwhile, Napoleon had reached Saint-Dizier, 120 miles to the east, but realized that he had failed to divert the Allies. He hurriedly marched back to save his capital, but was too late and, when he decided to try and retake it, was forced by his subordinates to recognize the futility of further fighting, which threatened both civil war and the destruction of the city. Already, on 2 April, the Senate had declared that Napoleon was deposed and a provisional government had been formed. Napoleon abdicated, at first in favour of his son on 4 April and then unconditionally on the 6th. Under the Treaty of Fontainebleau (12 April), he was exiled to the Mediterranean island of Elba, which he was to rule as an independent principality. The Bourbons were recalled to France, with the brother of the last king, who had died under the guillotine in 1793, taking the throne as Louis XVIII.

Exile and Return to Power

Napoleon reached Elba on 4 May, where he was joined by 700 men of his Imperial Guard. But his position was financially insecure, for the Bourbons did not pay the pension stipulated under the Treaty of Fontainebleau, and his wife and son were prevented from joining him by his father-in-law, the Austrian Emperor. He noted the unpopularity of the restored Bourbon monarchy, which had to contend with post-war problems, including the reduction of the army to a peace footing and the reuniting of a weary and politically divided nation.

On 26 February 1815, after less than ten months on the island, Napoleon sailed from Elba in an audacious bid to regain power. He landed near Cannes on the southern coast of France on 1 March and marched on Paris with his small escort of Imperial Guardsmen. He issued a proclamation to the French army, calling on the soldiers to desert the Bourbons and return to his side and blaming his earlier defeats on treason:

> Soldiers! We have not been beaten. . . . Victory will advance at the charge, the eagle with the national colours will fly from steeple to steeple to the towers of Notre-Dame [in Paris] and then you will be able to boast of what you have done and of being the liberators of the fatherland.
>
> In your old age, you will be surrounded and esteemed by your fellow citizens and they will listen to you with respect as you describe your great deeds. You will be able to say with pride: 'And I, too, I was part of this Grand Army' which entered the walls of Vienna twice, and those of Berlin, Madrid and Moscow and which delivered Paris from the stain imprinted there by treason and the enemy's presence. Honour to these brave soldiers, the glory of the fatherland; and eternal shame to these criminal Frenchmen, whatever the social rank in which they happened to be born, who for twenty-five years fought alongside the foreigners to tear open the heart of the fatherland.

Napoleon's boldness was decisive, for he paralysed the Bourbons with fear and won over a succession of units to his side. At the Laffrey defile south of Grenoble, he met a battalion of the 5th Regiment of Line Infantry. 'Soldiers of the 5th, do you not recognize me?' he called. 'If any of you wishes to fire on his Emperor, here I am!'

The men dissolved into cheers.

On 20 March, Napoleon reached the Tuileries palace, a day after Louis XVIII had left Paris for exile in the United Netherlands. Count Antoine Marie Lavallette, the Director-General of the postal services, recalled:

> Hardly had he stepped out on to the ground than there was a shout of 'Long live the Emperor!' It was like a thunderclap and came from the half-pay officers who were squashed to the point of suffocation in the entrance hall and packed the staircase. The Emperor was wearing his famous grey overcoat. I went towards him and the Duke of Vicenza [General de Caulaincourt] shouted to me: 'In God's name, get in front and clear a way forward for him.'

He began to climb the staircase. I went one step in front, walking backwards and watching him with deep emotion. My eyes were bathed in tears and in my excitement I repeatedly exclaimed: 'What! It's you, it's you! At last it's you!'

As for him, he walked up slowly, with his eyes closed, his hands stretched in front, like a blind man, and his happiness revealed only by his smile. When he reached the landing of the first floor, the ladies wanted to go and approach him, but a flood of officers rushed from the floor above across their path and would have crushed them had they been less agile. At last, the Emperor was able to enter his apartments; the doors were closed again with difficulty and the crowd dispersed, happy at having glimpsed him.

Napoleon immediately had to raise an army to resist a powerful Allied coalition. The rest of Europe had declared him an outlaw and planned to invade France in the summer. Napoleon decided to strike a pre-emptive blow against two of their armies, which were assembling in the Low Countries. Their commanders were among the foremost generals of the age: Field Marshal the Duke of Wellington and the Prussian Field Marshal Prince Gebhard Leberecht von Blücher.

Part Two

Wellington

Chapter 6

Formative Years

Wellington was born in Ireland in the spring of 1769 as Arthur Wesley, the third surviving son of Garret Wesley, first Earl of Mornington, and Anne Hill, the daughter of Arthur Hill, Viscount Dungannon. His family belonged to the Anglo–Irish Protestant Ascendancy, the minority caste based at Dublin that dominated the mass of Catholic Irish peasants. This background fostered self-reliance, strength of character and a natural authority. Yet Arthur was slow to demonstrate these qualities or develop his latent talents. Napoleon, who was born in the same year, became a general at twenty-four after helping to recapture the French port of Toulon in December 1793, at a time when Arthur was still a lieutenant-colonel who had yet to see active service.

'Food for powder and nothing more'

Arthur's formal education as a boy was haphazard and contributed little to his later success, in contrast to Napoleon's logical progression through some of the best educational institutions in France. After attending the Diocesan School at Trim in County Meath in Ireland and then a preparatory school at Chelsea in London, he spent three undistinguished years at Eton. The popular notion that he later exclaimed that the Battle of Waterloo was won on the school's playing fields is a myth. He was solitary and introverted, like Napoleon at Brienne. He preferred to play by himself, but had occasional fights, one of which he provoked by throwing stones at a boy swimming in the Thames river. He had inherited his father's love of music and played well on the fiddle, but showed few signs of any other ability. He was shy, idle and often unwell.

Like Napoleon, Arthur lost his father at a young age. The Earl of Mornington's death in 1781 strained the family's finances and, three years later, Arthur was withdrawn from Eton at the age of fifteen and taken by his mother to Brussels, where he received private tuition from a barrister called Louis Goubert. Arthur's mother was a formidable woman, imbued, like Napoleon's, with common sense, but, unlike her, lacking in maternal affection. She bluntly decided that her 'awkward son Arthur' was fit only for a military career ('food for powder and nothing more') and in 1786 sent him to the Royal Academy of Equitation at Angers in pre-Revolutionary France, which would serve as a finishing school before he joined the British army. It is one of the ironies of history that Wellington should have been taught at a French academy, but at the time it was not unusual for young Britons keen on a military career to seek preparation in superior institutions abroad. Arthur spent a year at Angers, where he learnt horse riding and fencing, pursued his academic studies and mastered French, while losing much of his former shyness. 'He really is a very charming young man,' wrote his mother, 'never did I see such a change for the better in any body.'

The Wesley family fortunes rested on Richard, the academically brilliant eldest brother who already looked set for an outstanding political career. Indeed, although relations between the two were later strained, it was primarily to Richard that Arthur owed his start in life and he would not fully emerge from his shadow until 1812, when Richard wrecked his career with an ill-judged resignation as Foreign Secretary. Richard sought a suitable position for Arthur and wrote to the Lord Lieutenant of Ireland: 'Let me remind you of a younger brother of mine, whom you were so kind as to take into consideration for a commission in the army – He is here at this moment and perfectly idle. It is a matter of indifference to me what commission he gets so long as he gets it soon.'

In March 1787, Arthur was gazetted to an ensigncy in the 73rd (Highland) Regiment of Foot. In the British army of the time, it was possible for ambitious young men with sufficient wealth and influence to purchase successive steps up the officer hierarchy to the rank of lieutenant-colonel, after which promotion was solely by seniority (the length of time served in a rank). The system had its faults but allowed keen young men to come to the fore instead of stagnating for years as a subaltern. Arthur in the six years between March 1787 and September 1793 rose five steps, from ensign to lieutenant-colonel, in seven different regiments. He saw little actual service with these units, for at the same time he was engaged in political and other pursuits, in much the way that the young Napoleon was able to spend long periods of leave in Corsica. Family influence secured his appointment in November 1787 as ADC to the Lord Lieutenant of Ireland and his five and a half years in this role gave him invaluable experience at the centre of power in Dublin. He was also elected in April 1790 to represent the family seat of Trim in the Irish House of Commons and held it, until the dissolution of June 1795, to the satisfaction of Richard, who praised his judgement, amiable manners, equanimity and firmness. (The Irish Parliament would be abolished under the Act of Union of 1800, which united Britain and Ireland following the unsuccessful rebellion of 1798.)

Arthur was already outgrowing his youthful idleness as he assumed more responsibilities. As he later recalled, he 'was not so young as not to know that since I had undertaken a profession I had better try to understand it'. Further impetus was given in the spring of 1793 when his bid to marry Kitty Pakenham was rejected by her brother, the third Baron Longford. The rebuff, which was due to his financial insecurity and apparent lack of prospects, apparently made him give up his more frivolous pursuits, burn his violin and dedicate himself to his career.

Baptism of Fire: the Low Countries, 1794–5

By now, the Revolution had broken out in France and plunged Europe into two decades of conflict. The French went to war with Austria and Prussia in 1792 and occupied most of the Austrian Netherlands (present-day Belgium). For Britain, this was a key region both strategically and commercially, and relations worsened with the execution of King Louis XVI on 21 January 1793. After the French declared war on Britain on 1 February, the Duke of York was sent with an army to help the Austrians regain Flanders.

In September 1793, Arthur became Lieutenant-Colonel of the 33rd (or the 1st Yorkshire West Riding) Regiment of Foot and in June 1794 sailed with his regiment from Cork in southern Ireland to help reinforce the Duke of York. The Allies had driven the French back in 1793, but retreated from the Austrian Netherlands after defeats at Tourcoing and Fleurus in May and June 1794. The 33rd initially landed at Ostend, but then re-embarked as the French approached and moved by sea to Antwerp in order to join the rest of the Duke of York's army.

By the end of July 1794, the British, abandoned by their Austrian allies and now heavily outnumbered, had withdrawn into Holland. Arthur saw action for the first time on 15 September. The Duke of York ordered Major-General Ralph Abercromby to retake Boxtel, an important advance post near Bois-le-Duc. Abercromby pushed back the French pickets, but retreated after encountering strong French units. As he withdrew, some of his formations became disordered by the difficult terrain. Arthur saw French cavalry advancing to exploit the situation and coolly deployed the 33rd in line across their path. He allowed the disordered British troops to pass and then closed his files and repulsed the French with a volley at close range.

The Duke of York subsequently withdrew to a new defence line on the north bank of the Waal river. Arthur described on 20 December how:

> At present the French keep us in a perpetual state of alarm; we turn out once, sometimes twice, every night; the officers and men are harassed to death, and if we are not relieved, I believe there will be very few of the latter remaining shortly. I have not had the clothes off my back for a long time, and generally spend the greater part of the night upon the bank of the river, notwithstanding which I have entirely got rid of that disorder which was near killing me at the close of the summer campaign. Although the French annoy us much at night, they are very entertaining during the daytime; they are perpetually chattering with our officers and soldiers, and dance the *carmagnol* upon the opposite bank whenever we desire them; but occasionally the spectators on our side are interrupted in the middle of a dance by a cannon ball from theirs.

Arthur was involved in several actions during the winter, for the French were able to attack over the frozen rivers. The British army had to resume its retreat on 15 January 1795 and in April was evacuated by sea from the mouth of the Weser river in northern Germany. Arthur had already returned to England on leave early in March and was so disenchanted by his first experience of campaigning that he nearly abandoned his military career. Fortunately, his applications for alternative, and more lucrative, civil posts proved fruitless and he returned to the 33rd Regiment in July.

Arthur later claimed that: 'I learnt more by seeing our own faults, and the defects of our system in the campaign of Holland, than anywhere else.' Above all, he had noted the damage done by inadequate and disorganized logistics to the discipline, health, morale and cohesion of an army. He also believed that senior officers should have visited their outposts regularly to see the situation for themselves. In short, he later recalled, 'I learnt what one ought not to do, and that is always something.' But it is easy to exaggerate the British army's failings in the Low Countries, particularly as Arthur had missed the more successful early stages of the campaign and instead had witnessed the difficulties caused by the bitter winter of 1794–5. The sudden expansion of Britain's small peacetime army to meet the challenges of war had inevitably resulted in problems, but these would be overcome as the army gained experience and underwent reform. The outcome of the campaign owed more to the numerical inferiority of the

British, and inadequate support from their allies, than to internal failings. The individual regiments had proved their superior quality in action and had won some significant victories over the French. Arthur himself stated: 'No one knew anything of the management of an army, though many of the regiments were excellent: the 33rd was in as good order as possible.' It was on the soundness of the British regimental system that Arthur would build his later success in the Peninsula and at Waterloo.

Chapter 7

India, 1797–1805

Since the start of the war, Britain had also been fighting the French in the West Indies. These islands produced sugar, coffee and cotton and were crucial to Britain's trade and finances and hence to her war effort. But they were notoriously lethal and thousands of troops were carried off by yellow fever every year. A series of reverses resulted in 33,000 British reinforcements being sent to the West Indies in the autumn of 1795 under Major-General Abercromby. They included Arthur and the 33rd, but fortunately the ships carrying the regiment were twice driven back to England by storms. By the time the 33rd was ready to sail once more, its destination had been changed to India.

Arthur was promoted to the rank of colonel in May 1796. His eight-month passage by sea to India, including a break at the Cape of Good Hope, was a crucial preparatory period in his career, for he took with him an extensive library and set aside a couple of hours each day to study, a rule he kept throughout his life. In July 1801, he wrote:

> I know but one recipe for good health in this country [India], and that is to live moderately, to drink little or no wine, to use exercise, to keep the mind employed, and, if possible, to keep in good humour with the world. The last is most difficult, for, as you have often observed, there is scarcely a good-tempered man in India.

His library was particularly strong on the history, administration and wars of India and also contained books of a wider scope, for example on economics, law, philosophy and theology, but little light reading. He studied the history of war, including Julius Caesar's *Commentaries* and the works of Frederick the Great, Marshal de Saxe and the military theorist Major-General Lloyd and, for more recent events, read the writings of the French Republican General Charles Dumouriez, who had fought the Austrians in the Low Countries before deserting in 1793.

Arthur was, in fact, compensating for something that, to his lasting regret, he never had. He believed that officers had double the chance of becoming first-rate soldiers if in addition to a military education they had the broader outlook that was cultivated by a university. 'I would give more than I can mention,' he later remarked, 'that I had had a university education.'

Arthur had matured from an idle and unprepossessing youth into a hardworking and well-read young officer. He had been a late developer, but compensated for this by the systematic, determined and comprehensive way in which he educated himself through intensive reading. His steadier development contributed to his common sense and his awareness of the limits to what was possible, qualities in which Napoleon became increasingly deficient.

Arthur brought to India a willingness to learn, painstaking attention to detail and a thorough approach to problem-solving in which he would gather all available information before making well-reasoned judgements. He would automatically have a higher profile in India, where there were fewer than 4,000 Britons (not including enlisted soldiers and sailors) among a population of about 140 million. India offered more extensive and novel opportunities to develop his talents and exercise independent command than were available at home.

Arthur and the 33rd arrived in India in February 1797. The subcontinent consisted of a patchwork of native states, notably the loose Maratha Confederation of Hindu warlords in the north and centre and, in the south, two Muslim princes, the Nizam (or King) of Hyderabad and Tipoo Sultan of Mysore. The British East India Company had begun trading in this region in the early 1600s and had evolved from a commercial organization into a major power in its own right. It had three main territories, or presidencies: Madras on the east coast, Bombay on the west and, the most important of all, Bengal in the north-east. Each presidency had an army of native troops, or sepoys, commanded by European officers. The Company supplemented these forces by hiring units of the British army, such as Arthur's 33rd Regiment.

The supreme British executive in India was the Governor-General, based in Bengal, who was answerable both to the British Parliament through the Board of Control and to the stockholders of the Company through its Court of Directors. Corruption was widespread amongst the Company's servants and considerable riches and political influence were sometimes acquired, even by those who restricted themselves to legitimate means. But service in India could also be tedious and unhealthy and Europeans were more likely to die than make a fortune there.

The French had bitterly contested the British position in India until their defeat in the Seven Years' War (1756–63). The remaining French trading posts were occupied on the outbreak of war in 1793, but a potential threat remained, as French mercenaries were advising some native rulers and helping to train their units as disciplined formations using European drill.

Arthur was based initially at Calcutta in Bengal. He impressed the Governor-General, Sir John Shore, with his ability and common sense and advised him unofficially, while also engaged in his regimental duties. In August 1797, he sailed with the 33rd as part of an expedition to capture Manila in the Spanish-owned Philippines. Spain had been a French ally since October 1796, but lost her fleet at the Battle of Cape St Vincent on 14 February 1797, a defeat which increased the vulnerability of her colonies. However, the expedition was recalled after reaching Penang in what is now Malaysia, because of concern about the intentions of Tipoo of Mysore. Arthur returned to Calcutta in December and took three months' leave at the start of 1798 to visit Madras and acquaint himself with the local terrain and personnel, in anticipation of seeing active service there in a war against Tipoo.

Arthur's eldest brother, Richard, arrived at Calcutta in May as the new Governor-General. He was accompanied by another brother, Henry, as his private secretary and it was at this time that he changed the family name to Wellesley. The ambitious Richard was determined both to advance the interests of his country and make his family a politically influential force, much as the Bonapartes became under Napoleon's leadership. He gave Arthur heavy responsibilities and opportunities for advancement

WELLINGTON IN INDIA, 1797-1805

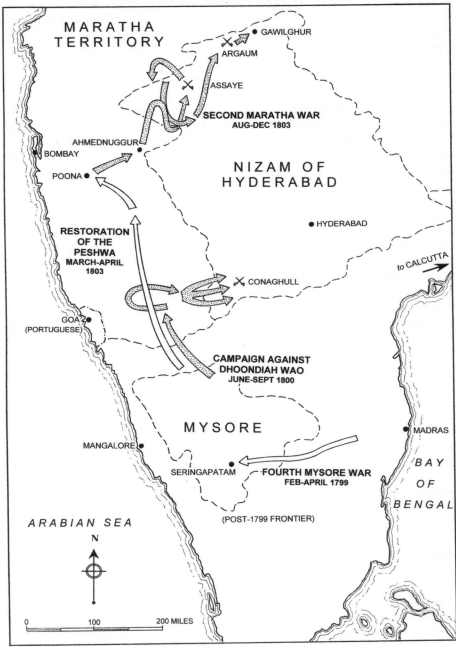

MARATHA
TERRITORY

GAWILGHUR

ARGAUM

ASSAYE

SECOND MARATHA WAR
AUG-DEC 1803

AHMEDNUGGUR

BOMBAY

POONA

NIZAM OF
HYDERABAD

HYDERABAD

RESTORATION
OF THE
PESHWA
MARCH-APRIL
1803

to CALCUTTA

CONAGHULL

GOA
(PORTUGUESE)

CAMPAIGN AGAINST
DHOONDIAH WAO
JUNE-SEPT 1800

MYSORE

MADRAS

MANGALORE

SERINGAPATAM

FOURTH MYSORE WAR
FEB-APRIL 1799

BAY

OF

BENGAL

(POST-1799 FRONTIER)

ARABIAN SEA

N

0   100   200 MILES

and undoubtedly ensured that he rose faster than he would otherwise have done. But Arthur's experience and skills would have ensured his eventual success under most governor-generals. Richard relied heavily on him for military and political advice and wrote in 1800: 'I employ you because I rely on your good sense, discretion, activity, and spirit. I cannot find all those qualities united in any other officer in India.'

Richard was intent on thwarting any French bid to undermine the British position. A French expedition under Napoleon landed in Egypt in 1798 and many Britons feared that India was his ultimate target. Richard believed that it was necessary to act offensively to forestall French attempts to help native powers. Britain had lost her American colonies as recently as 1783, following French intervention in the American War of Independence. The India Act of 1784 had declared territorial expansion in the subcontinent to be repugnant to the wish, the honour and the policy of Britain, but Richard pursued a more imperialistic policy, taking advantage of the distraction provided by the French Revolutionary wars and his distance from London (it took four to eight months for communications to arrive in the days of sail).

Richard skilfully exploited the disunity and mutual distrust of the native states. He extended British influence by using subsidiary treaties, under which Indian rulers paid for East India Company troops to protect them from their enemies. The British had hitherto used subsidiary treaties to secure satellite states for defensive purposes, but Richard turned them into a preliminary to using force against a third party. The first occasion was when he secured a subsidiary alliance with the Nizam of Hyderabad by exploiting his fear of his powerful neighbours, the Marathas and Tipoo of Mysore. The Nizam expelled his French advisers and in 1799 would join the British in a pre-emptive strike against the troublesome Tipoo.

Mysore

The British had already fought three wars against Mysore and had narrowly avoided the loss of Madras in the first two (1767–9 and 1780–4). In the third (1790–2), Lord Cornwallis had invaded Mysore and forced Tipoo to sue for peace. Tipoo hated the British and sought French help in recovering the territories he had been forced to cede. In 1798, the French Governor of the island of Mauritius in the Indian Ocean proclaimed an alliance between France and Mysore. The French had an interest in creating trouble for the British in India, but could not immediately support their threats with force. Nonetheless, the perceived threat was enough to trigger, and justify, a British pre-emptive strike against Tipoo.

Arthur played an important role in the preparations for this conflict, the Fourth Mysore War. He was involved in both the military and diplomatic groundwork at Madras, where he organized the main army of 21,000 men due to take the offensive from the east. Another army of 6,000 would invade Mysore from the west. In January 1799, Arthur handed over command of the main army to Lieutenant-General George Harris, the commander-in-chief at Madras, who praised his 'judicious and masterly arrangements in respect of supplies'.

War was declared on 22 February. Arthur was attached to an army supplied by the Nizam of Hyderabad and had effective command of it. Stiffened by the addition of the 33rd Regiment, it reinforced Harris's force and accompanied his advance. After two successful actions, Harris arrived before Tipoo's capital, Seringapatam, on 3 April.

Two days later, Arthur suffered a setback when ordered to clear enemy outposts from a clump of trees called Sultanpettah Tope so as to allow the siege to begin. The attack was made at night and was repulsed after the troops became hopelessly disordered as they contended with the darkness, enemy counter-attacks and the difficult terrain. Arthur was unable to control the action and returned to report his failure to Harris in considerable agitation. It had been a minor defeat, but taught him an important lesson: 'I have come to a determination; when in my power, never to suffer an attack to be made by night upon an enemy who is prepared and strongly posted, and whose posts have not been reconnoitred by daylight.'

The experience also contributed to his understanding of men who meant well, but made a mistake or temporarily lost their nerve. He later remarked that all soldiers broke at some stage and that he had no objection to them running to the rear so long as they came back again. Captain John Stepney Cowell, a Coldstream Guards officer who served under him in the Peninsula, added:

> No man however was more fair and considerate towards a first failure of others in a military attempt than Lord Wellington. A staff-officer, attached to head-quarters, informed me he had heard him declare that a man failing *once* (under certain circumstances) should not preclude his being tried again; and on one occasion he added, 'Where should I have been had I not had a second trial at Seringapatam?'

Next morning, Arthur again attacked and this time successfully cleared Sultan-pettah Tope. The siege of Seringapatam then went ahead and culminated in the storming of the city on 4 May. Tipoo died gallantly during the fighting. Arthur as commander of the reserve left in the trenches was not personally engaged, but was appointed Governor of the captured city, to the fury of Major-General David Baird who had led the storming and who was disappointed at not obtaining the post himself, though he lacked the necessary tact and patience. Half of Mysore was annexed and divided between the East India Company, the Nizam and the Marathas. The land-locked rump became a British subsidiary state under a restored Hindu dynasty in the person of a five-year-old rajah.

Harris withdrew his army in July, leaving Arthur in military command in Mysore and in control of the civil administration. Arthur worked closely with the Resident, Lieutenant-Colonel Barry Close, and Indian colleagues. For the first time, he had an independent command and he reported directly to his brother, the Governor-General. He exercised his new military and diplomatic responsibilities firmly but fairly. He waged successful counter-insurgency operations to pacify Mysore, the keynote being his campaign against a band of freebooters up to 40,000 strong under Dhoondiah Wao, the self-styled King of the Two Worlds (Heaven and Earth). Adventurers in India often used such claims of divine status, and the prospect of plunder, to gather thousands of followers. Prestige was all-important and it could be undermined by bold and aggressive action. Arthur relentlessly harried Dhoondiah and tried to head him off by dividing his own forces into several prongs. He meticulously organized his logistics to keep his force well supplied, disciplined and mobile. As a result, Dhoondiah's followers began to desert under the pressure. Arthur eventually caught up with him and overthrew his remaining men at Conaghull on 10 September 1800 with a decisive cavalry charge. Dhoondiah was slain, but the victorious Arthur made himself responsible for the dead man's four-year-old son and ensured that he had a good start in life.

In November 1800, Arthur was sent to Trincomalee in the island of Ceylon (now Sri Lanka) to organize an expedition of over 5,000 troops. It was intended either to destroy the French privateers operating from the island of Mauritius or to attack the rich colony of Batavia (Java) in the East Indies, whose Dutch masters were allied to France. The destination was finally switched to Egypt, which Napoleon had occupied in 1798. Napoleon himself had returned to France a year later, but had left his army behind. The British government wanted to evict the French, using a British army based in the Mediterranean under Sir Ralph Abercromby, seconded by the expedition from India which would land on the Red Sea coast.

Arthur expected to command the expedition, but was superseded in January 1801 by Major-General David Baird, who had protested vigorously at the prospect of being passed over once again in favour of the Governor-General's brother. Arthur bitterly resented his supersession, for although only a colonel he was confident of his capabilities and had organized the expeditionary force in the first place. The episode caused a temporary rift with his brother Richard, but Arthur resigned himself to accompanying the expedition as second-in-command, for, as he wrote: 'I am not quite satisfied with the manner in which I have been treated; however, I have lost neither my health, spirits, or temper. ... I have never had much value for the public spirit of any man who does not sacrifice his private views and convenience when it is necessary.'

As it happened, he had to stay behind after contracting fever and the Malabar Itch, a nasty form of ringworm, and this saved his life, for the ship on which he would have sailed sank with no survivors. Furthermore, the unfortunate Baird arrived too late in Egypt to see action before the capitulation of the French army, while Arthur soon won further distinction in India.

War with the Marathas

Arthur returned to Seringapatam in May 1801. He completed the pacification of Mysore, during which he led an expedition to hunt down and hang the Rajah of Bullum, a hostile chief intent on establishing himself as an independent ruler. In December 1802, Arthur learnt that he had been promoted to major-general and the following year he added to his reputation in the Second Maratha War (1803–5).

The Maratha states had emerged in northern and central India during the collapse of the Mughal Empire in the seventeenth century. They formed a loose confederation under the Peshwa, or hereditary chief minister, Bajee Rao II, but in reality were rarely united and often at odds. The most important Maratha chiefs included Jeswunt Rao Holkar of Indore; Dowlut Rao Scindia of Gwalior; and Bhonsla, Rajah of Nagpur (also known as the Rajah of Berar).

Richard wanted to break the power of the Marathas and neutralize the threat they posed to the British position in the subcontinent. He had already prepared for this move diplomatically in 1801 when he ruthlessly annexed large tracts of the Nawab of Oudh's lands next to Bengal in the far north. This helped isolate the Marathas and exposed them to British attack from both north and south. Maratha disunity provided Richard with a chance to intervene in their affairs. Holkar defeated the Peshwa and his ally Scindia in October 1802. Under the Treaty of Bassein, Richard established British influence over the deposed Peshwa by agreeing to restore him in return for a subsidiary alliance.

In March 1803, Arthur entered Maratha territory from Mysore in the south with 10,000 men and advanced on the Peshwa's capital, Poona, which lay 80 miles south-east of Bombay. He had meticulously organized his supplies and entered Poona without resistance on 20 April. He covered the final 60 miles with his cavalry in thirty-two hours to save the city from being plundered or burnt when it was abandoned.

Holkar withdrew to avoid a confrontation. But the likelihood of war grew, for Scindia and the Rajah of Berar resented the British intrusion in Maratha affairs, not least as it had destroyed their own influence over the Peshwa. Richard recognized the difficulties in negotiating from Calcutta and on 26 June delegated political and military powers to the local commanders, Arthur in the central Indian plateau of the Deccan and General Gerard Lake in Hindustan in the north.

By August, fruitless negotiations had made war unavoidable. The British launched two concerted offensives against Scindia and the Rajah. In the north, Lake marched from Cawnpore with 14,000 men against Delhi and Scindia's main, French-trained army under General Pierre Perron. Over 600 miles to the south, Arthur advanced from Poona against the remaining Maratha forces. Arthur had 11,000 troops under his immediate command, along with an attached body of over 9,000 men under Colonel James Stevenson. He used Stevenson's troops to cover the Nizam of Hyderabad's territory, while he himself tried to force a decisive battle on his opponents.

On 8 August, Arthur stormed the town of Ahmednuggur, causing one of his allies to remark in admiration: 'These English are a strange people and their General a wonderful man. They came here in the morning, looked at the *pettah* [town]-wall, walked over it, killed all the garrison, and returned to breakfast.'

Using Ahmednuggur as a forward supply base, Arthur advanced to clear the northern parts of the Nizam's dominions following Maratha incursions. He realized that the key to success would be to take the war to the enemy and he informed Lieutenant-Colonel Close:

> We must get the upper hand, and if once we have that, we shall keep it with ease, and shall certainly succeed. But if we begin by a long defensive warfare, and go looking after [our] convoys which are scattered over the face of the earth, and do not attack briskly, we shall soon be in distress.

On 23 September, he encountered a strongly posted force of at least 40,000 Marathas at the village of Assaye. He had only 7,000 troops immediately to hand, for Stevenson's detachment was over 10 miles away, but he resolved to attack at once since British prestige was at stake and his only chance of success lay in bold and aggressive action. He forded a river to attack the Marathas' flank, but found that they were better trained and equipped than he had supposed, as they managed to change front in time to face the direction of his advance. He pressed home his attack in the face of an unexpectedly heavy fire, but one of his subordinates blundered and led a direct assault on the strongly defended village of Assaye. Fortunately, Arthur broke the Marathas further south and drove them from the field with the loss of nearly all their artillery. His Brigade-Major, Lieutenant Colin Campbell, wrote:

> The General was in the thick of the action the whole time. . . . No man could have shown a better example to the troops than he did. I never saw a man so cool and collected as he was the whole time, though I can assure you, till our troops got orders to advance, the fate of the day seemed doubtful.

Arthur suffered over 1,500 casualties at Assaye, nearly a quarter of those present. He himself had a horse killed under him and another piked and that night was left exhausted and plagued by nightmares. He later wrote to Stevenson: 'I acknowledge that I should not like to see again such a loss as I sustained on the 23rd September, even if attended by such a gain.' Despite its cost, the Battle of Assaye firmly established Arthur's ascendancy over the Marathas and boosted the British reputation for invincibility. Arthur and Stevenson subsequently captured Scindia's main strongholds and then advanced on the Rajah of Berar's mountain fortress of Gawilghur. By now, Lake had also defeated Scindia's forces in Hindustan and taken Delhi. On 29 November, Arthur won another victory at Argaum, this time for the loss of fewer than 400 men. He completed his success by storming Gawilghur on 15 December and negotiating conciliatory peace treaties with Scindia and the Rajah of Berar by the end of the month.

Holkar had remained aloof during this fighting, for he had an interest in seeing the British defeat his bitter rival, Scindia. But now that Scindia had become a British ally, Holkar prepared for war. In April 1804, Richard ordered Lake to begin hostilities against him. Lake advanced into Holkar's territory, but a detachment of 12,000 sepoys was routed in August 1804 after its lacklustre commander, Colonel William Monson, lost his nerve and retreated. This humiliating reverse was avenged by Lake three months later at Farruckabad and Holkar finally surrendered in December 1805.

Arthur played no role in defeating Holkar, for a famine in the Deccan made it logistically impossible for him to take the offensive. By now, he had been in India for seven years and was concerned at the strain on his health. He also believed that his services had not been sufficiently recognized by the authorities in England. He wrote in June 1804: 'I think I have served as long in India as any man ought who can serve anywhere else; and I think that there appears a prospect of service in Europe in which I should be more likely to get forward.'

After his lacklustre youth, he had become a highly motivated man, driven by an ambition to distinguish himself in the service of his King and Country and in the process to earn the rewards of respect and financial independence. His ambition, unlike Napoleon's, was subordinated to his country's interests and was a positive, not destructive, force. He was forceful in defending his interests or in protesting when he thought himself unjustly treated, but the essential bedrock of his adult life lay in the concepts of duty and public service.

Arthur sailed for England in March 1805. By then, Richard's aggressive policy had extended British control, direct and indirect, right down the eastern coast and across the entire southern part of India. Following the Third Maratha War (1817–19), British paramountcy would be complete. But Richard had made enemies through the ambition, high-handedness and expense of his policies and was recalled by the East India Company. India could be a springboard to the highest political power in England, but also entailed serious risks, as had been shown by the impeachment of

Warren Hastings, a previous Governor-General. Hastings's seven-year trial had ended in acquittal but had ruined him financially. Richard left India in August 1805 and was eventually cleared of all charges against him relating to his service in India.

Arthur was knighted in September 1804 and was able to repay his debts as a result of the prize money that he had won through his Indian triumphs. He had also trained his mind through study and toughened himself with physical exercise, especially riding. After Waterloo, an old friend expressed surprise at his physical strength and endurance, which contrasted sharply with his indifferent health in early life. 'Ah, that is all India,' he replied. 'India effected a total change in my constitution.'

Arthur had proved himself in political and diplomatic negotiations and had emerged as an outstanding administrator and logistician. He recognized that meticulous attention to logistics was essential to sustain a campaign in the physically difficult conditions of India. He hired bullocks to carry supplies, but also relied on travelling bazaars which accompanied his army and were supplied by *brinjarries*, or hereditary grain merchants. These logistical arrangements gave him an unprecedented mobility. He wrote: 'The only mode by which we can inspire either our allies or our enemies with respect for our operations will be to show them that the army can move with ease and celerity at all times and in all situations.' This enabled him to take the war to the enemy, as did the importance he attached to intelligence. He ran three intelligence departments in India to enable him to compare the information received for accuracy and he paid well to reward and encourage reliable sources. He used the native *hircarrahs*, or professional messengers, to carry letters, obtain intelligence and act as guides and he himself reconnoitred whenever possible.

The British had only a limited technological superiority over their enemies in India and depended on the boldness, determination and skill of their commanders. Arthur had become accustomed to attacking boldly, for a small but disciplined army, well-led and with a reputation for invincibility, could overthrow a much larger native force. But the experience he had gained both on the battlefield and in the wider aspects of command should not be seen merely as a preparation for his more famous achievements in Europe. He had played a key role in the creation of British India and for this reason alone would have earned himself a place in history.

Chapter 8
Interlude, 1805–8

Arthur reached England on 10 September 1805 and two days later met Vice-Admiral Horatio Nelson by chance at the Colonial Office in London. He later recalled how Nelson immediately engaged him in conversation, but 'it was almost all on his side, and all about himself, and, really, in a style so vain and silly as to surprise and almost disgust me'. Nelson was at the height of his fame, while Arthur had established a reputation only in India. But eventually Nelson left the room, learnt who Arthur was and returned to continue the conversation in a very different tone, showing a surprising knowledge of a wide range of topics. Arthur realized that Nelson was 'really a very superior person' and thought that he had never had a more interesting conversation. Nelson left the next day to join his flagship at Portsmouth and a month later was killed while crushing Napoleon's fleet at Trafalgar (21 October).

In that era, government ministers had no formal body, such as the Chiefs of Staff Committee of the Second World War, to provide professional military advice. Instead, they informally consulted officers, like Arthur, whom they knew and trusted. Arthur gave advice on a range of military matters and not simply on questions related to India. The chief minister, William Pitt the younger, found him:

> quite unlike all other military men with whom I have conversed. He never makes a difficulty or hides his ignorance in vague generalities. If I put a question to him he answers it distinctly; if I want an explanation, he gives it clearly; if I desire an opinion, I get from him one supported by reasons that are always sound. He is a very remarkable man.

In November 1805, Lieutenant-General Lord Cathcart led an expedition to northern Germany in support of Allied moves against France, where Napoleon had seized power and crowned himself Emperor. Arthur commanded one of Cathcart's brigades, but was disappointed in not seeing active service: the expedition had to be withdrawn in February 1806, two months after Napoleon decisively defeated the Austrians and Russians at Austerlitz in distant Moravia, thereby smashing the Allied coalition ranged against him.

Arthur was then given command of a brigade based at Hastings, although the invasion scare of 1803–5 had died down following Nelson's victory at Trafalgar. He did not resent this posting, even though he had held larger, independent commands in India: 'I am *nimmukwallah*, as we say in the East; that is, I have ate of the King's salt, and, therefore, I conceive it to be my duty to serve with unhesitating zeal and cheerfulness, when and wherever the King or his government may think proper to employ me.' He was also appointed to the Colonelcy, or proprietorship, of the 33rd Regiment, which would be given the title The Duke of Wellington's Regiment after he died.

Arthur finally married Kitty Pakenham at Dublin in April 1806, but found that they were ill-matched in temperament and intellect. Kitty's vagueness and timidity grated with his decisive self-confidence and her limited capabilities as a hostess discouraged him from entertaining guests at his home. He bluntly admitted to a friend in 1822: 'I married her because they asked me to do it & I did not know myself. I thought I should never care for anybody again, & that I shd. be with my army &, in short, I was a fool.' Nonetheless, their marriage produced two sons and lasted until Kitty's death in 1831.

Arthur also entered the House of Commons as a Member of Parliament, his main motive being to help defend his brother Richard against political attacks related to his service in India. In March 1807, King George III asked the Duke of Portland to form an administration. Arthur was offered the post of Chief Secretary to the Lord Lieutenant of Ireland. Before accepting, he checked that it would not prevent his employment on active military service: 'The Ministers have told me that they consider me at liberty to give up the office in Ireland whenever an opportunity of employing me professionally will offer, & that my acceptance of this office, instead of being a prejudice to me in my profession, will be considered as giving me an additional claim to such employment.' As Chief Secretary, Arthur was based at Dublin Castle. Ireland needed a strong hand in the aftermath of the crushed rebellions of 1798 and 1803. His duties included organizing election campaigns and dispensing the patronage vital to maintaining the administration's political influence. He also examined the defences of Ireland in case of a French invasion or another uprising.

Arthur remained determined to see active service again, even in a subordinate position. His chance came in the summer of 1807, after Napoleon secured an alliance with Russia at Tilsit and thus isolated Britain. Napoleon wanted to seize the neutral Danish fleet as he sought to overwhelm the Royal Navy. But the British government pre-empted him by sending Lord Cathcart with an expedition to Copenhagen. Arthur was given command of a division, covered the siege of the city and routed a relief attempt by a largely untried militia force at Kiøge on 29 August. With a team of commissioners, he negotiated the city's capitulation on 7 September on Cathcart's behalf, after which the expedition sailed home with the Danish ships.

In April 1808, Arthur was promoted to lieutenant-general. His next command was an expedition intended to support rebels in the Spanish colonies of Latin America. But Napoleon's intervention in the Iberian peninsula in 1807 caused revolts to explode across Spain and converted her into a British ally. Arthur's expedition was therefore diverted to the Peninsula.

The war in the Peninsula would saddle Napoleon with a permanent conflict at the western end of his Empire and transform Arthur into the foremost British general of the age. Before leaving London to join his command at Cork in southern Ireland, he dined with a friend, John Wilson Croker. He seemed lost in thought and, on being asked what he was thinking, replied:

> Why, to say the truth, I am thinking of the French that I am going to fight. I have not seen them since the campaign in Flanders [in 1794–5], where they were capital soldiers, and a dozen years of victory under Buonaparte must have made them better still. They have besides, it seems, a new system of strategy, which has outmanoeuvred and overwhelmed all the armies of

Europe. 'Tis enough to make one thoughtful; but no matter: my die is cast, they may overwhelm me, but I don't think they will outmanoeuvre me. First, because I am not afraid of them, as everybody else seems to be; and secondly, because if what I hear of their system of manoeuvres be true, I think it a false one as against steady troops. I suspect all the continental armies were more than half beaten before the battle was begun. I, at least, will not be frightened beforehand.

Chapter 9

The Peninsular War, 1808–11

Victories in Portugal: 1808

Arthur sailed from Cork with 9,000 British troops and decided to land in Portugal. The French occupation forces in the country had been cut off by the revolts in Spain and had withdrawn to the vicinity of Lisbon. On 1 August, Arthur began landing at Mondego Bay, 100 miles to the north, and was joined by 5,000 soldiers from Gibraltar. But he learned that he would soon be superseded in command. The British government had realized that the French had more troops in Portugal than originally thought, that the British expeditionary force had to be heavily reinforced and that Arthur could not reasonably be kept in command of the larger army as he lacked seniority. Instead, Lieutenant-General Sir Hew Dalrymple would take over as commander-in-chief, with Lieutenant-General Sir Harry Burrard as his second-in-command.

Arthur marched southwards in the hope of defeating the French while he was still in charge and on 17 August encountered 4,400 French troops under General Henri Delaborde near the village of Roliça, 60 miles from Mondego Bay. He won this initial battle with a vigorous attack and then advanced another 13 miles to the mouth of the River Maceira to cover the disembarkation of 4,000 reinforcements from England.

Burrard also arrived off the coast and, realizing that the self-confident Arthur was underestimating the strength of the French, ordered him to remain on the defensive. Since Burrard did not immediately land, Arthur was still in command the next day, the 21st, when General Andoche Junot attacked his position at Vimeiro with 13,000 French troops. Arthur shifted his army to check Junot's obvious attempt to outflank him and completely checked a succession of assaults, inflicting 2,000 casualties for the loss of just 720 men.

An immediate pursuit might have rolled the French back and liberated Lisbon, 35 miles to the south, but Arthur was prevented from doing so by the lacklustre Burrard, who had landed and joined him while the battle was in progress. The following morning, Dalrymple also arrived and the situation immediately became mired in controversy when the French sought an armistice. The fifty-eight-year-old Dalrymple had been on active service for only one of his forty-five years in the army and lacked self-confidence. He negotiated the Convention of Cintra, which was signed on 30 August, whereby the French troops in Portugal would be repatriated on British ships with their arms and baggage and left free to fight again. The convention cleared the French from the country without the need for further fighting, but proved intensely unpopular in both Britain, where the issue became politicized, and Portugal, whose representatives had not been consulted. Arthur wrote in frustration to his brother William:

> I wish I was away from this army. Things will not flourish as we are situated.
> ... There is no more confidence in me on the part of the Chiefs than if I had

WELLINGTON IN THE PENINSULA, 1808-14

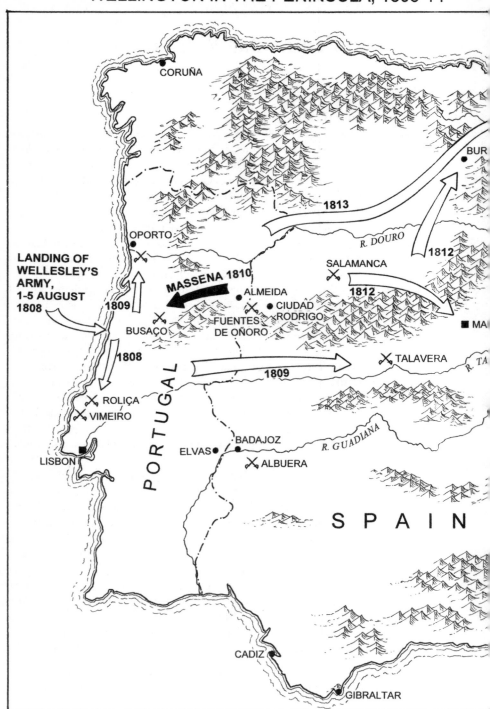

CORUÑA

BUR

1813

R. DOURO

OPORTO

SALAMANCA

**LANDING OF
WELLESLEY'S
ARMY,
1-5 AUGUST
1808**

1812

MASSENA 1810

ALMEIDA

1812

1809

CIUDAD
RODRIGO

FUENTES
DE OÑORO

BUSAÇO

MA

1808

TALAVERA

R TA

1809

PORTUGAL

ROLIÇA

VIMEIRO

BADAJOZ

R. GUADIANA

LISBON

ELVAS

ALBUERA

S P A I N

CADIZ

GIBRALTAR

FRANCE

R. ADOUR

BAYONNE

⚔ ORTHEZ

1814 →

⚔ TOULOUSE

⚔ FIGHTING IN
THE PYRENEES

TIAN

R. GARONNE

⚔ SORAUREN

PAMPLONA

R. EBRO

THE PYRENEES

BARCELONA

N

VALENCIA

BALEARIC
ISLES

*MEDITERRANEAN
SEA*

0   50   100 MILES

been unsuccessful. . . . The General [Dalrymple] has no plan, or even an idea of a plan, nor do I believe he knows the meaning of the word *Plan*. . . . These people are really more stupid and incapable than any I have yet met with; and if things go on in this disgraceful manner I must quit them.

Arthur returned home in October and Burrard and Dalrymple were soon recalled. All three generals faced a Court of Enquiry (November–December) and Arthur was wholly vindicated, while the other two never saw active service again.

In Arthur's absence, command of the British army in Portugal fell to a new commander, Lieutenant-General Sir John Moore. Leaving 10,000 men to protect Lisbon, Moore advanced with the rest to support the Spaniards. But the Spanish armies collapsed when Napoleon intervened in the Peninsula with massive reinforcements in November. Moore initially ordered his army to retreat back to Portugal, but then decided to strike at Napoleon's communications instead, in the hope of disrupting his operations and invigorating Spanish resistance. After defeating elements of a detached French corps at Sahagun, 150 miles north-west of Madrid, on 21 December, he learnt that he had provoked Napoleon into moving against him and fell back to the north-western coast of Spain. Moore escaped Napoleon's attempt to trap him, but lost 6,000 men in his midwinter retreat through the Cantabrian mountains. He himself was mortally wounded in a battle outside the port of Coruña on 16 January 1809, but by repulsing the French attacks under Marshal Soult, he enabled his army to be evacuated safely by sea.

Moore had won an outstanding reputation as both a fighting general and a trainer of troops, but he lacked Arthur's robust self-confidence in questions of strategy and had stated that Portugal would be indefensible if the French succeeded in Spain. Arthur disagreed and argued his case in a famous memorandum dated 7 March 1809:

I have always been of opinion that Portugal might be defended, whatever might be the result of the contest in Spain, and that in the meantime measures adopted for the defence of Portugal would be highly useful to the Spaniards in their contest with the French. . . . My opinion was that, even if Spain should have been conquered, the French would not be able to overrun Portugal with a smaller force than 100,000 men.

After intense debate, the British government decided to maintain its commitment to the Peninsula and to send Arthur with reinforcements to join the 10,000 British troops still in Portugal.

It was a crucial decision. Since the outbreak of war with France in 1793, Britain had been searching for an effective means of countering French power on the Continent. In the Iberian peninsula, she found a theatre in which her small available field army could help drain Napoleon's resources and inspire resistance to him in occupied Europe. The Peninsula was remote from Paris and, with its difficult terrain and poor communications, difficult for the French to occupy. The bulk of the French troops were tied down throughout the occupied regions by guerrillas and the Spanish regular forces and thus unable to concentrate all their resources against the British army, which had an impact out of proportion to its size.

Return to Portugal: 1809

Arthur reached Lisbon on 22 April 1809. He had a total of 23,000 British troops and would soon be able to increase his strength with Portuguese manpower, as a British officer, Lieutenant-General William Carr Beresford, had been appointed to regenerate the Portuguese army as an effective fighting force.

Arthur's immediate mission was to secure Portugal and he advanced against a French corps under Marshal Soult that had invaded the northern provinces in the wake of the Battle of Coruña. Soult had occupied the city of Oporto on the Douro river and had destroyed the bridge, removed boats from the south bank and posted troops to watch for any attempts to cross the river between Oporto and the sea. But Portuguese civilians retrieved some wine-barges and thus enabled Arthur on 12 May to cross the river to the east of Oporto, where he was hidden by cliffs from French observation. By the time Soult reacted, Arthur had secured a bridgehead on the north bank. After failing in their counter-attacks, the French retreated and were driven from Portugal with the loss of 4,000 men and all their artillery.

Despite his success, Arthur was disappointed by the indiscipline of his troops and complained on 31 May:

> The army behave terribly ill. They are a rabble who cannot bear success any more than Sir John Moore's army could bear failure. I am endeavouring to tame them; but, if I should not succeed, I must make an official complaint of them, and send one or two corps home in disgrace. They plunder in all directions.

As the war progressed, Arthur gradually reduced such problems. His army grew in experience and self-confidence, while the French became demoralized by a succession of defeats. At this time, he also formed his army into divisions. Hitherto, his infantry battalions had simply been grouped into brigades, but the growth in the army's size made it necessary to combine two or more brigades into permanent divisions for greater cohesion, flexibility and control.

On 11 June, Arthur obtained permission from the British government to intervene inside Spain. Napoleon was preoccupied with a crisis in central Europe, where he had been attacked by Austria, and for the time being would not be able to send reinforcements to the Peninsula. Arthur planned to unite with a Spanish army under Don Gregorio Garcia de la Cuesta, defeat an exposed French corps under Marshal Claude Victor and liberate Madrid. But the venture was over-ambitious and too dependent on his Spanish allies, who proved unreliable and unable to fulfil their promises to keep him supplied. Victor was able to withdraw to safety and the French then concentrated 46,000 troops against Arthur and Cuesta's combined total of 55,000. A battle ensued at Talavera, 70 miles south-west of Madrid, on 27–8 July. Arthur bore the brunt of the action with his British troops and repelled all the French assaults. But he lost a quarter of his strength and had to retreat after the battle as he had almost exhausted his provisions and faced the threat of being cut off from Portugal by Marshal Soult, who was marching south with three corps from north-western Spain.

Although Arthur reached the safety of the Portuguese border, the Talavera campaign had been a disappointing failure. It was partly to counter criticisms of the setback by political opponents of the British government that Arthur was created Baron Douro of Wellesley and Viscount Wellington of Talavera in recognition of his battlefield victories. He now signed his name as Wellington, although it was not until 1814, after further steps in the peerage, that he became a duke.

Lieutenant Joseph Moyle Sherer of the 34th (or the Cumberland) Regiment of Foot vividly caught Wellington's appearance at this time when he described a review of the 2nd Division in October 1809:

> I was in the highest possible spirits, eager to behold the hero, and as he passed very slowly down the line, observing the men with a keen scrutinising look, I had the fullest opportunity for indulging my curiosity. I was much struck with his countenance; and, in his quick-glancing eye, prominent nose, and pressed lip, saw, very distinctly marked, the ready presence of mind, and imperturbable decision of character, so essential in a leader ...

The French Invade Portugal: 1810

Napoleon now turned his attention back to the Peninsula. He had defeated Austria at the Battle of Wagram in the summer of 1809 and secured a victorious peace with the Treaty of Schönbrunn on 14 October. He was left unchallenged in central Europe and in the winter of 1809–10 began sending 138,000 reinforcements to Spain. The French inflicted a string of defeats on the Spanish regular armies and overran Andalusia in the south in January and February 1810.

Napoleon also sent Marshal Massena to take command of the newly formed French Army of Portugal, cross the border from Spain and drive Wellington into the sea. Massena had won a glittering reputation against the Austrians and Russians in the French Revolutionary Wars. Wellington later admitted that 'when Massena was opposed to me, in the field, I never slept comfortably', even though the fifty-two-year-old French marshal had become burnt out and looked nearer sixty.

Wellington had yet to establish unquestioned confidence in himself either in his army or at home. Many doubted his ability to maintain his position in Portugal, but he had already begun preparations to resist an invasion. In October 1809, for example, he had ordered the secret construction of fortifications, the Lines of Torres Vedras, to seal off Lisbon in case the rest of the country was overrun. In February 1810, he boosted his overall numbers by integrating Portuguese brigades into his infantry divisions. The Portuguese provided Wellington with about one-third of his field army for the rest of the Peninsular War. At this time, Wellington also created the crack Light Division to act as his army's advance or rearguard and to screen its operations.

By the summer of 1810, the French had 360,000 troops in Spain, but had to hold down occupied regions and guard their communications, leaving Massena with only 65,000 for the invasion of Portugal. He opened an invasion route in the north by taking the twin frontier fortresses of Ciudad Rodrigo and Almeida from their Spanish and Portuguese garrisons in July and August. Then, misled by faulty maps, he advanced along one of the worst possible routes, which delayed his progress and damaged his wheeled transport.

Wellington fell back and concentrated most of his army on a magnificent defensive position, a steep ridge at Busaco, across Massena's path. He placed his troops on the reverse slopes of the ridge, sheltered from observation and artillery fire. Consequently, when Massena attacked on 27 September, he was unaware of Wellington's exact dispositions. The steep and broken terrain made it difficult for the French to coordinate their attacks, so they were defeated piecemeal. Wellington had built a lateral road running behind the crest of the ridge and used it to bring reinforcements quickly to meet the assaults. His battalions counter-attacked in lines two ranks deep, in which every man could fire his musket. The French tended to advance in columns for ease of manoeuvre, but only the front three ranks of a column could fire without hitting their comrades in front and they usually had no time to deploy. Volleys smashed the cohesion of the French columns, which broke and fled as the British cheered and launched a bayonet charge.

Lieutenant Sherer heard Wellington giving orders at Busaco and noted:

> I was particularly struck with the style of this order, so decided, so manly, and breathing *no* doubt as to the repulse of any attack; it confirmed confidence. Lord Wellington's simplicity of manner in the delivery of orders, and in command, is quite that of an able man. He has nothing of the truncheon about him; nothing foul-mouthed, important, or fussy: his orders on the field are all short, quick, clear, and to the purpose.

The Battle of Busaco raised morale within the army and at home and gave combat experience to the newly integrated Portuguese units. Lieutenant George Simmons of the 95th Regiment of Foot (Riflemen) wrote: 'The Portuguese, led on by English officers, fight like tigers. They have behaved astonishingly well. I have witnessed several regiments of them come on with the greatest enthusiasm.' Wellington had apparently hoped to check the French invasion at Busaco, but Massena subsequently manoeuvred round his northern flank and obliged him to retreat all the way to Lisbon. Wellington withdrew within the Lines of Torres Vedras, which Massena, mindful of his defeat at Busaco, wisely declined to attack. Wellington had ordered that as far as possible, supplies should be destroyed or brought within the Lines, although it proved impossible to ensure that these instructions were always carried out. After a month, Massena fell back from before the Lines to an area near Santarém, 28 miles to the north, where his troops survived on what provisions they could find for the next four months.

Napoleon, who monitored the course of events from Paris, admired Wellington's ruthlessness:

> There's a man for you. He is forced to flee before an army that he dares not confront, but he establishes a desert of eighty leagues between himself and the enemy. He slows its march, weakens it by all manner of deprivations and knows how to ruin it without fighting it. In Europe, only Wellington and I are capable of carrying out these measures.

Finally, on 5 March 1811, Massena had to begin a full-scale retreat. Wellington, who had been reinforced during the winter, pursued and fought a series of minor actions against Massena's rearguard, notably at Pombal, Redinha, Casal Nova, Foz d'Arouce and Sabugal. He outran his supplies and could not risk undermining the discipline of his army by pressing the French more closely. Nonetheless, Massena was obliged to withdraw from Portugal, having lost 25,000 men in his disastrous invasion, almost all of them through starvation, disease and guerrilla attacks rather than in battle. The outcome had triumphantly vindicated Wellington's strategy and reinforced his authority within his army. His scorched-earth policy has been criticized for the suffering it inflicted on the Portuguese people, but it was a traditional Portuguese response to Spanish invasion and the alternative would have been the even greater evil of permanent French occupation.

Massena re-organized his forces and returned to the offensive after just three weeks. He intended to relieve the French garrison in the fortress of Almeida, 5 miles inside Portugal, and therefore attacked Wellington at the frontier village of Fuentes de Oñoro on 3 and 5 May. He eventually outflanked Wellington in the south, but merely caused him to pull back his southern flank to a stronger position. Massena retreated three days later, while the garrison of Almeida abandoned the fortress and escaped with heavy losses. Napoleon subsequently replaced Massena in command of the Army of Portugal with Marshal Auguste Marmont, a younger and keener man.

Wellington had secured Portugal as a base for his future operations, but the situation in the Peninsula as a whole remained uncertain. The French occupation forces were still being reinforced and were gradually tightening their grip on Spain by defeating the Spanish regular armies, conquering hitherto unoccupied districts and pacifying regions that they already held.

Stalemate: 1811

The immediate situation confronting Wellington on the Portuguese frontier was one of stalemate and this lasted for the rest of 1811. The French had six armies in Spain and the three nearest Wellington were the Armies of the North, Portugal and the South. The French had to disperse their forces and live off the country, but could check Wellington, should he take the offensive, by concentrating any two of their armies against him.

There were two main invasion routes across the mountainous border between Portugal and Spain and each was guarded by a pair of frontier fortresses. Wellington's possession of Almeida in the north and Elvas in the south helped ensure the security of Portugal. But he would not be able to thrust into Spain, should such an opportunity present itself, until he had seized the two fortresses on the Spanish side of the frontier: Ciudad Rodrigo in the north and Badajoz in the south.

In March 1811, Wellington detached 19,000 men under Beresford to besiege Badajoz, while he himself remained in the north. Marshal Soult moved against Beresford with part of the Army of the South to try and raise the siege. Beresford concentrated in a covering position at Albuera, 12 miles south-east of Badajoz, where on 16 May he repelled Soult in some of the hardest fighting of the war. Beresford suffered 5,900 casualties and was widely criticized for his conduct of the action.

Wellington arrived with reinforcements after Albuera and visited the wounded. 'Men of the 29th [Regiment],' he told some of them, 'I am sorry to see so many of you here.'

'If you had commanded us, my Lord,' replied a soldier, 'there wouldn't be so many of us here.'

Wellington resumed the siege of Badajoz, but had an antiquated siege train and desperately few trained engineers. He was unable to capture the city before Marmont brought the Army of Portugal south to join Soult. Heavily outnumbered by their combined forces, Wellington had to abandon the siege in the middle of June and withdraw 9 miles to a defensive position on the Caia river near Elvas.

By this stage, the French were wary of attacking Wellington except in favourable circumstances and they did not venture to do so on the Caia, despite their advantage of numbers. Wellington wrote to a friend on 26 June: 'They have been looking at us for a week and the more they looked at us the less they like us and I believe that I should get over the crisis of this moment without a battle, of which we can at present ill spare the necessary loss, however confident I am of the result.' After three weeks the French dispersed again to find supplies and re-establish their control over areas that they had temporarily abandoned in order to concentrate against Wellington.

Since the French had relieved Badajoz, Wellington now blockaded Ciudad Rodrigo in the north. He was again foiled when two French armies, those of the North and Portugal, concentrated 60,000 men against him in late September. Wellington, who had only 46,000 troops available, abandoned the blockade and fell back to the safety of more mountainous country to the south-west. He occupied a strong position near the Coa river, where the French again failed to attack before they were obliged to disperse.

Chapter 10

The Peninsular War, 1812–14

Wellington Takes the Offensive: 1812

By the end of 1811, Napoleon was preparing a massive invasion of Russia with more than half a million men, following the breakdown of the alliance he had made with Tsar Alexander I four years earlier. Napoleon's plans ruled out reinforcements for the Peninsula and, indeed, actually resulted in 27,000 troops being removed from Spain.

Despite this, Napoleon ordered the Army of Aragon under Marshal Louis Suchet to conquer the eastern province of Valencia. Marmont was obliged to detach 10,000 men to support Suchet and also had to take over responsibility for more territory in the north. As a result, the French had fewer troops directly opposed to Wellington. Napoleon had upset the stalemate that had prevailed throughout 1811.

Before Wellington could strike into Spain, he still had to take the border fortresses of Ciudad Rodrigo and Badajoz. At least he now had a proper siege train, even if he still lacked adequate numbers of engineers. He surprised Marmont by moving against Ciudad Rodrigo early in January 1812 and stormed it on the 19th before it could be relieved.

Wellington then marched the bulk of his army southwards and besieged Badajoz in March. One of his soldiers, Private Edward Costello of the 95th Regiment, wrote that Wellington occasionally visited the trenches to inspect them or observe the enemy:

> One day when [Tom] Crawley and myself were working near each other in the trenches, a shell fell inconveniently close to us. Tom was instantly half buried in mud, awaiting the explosion. Perceiving it had sunk itself deep into the earth, the fuse being too long, I intended availing myself of the opportunity, to play a trick upon Crawley, by throwing a large lump of clay on his head directly the shell exploded, and so make him believe himself wounded. To obtain the clod I sprang at the other side of the trench, but exposed myself to a shot from the walls of the town, which immediately came in the form of grape, splashing me with mud from head to foot, and forcing me to throw myself back into the trench upon Crawley, who, in his fears, made sure that a shell had fixed itself upon his rear, and roared like a bull; in an instant, however, the sunken missile really burst; on the smoke dispersing, who should I behold but the Duke himself, crouched down, his head half averted, drily smiling at Crawley and me.

Badajoz was a more formidable fortress than Ciudad Rodrigo and Wellington lost over 4,600 men in the siege. The city was finally stormed on 6 April and then sacked by those of the crazed troops who survived the slaughter in the breaches. Wellington later recalled in disgust how he entered a cellar and saw some soldiers lying on the floor so drunk that the wine was actually flowing from their mouths. Private Costello wrote that on the morning afterwards:

> The town was still in great confusion and uproar, although every available means had been taken to suppress it. In one of the streets I saw the Duke of Wellington, surrounded by a number of British soldiers, who, holding up bottles with the heads knocked off, containing wine and spirits, cried out to him, a phrase then familiarly applied to him by the men of the army, 'Old boy! will you drink? The town's our own – hurrah!

With the border fortresses in his hands, Wellington now held the initiative. In June, he advanced into the interior of Spain from Ciudad Rodrigo and reached the city of Salamanca. Marmont concentrated the Army of Portugal and began a series of skilful manoeuvres in which he tried to cut Wellington's line of retreat to Portugal. Wellington evaded these traps, but, being unable to entice Marmont into attacking him in a strong position, resigned himself to having to fall back to Portugal. Then, on 22 July, just as he was beginning to withdraw, he noticed that Marmont in his eagerness to outflank him had allowed his army to become over-extended. Wellington galloped off to unleash a brilliant counter-stroke by personally giving the necessary orders to his divisional commanders.

A devastating attack by the 3rd Division against the head of Marmont's army opened the Battle of Salamanca. The fighting spread as Wellington's other divisions attacked in succession from west to east. Both Marmont and his successor in command were wounded one after the other and a belated counter-attack organized by General Bertrand Clausel was beaten back. By the end of the battle, Wellington had inflicted about 12,500 casualties and a massive defeat on the French for the loss of 5,000 of his own men. Two days later, he wrote to the Secretary of State for War and the Colonies: 'I hope you will be pleased with our battle, of which the dispatch contains as accurate an account as I can give you. There was no mistake; every thing went on as it ought; and there never was an army so beaten in so short a time.'

After Salamanca, Wellington enjoyed a permanent moral ascendancy over the French. One of their divisional commanders, General Maximilien Foy, wrote in admiration:

> Of the battles that the English have won in our times, that of Salamanca is the most skilful, the largest in numbers of troops engaged and the most important in results. It places Lord Wellington almost as high as the Duke of Marlborough. Up to now, we have come to know his caution, his eye for a position and his skill in taking advantage of it. But at Salamanca he showed that he was a great and able master of manoeuvre. He kept his dispositions hidden for almost the whole day and waited for us to make our move before revealing his. He played without taking risks. He fought in the oblique order [with his attack falling on one flank and rolling up the French line] – it was a battle in the style of Frederick the Great.

The immediate result of Salamanca was to open the road to Madrid and Wellington triumphantly entered the city on 12 August. He remained there for a fortnight. Then, leaving 43,000 troops under Lieutenant-General Sir Rowland Hill to cover the city, he took the remaining 35,000 to seize Burgos, over 125 miles to the north. By capturing Burgos, Wellington could jeopardize the entire French position in the Peninsula, as it lay on their main line of communications. It could also help secure his position deep inside Spain by checking any counter-offensive by French forces based in the north.

But Wellington had seriously underestimated the strength of the castle on the hill above Burgos and lacked sufficient engineers and siege equipment. The castle, ably defended by the French General Louis Rey, defied a series of assaults starting on 19 September. The attacks were made by inadequate numbers of troops through a misguided concern to limit casualties, and their failure demoralized Wellington's men. Dr James McGrigor, Wellington's senior medical officer, was with him during this frustrating time:

> In my usual morning visits to his lordship with reports of the sick and wounded of the army, when I met the heads of the departments, and likewise the chief engineer, who had nothing but an unfavourable report to give, Lord Wellington was often in bad humour, for everything went wrong with him. This, therefore, was the period in his life when fortune seemed to turn her back upon him. At length, after daily losses of numbers of men and officers, discontent was not silent even among the officers themselves; for they saw that, without means, particularly in artillery, they were knocking their heads against stone walls without the least prospect of making any impression upon them.

The French withdrew from southern Spain in order to concentrate their armies and counter the threat to their communications. By now, Wellington had lost more than 2,000 men at Burgos. Faced with overwhelming enemy numbers in the field, he had to break off the siege on 19 October and fall back to the Portuguese frontier.

Discipline broke down, especially in the final stages of the retreat when heavy rain and the temporary failure of the army's logistics resulted in widespread disorder, looting and drunkenness. Wellington was furious and severely criticized the behaviour of his men in a memorandum of 28 November, addressed to his senior subordinates:

> It must be obvious, however, to every Officer, that from the moment the troops commenced their retreat ... the Officers lost all command over their men. Irregularities and outrages of all descriptions were committed with impunity; and losses have been sustained which ought never to have occurred.
>
> Yet the necessity for retreat existing, none was ever made in which the troops made such short marches; none on which they made such long and repeated halts; and none on which the retreating armies were so little pressed on the rear by the enemy.

The essence of this complaint was undeniably true, but in the anger of the moment, Wellington exaggerated certain points and failed to exempt from his blanket condemnation those units that had upheld their discipline. The memorandum soon became known throughout the army and caused considerable ill-feeling.

Just four months after the triumph of Salamanca, the campaign of 1812 had ended in bitter disappointment.

The Breakthrough: 1813

Wellington spent the winter bringing his army to a peak of fitness and training and was reinforced to a total of 80,000 British and Portuguese troops. Following his appointment as generalissimo of the Spanish armed forces, he would also have over 21,000 Spaniards directly attached to his field army. He introduced tents to enable his men to bivouac more healthily and portable tin kettles to replace the heavy and inefficient iron cauldrons. He improved the medical arrangements and established the British army's first permanent military police force by setting up the Staff Corps of Cavalry.

The strategic situation had also improved. In concentrating against Wellington to relieve Burgos, the French had been obliged to abandon southern Spain and they never reoccupied it. Napoleon further reduced his forces in the Peninsula as he withdrew troops to central Europe in the wake of his disaster in Russia in 1812. Prussia joined Russia in the field in the spring of 1813, while Austria declared her neutrality.

Wellington returned to the offensive in May 1813. He feinted frontally against Salamanca and then surprised the French by turning their northern flank with his main thrust. To do so, he marched the bulk of his army through the mountains of northern Portugal, which the French had assumed were impassable for large bodies of troops. He then maintained the momentum of his advance along the north bank of the Douro river, relentlessly outflanking each position occupied by the French, including Burgos, and hustling them back before they could concentrate sufficient forces to stop him. Captain Harry Smith of the Light Division wrote: 'Our Division halted the next day [20 June], but the army never did, from the day of breaking up its cantonments until they fought the battle of Vittoria. It was a most wonderful march, the army in great fighting order, and every man in better wind than a trained pugilist.'

On 21 June, after thrusting 200 miles across northern Spain, Wellington swept round and fell on the French in the valley outside the city of Vitoria. By the end of the day, he had smashed them decisively and seized a vast quantity of equipment and baggage, including 150 guns. It was one of his finest achievements. It won him promotion to Field Marshal and a European reputation, for it reinvigorated the Continental Allies at a time when they were about to launch a new campaign against Napoleon in the autumn after a two-month armistice. General von Blücher, commanding the Army of Silesia, wrote exuberantly on 24 July after hearing of the victory: 'Long live Wellington! That's how we, too, must fight the French. We can do it also, if we are strong.'

Vitoria might have been an even greater victory, but Wellington was unable to cut all the French escape routes. He was also prevented from exploiting it with a vigorous pursuit, partly because of logistical constraints and partly because of the looting and indiscipline of some of his troops. He complained bitterly:

> We started with the army in the highest order, and up to the day of battle nothing could get on better; but that event has, as usual, totally annihilated all order and discipline. The soldiers of the army have got among them about a million sterling in money, with the exception of about 100,000 dollars

which were got for the military chest. The night of the battle, instead of being passed in getting rest and food to prepare them for the pursuit of the following day, was passed by the soldiers in looking for plunder. The con-sequence was that they were incapable of marching in pursuit of the enemy, and were totally knocked up.

Wellington now sought to consolidate his achievement by taking the fortresses of San Sebastian on the coast and Pamplona 40 miles inland, both on the Spanish side of the Pyrenees. Meanwhile, Napoleon ordered Marshal Soult to restore the situation in the Peninsula and entrusted him with all the French forces directly opposed to Wellington. Soult soon rallied these troops following their defeat at Vitoria and on 25 July took the offensive, attacking through the Pyrenees and driving back Wellington's outlying divisions towards Pamplona.

Wellington had been forced to disperse his army on a wide front to cover his operations against both Pamplona and San Sebastian. On 27 July, he reached the village of Sorauren, 4 miles outside Pamplona, to assume personal command of his troops there. His arrival was greeted by a tremendous bout of cheering and induced Soult to postpone an attack to the following day. Lieutenant James Mills of the 40th (or the 2nd Somersetshire) Regiment of Foot commented:

> On all occasions, in the field or on the line of march, when recognised by any of the men as he rode past, his lordship was invariably greeted with a burst of welcome and enthusiastic cheers – a just and sincere tribute from the humbler ranks to the hero of so many victories. But to-day these acclama-tions were still more marked and hearty as he showed himself near the brigades; and I cannot adequately express the sense of confidence and assurance that was revived by his mere presence in the midst of a single division of his army. Cheers upon cheers were vehemently raised along the whole line, which were only lulled to quiet by the joyous conviction that all would yet go well.

When Soult attacked on the next day, the 28th, he was repulsed in the First Battle of Sorauren. Two days later, in the Second Battle, Wellington switched to the offensive and drubbed Soult's army as it began to retreat back to France. Soult's disastrous offensive, the actions of which are known collectively as the Battle of the Pyrenees, had lasted nine days and had cost over 13,500 French casualties. Wellington had lost half that number.

Wellington had entrusted the siege of San Sebastian to Lieutenant-General Sir Thomas Graham. The town had defied an initial attempt to storm it on 25 July, but fell on 31 August. The French garrison of Pamplona was starved into surrender two months later.

Wellington was now ready to resume the offensive and fight his way over the Pyrenees. Captain Harry Smith, a brigade-major in the Light Division, explained that the army stood on the Bidasoa river, which marked the frontier with France:

> We were in this line for some time, daily watching the enemy making works with extraordinary vigour and diligence, which we knew ere long we should have the glory (the pleasure, to most of us) to run our heads against, for such

WELLINGTON INVADES FRANCE, OCTOBER-DECEMBER 1813

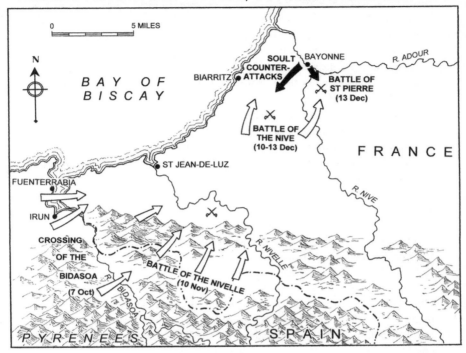

was the ardour and confidence of our army at this moment, that, if Lord Wellington had told us to attempt to carry the moon, we should have done it.

On 7 October, Wellington surprised the French by crossing the Bidasoa at Fuenterrabía near the sea, where they thought the river was impassable. He himself had discovered from local shrimpers that it could be forded at low tide.

Soult withdrew 6 miles and fortified a new position on the heights above the Nivelle river. Wellington attacked on 10 November, but this time merely demonstrated in the west, where Soult was disproportionately strong, and broke through further inland. An officer of the 95th Regiment, Jonathan Leach, vividly described the battle:

> It is impossible to conceive a finer sight than the general advance of our army from the Pyrenean passes against the French position. Almost as far as the eye could reach, was seen one sheet of flame and smoke, accompanied with an incessant fire of light troops, and frequent volleys of musquetry, as the lines and columns approached the entrenchments.

Captain Harry Smith recorded an interesting discussion between Wellington and some of his subordinates a few days before the Battle of the Nivelle and his account shows Wellington in a different light from the aloof and uncommunicative commander of popular legend:

The enemy, not considering this [mountainous] ground strong enough, turned to it with a vigour I have rarely witnessed, to fortify it by every means art could devise. Every day, before the position was attacked, Colonel Colborne [the commander of the 52nd Regiment] and I went to look at their progress; the Duke himself would come to our outpost, and continue walking there a long time. One day he stayed unusually long. He turns to Colborne, 'These fellows think themselves invulnerable, but I will beat them out, and with great ease.'

'That we shall beat them,' says Colborne, 'when your lordship attacks, I have no doubt, but for the ease –'

'Ah, Colborne, with your local knowledge only, you are perfectly right; it appears difficult, but the enemy have not men to man the works and lines they occupy. They dare not concentrate a sufficient body to resist the attacks I shall make upon them. I can pour a greater force on certain points than they can concentrate to resist me.'

'Now I see it, my lord,' says Colborne.

The Duke was lying down, and began a very earnest conversation. General Alten, Kempt, Colborne, I, and other staff-officers were preparing to leave the Duke, when he says, 'Oh, lie still.'

After he had conversed for some time with Sir G. Murray [his Quartermaster-General], Murray took out of his sabretache his writing-materials, and began to write the plan of attack for the whole army. When it was finished, so clearly had he understood the Duke, I do not think he erased one word. He says, 'My lord, is this your desire?'

It was one of the most interesting scenes I have ever witnessed. As Murray read, the Duke's eye was directed with his telescope to the spot in question. He never asked Sir G. Murray one question, but the muscles of his face evinced lines of the deepest thought. When Sir G. Murray had finished, the Duke smiled and said, 'Ah Murray, this will put us in possession of the fellows' lines. Shall we be ready to-morrow?'

'I fear not, my lord, but next day.'

As a result of the Battle of the Nivelle, Wellington broke out of the Pyrenees. He would now be able to spend the winter on less exposed ground south of the city of Bayonne near the Atlantic coast. On 9 December, he consolidated his position by pushing his right wing across to the east side of the Nive river, partly to threaten Soult's communications with the interior of France and partly to obtain the food and forage available on this bank while simultaneously denying them to the French.

Soult responded with a series of counter-attacks on either side of the Nive between 10 and 13 December. On the first three days, Wellington checked the French assaults on the west bank. On the last day, part of his army under Lieutenant-General Sir Rowland Hill was attacked on the east bank in the Battle of St Pierre. Hill was danger-ously outnumbered, but repulsed the French. Wellington arrived with reinforce-ments at the end of the battle, but declined to take personal command and left Hill to complete his hard-won victory.

Soult's counter-attacks on the Nive had been completely defeated with the loss of 7,000 men. He never again took the offensive for the rest of the war.

The End of the War: 1814

A two-month lull ensued during the winter. Wellington was careful to coordinate his operations with the progress of the wider war against Napoleon. In October, the Continental Allies, led by Austria, Prussia and Russia, had defeated Napoleon in a massive, four-day battle at Leipzig. They subsequently drove him from central Europe and crossed the Rhine into eastern France by the beginning of January 1814. Wellington wanted to support them with an advance of his own in the south, but had to take care not to over-extend himself. If Napoleon managed to win a victory in the north, he might secure a local armistice and then reinforce Soult.

Wellington took the offensive in the middle of February 1814, once better weather had improved the roads, and thrust eastwards, away from the Atlantic coast. He thereby forced Soult to retreat from Bayonne, which he promptly had invested by a detachment of over 18,000 men under Lieutenant-General Sir John Hope.

By now, Wellington had brought his army to a peak of efficiency and later remarked: 'I always thought that I could have gone anywhere and done anything with that army. It was impossible to have a machine more highly mounted and in better order.' For their part, his men trusted him implicitly as a guarantee of victory. The Reverend George Gleig was a young officer in the 85th (or the Bucks Volunteers) Regiment of Foot (Light Infantry) when he first saw Wellington in 1813. He later described the scene in his novel *The Subaltern*, which he based on his experiences:

> He who rode in front [Wellington] was a thin, well-made man, apparently of the middle stature, and not yet past the prime of life. His dress was a plain grey frock, buttoned close to the chin; a cocked hat, covered with oilskin; grey pantaloons, with boots buckled at the side; and a steel-mounted light sabre. ... There was in his general aspect nothing indicative of a life spent in hardships and fatigues; nor any expression of care or anxiety in his countenance. On the contrary, his cheek though bronzed with frequent exposure to the sun, had on it the ruddy hue of health, while a smile of satisfaction played about his mouth, and told, more plainly than words could have spoken, how perfectly he felt himself at his ease. Of course I felt, as I gazed upon him, that an army under his command could not be beaten; and I had frequent opportunities afterwards of perceiving how far such a feeling goes towards preventing defeat.

On 27 February, Wellington attacked Soult at Orthez, 40 miles inland. Soult was strongly posted on the hills above the town and checked the initial assaults. Wellington skilfully adjusted his plan, resumed the attack and routed the French. He himself was slightly wounded at the end of the battle, when a shot struck his sword hilt and drove it against his thigh, making riding difficult for over a week.

Wellington detached forces to occupy Bordeaux, 75 miles to the north, after hearing that the mayor was prepared to oppose Napoleon. He himself continued eastwards and on 26 March, after several minor actions, arrived before Toulouse. Soult prepared to defend the city, taking advantage of the rivers and canals which covered it. Wellington crossed the Garonne river, so he could assault the Calvinet heights, which commanded Toulouse from the east. Soult, conscious of the city's vulnerability on this side, fortified the hills and Wellington later claimed that 'in the whole of my experience, I never saw an army so strongly posted as the French at the battle of Toulouse.'

Wellington attacked on three sides of the city on 10 April, feinting in the west and making his main effort against the heights in the east. The coordination of his assaults broke down, for he found it impossible personally to control the whole of his army when it was so extended. Some of his units, especially the Spanish infantry, were bloodily repulsed, but by the end of the day, he had seized the crucial heights. Soult abandoned the city within thirty-six hours to avoid being trapped inside it.

Ironically, the Battle of Toulouse need not have been fought, for Napoleon had already abdicated, following the occupation of Paris by the Continental Allies on 31 March. Wellington received the news only on 12 April. Soult agreed to an armistice five days later, after the isolated French garrison of Bayonne had made a pointless and unsuccessful sortie on the 14th, causing another 1,500 casualties.

The Peninsular War was finally over. Wellington had defeated some of Napoleon's foremost generals, including six of his marshals, all of whom had initially made the mistake of underestimating him. His victories had bolstered the position of the British government, which was resolute in prosecuting the war against Napoleon and supporting the Continental Allies financially so they could maintain their armies in the field. Napoleon's fate was decided primarily in Russia and central Europe, where he was pitted against the massive Allied armies in 1812–14. But the Peninsula was a crucial secondary theatre that overstretched Napoleon's resources. Wellington helped tie down up to a quarter of a million of Napoleon's troops, whose presence in central Europe would at the very least have prolonged the war. Wellington inflicted heavy casualties, undermined French prestige and morale, kept alive Spanish resistance and reinvigorated the Allied coalition with the success of his campaigns.

On 14 June, after a diplomatic mission to the newly restored Spanish King Ferdinand VII at Madrid, Wellington bade farewell to his army at Bordeaux. He had been created Marquis of Douro and Duke of Wellington in May and took his seat in the House of Lords on his return to England. In August, he went to Paris as the British ambassador, but became the target of assassination attempts. In February 1815, he was transferred to take the place of the Foreign Secretary, Lord Castlereagh, in representing Britain at the Congress of Vienna, where the European powers were deciding the future of post-war Europe.

It was at Vienna, just one month later, that Wellington received the news of Napoleon's escape from exile on the island of Elba. Tsar Alexander I of Russia turned to him and said: 'It is for you to save the world again.'

Part Three

Blücher

Chapter 11

Formative Years

Gebhard Leberecht von Blücher, the Prussian commander-in-chief at Waterloo, was born on 16 December 1742 at Gross-Renzow near Rostock. At the time, Germany had yet to be united as a nation and was still fragmented into more than 300 separate states. Rostock lay on the Baltic coast in the Duchy of Mecklenburg-Schwerin and so Blücher was not, in fact, a native Prussian, just as Napoleon was a Corsican outsider and Wellington an Anglo-Irishman.

Youth

Blücher was born into a minor noble family and was the youngest of nine children. His father, Captain Christian Friedrich von Blücher, had served in a Mecklenburg cavalry regiment before transferring to the army of Hesse-Cassel and had resigned his commission in 1737, reputedly as he had acted as a second in a fatal duel. While in the army, he had married Dorothea Marie von Zülow, the daughter of a landed nobleman and former soldier.

Rostock, where Blücher grew up, was a busy and interesting place. It was an old Hanseatic city, with important trade links with Denmark, Sweden and Russia and a university that attracted a cosmopolitan mix of students.

Blücher had a happy childhood, but a poor education. He attended the main school in Rostock, but showed little aptitude for study. His spelling and grammar remained idiosyncratic all his life: for example he referred to the French as *Francosen* instead of *Franzosen* and instead of *Majestät* ('majesty') wrote *Majästedt, Magistedt* or *Magested*. He often omitted letters, syllables or even whole words, but he did acquire a good stock of Latin and even in old age still occasionally included a Latin word or quotation in his letters.

Yet his incomplete education should not be confused with stupidity. Napoleon, too, made frequent mistakes in spelling, partly because he had been born in Corsica and French was not his first language. Despite his grammatical mistakes, Blücher did not find it hard to put his thoughts in writing, for he often wrote long letters in his own hand. Unlike Napoleon, he tended to dictate only if he was ill. He was, in fact, naturally shrewd and intelligent and simply learned more from experience and meeting other people than from books. He respected more educated men and cultivated their friendship, but was open about his own limitations and knew what he could achieve through the force of his personality and ability to work with others. His very lack of education gave him a greater ability to talk naturally to his soldiers using clear and plain language. He could immediately find the right words for a situation and address his troops without preparation and his speech does not seem to have been hindered in any way by the idiosyncrasies that affected his writing.

Unlike Napoleon and Wellington, Blücher owed little of his success to family influence. He later remarked 'when I was young, people made short work of kids', and this was hardly surprising in his case, as his parents had a large family but little income. When Blücher was about fourteen, he and another brother were sent to live with his sister Margarete and her husband, Captain von Krackwitz, who had settled on the Swedish island of Rügen, 50 miles north-east of Rostock. Blücher's father wanted them to acquire the necessary experience to be farmers and to manage an estate.

Blücher enjoyed horse-riding, hunting, rowing and sailing as he explored the island with his brother or friends. He also became attracted to the idea of a military career. The Seven Years' War (1756–63) had broken out when Frederick the Great of Prussia made a pre-emptive attack on Austria. Sweden joined the coalition against Prussia and reinforced her troops on Rügen, which formed a base from which to move units across a narrow stretch of sea into Swedish Pomerania, a pocket of territory on the north German coast. Thus, Rügen formed part of a bridgehead on the Continent that the Swedes could use to attack Prussia from the north. But by the end of 1757, their troops had been driven back to the Pomeranian capital, Stralsund, and to Rügen.

As a result of the fighting, the Swedes realized that they needed light cavalry to supplement their cuirassier and dragoon regiments, but were unable to obtain any Cossacks or Hungarian hussars from their allies, Russia and Austria. In the spring of 1758, two noblemen from Rügen offered to raise a couple of hussar squadrons and among those who enlisted were Blücher and one of his older brothers, Siegfried.

Blücher's sister and brother-in-law tried to dissuade him, but he rejected their pleas by pointing out that he was determined to become a soldier and that the sooner he did so, the less time he would waste. Yet he was still only fifteen and hussars had a poor reputation and were seen as suitable only for adventurers and recruits from the lower classes. Since the cost of recruiting and mounting hussars was so low, casualties were affordable and hussars were used on raids and reconnaissances and whenever it seemed a waste to risk other, more precious, cavalry. Thus, like Wellington, Blücher began his military career on an unpromising note and it is easy to appreciate the concerns of his relatives. Yet, ironically, his service in the hussars would actually help his development as a soldier, by exposing him to more combat than he would otherwise have experienced. Advancement would also be easier than in more traditional regiments, whose officer ranks were dominated by the upper nobility.

In the summer of 1758, the two hussar squadrons from Rügen joined eight others recruited in Danzig, Lübeck and Sweden to form the Swedish Hussar Regiment. It was subsequently given the title of the Mörner Hussar Regiment in 1766, later renamed the Crown Prince's Hussar Regiment and disbanded in 1927.

'Grant him soon a nice little war'

Blücher therefore began his military career fighting against Prussia. The Swedish people lacked enthusiasm for the war and their operations after 1758 were unambitious and usually small in scale. Blücher received the first of several wounds in a minor action in September 1759 and then, on 29 August 1760, after more than two years of campaigning, he was taken prisoner in an action near the Kavelpass by a Prussian squadron that suddenly charged out of a wood.

By chance, Blücher turned out to be a distant relative of Colonel Wilhelm Sebastian von Belling, the commander of the Prussian hussar regiment that had captured him. (Blücher's father was the cousin of Belling's wife.) Belling wanted him to enter his regiment as a cornet and Blücher did so within a month, having quickly overcome his initial qualms about breaking his oath of allegiance to the King of Sweden. Ironically, he spent that winter in Rostock, for the Prussians had occupied the Duchy of Mecklenburg–Schwerin and his native city.

The adjustment to Prussian service was not as difficult for Blücher to make as it might seem, for the Swedish Hussar Regiment had been composed of a mixture of Swedes, Germans and Poles, had drilled according to Prussian regulations and had operated using German words of command. It was common at the time to transfer between different armies: for example, one of Blücher's brothers, Gustav, initially joined the Danish army, but later died fighting for the Russians against the Ottoman Turks. Another two brothers had fought for Prussia even when Blücher was fighting against her: Berthold was wounded at Kolin in 1757 and Burchard fell at Kunersdorf two years later.

Belling was the single most formative influence on the young Blücher and had a greater and more lasting impact on his character and development as a soldier than any one mentor had on either Napoleon or Wellington. In later life, Blücher often said that the unforgettable Belling had been like a true father to him.

Despite being a short, stocky and eccentric man, Belling was an inspirational leader. He seemed fearless, and insisted on leading from the front and riding a white horse, however conspicuous this made him to the Swedes on a battlefield. He played as hard as he fought and saw nothing unusual in sending his officers on a mission directly from a ball. He was also a devout man, read the Bible daily and regularly prayed before a battle. Afterwards, in his evening prayers, he would thank God for his preservation, ask for divine guidance for officers with whom he was displeased and His blessing for the whole regiment. 'You see, dear Heavenly Father, the sad plight of Thy servant Belling,' ran one of his favourite requests. 'Grant him soon a nice little war that he may better his condition and continue to praise Thy name, Amen.' It was undoubtedly from Belling that Blücher acquired his own strange mix of piety and ruthlessness.

Belling made Blücher his adjutant and his patronage was crucial to the development of his career. Blücher loved the life of a hussar, for it suited his bold, independent and aggressive temperament. He was promoted to First Lieutenant in June 1761, suffered a wound in the foot in October 1762 and fought a duel the following month while convalescing at Leipzig.

Belling was able to contain the Swedes without much difficulty with a small, mixed force of light cavalry and militia. When Swedish negotiators sought an armistice in 1762, Frederick the Great mockingly asked if he had really been at war with them. On being assured that he had, he replied, 'Oh, yes, I remember now, my Colonel Belling had some dealings with them.'[1]

By the end of the Seven Years' War in 1763, Blücher was still only twenty, but had been fighting for the past four years and found it difficult to adapt to peace and to the tedium of garrison life in various small towns. Instead of taking the opportunity to study and make up for his uneven education as Wellington did, Blücher indulged in gambling, drinking and womanizing, as well as duels and practical jokes. His wildness extended to trading stolen horses and possibly even helping to steal them, as a means of supplementing his pay. In many of his actions, whether horse rustling, breaking an oath of allegiance to the King of Sweden or violating an armistice, Blücher showed little conscience and in this respect was similar to Napoleon, for to them, the end justified the means.

Blücher was promoted to captain in 1771 and took part in the occupation of Poland, which was at the centre of a dispute between Prussia and Russia. Blücher responded to attacks by Polish partisans with ruthless reprisals, for he lacked the subtlety and patience for an effective counter-insurgency campaign. In 1772, he even had a priest shot in the belief that he had been responsible for the kidnap and brutal murder of one of his hussar sentries. This incident marred his regiment's reputation and nearly wrecked his career. His former patron, Belling, had retired and Blücher was passed over for promotion, partly because he was disliked by Belling's successor and partly, it seems, because he belonged only to the minor nobility. True to his impulsive character, Blücher wrote to Frederick the Great, asking leave to resign. He received no reply and wrote again in the spring of 1773:

> Permit me, with all due submission, to apprise Your Majesty how insupportable it is for me to see myself superseded by an officer who has no other essential merit whatever to boast of than being the son of the Margrave of Swedt.
>
> Your Majesty will therefore be graciously pleased to permit me to resign, sooner than expose myself to the most acute sensations during every hour of my life.

Frederick the Great reacted in his whimsical fashion:

> Captain von Blücher has leave to resign, and may go to the devil as soon as he pleases.

With his military career apparently at an end, Blücher's life changed dramatically. He was now in his early thirties and on 21 June 1773 he married Karolina von Mehling, the seventeen-year-old daughter of a landowner in East Prussia with whom he had been billeted in 1770. She bore him seven children, three of whom would survive to adulthood. After learning from his father-in-law how to be a farmer, Blücher bought and ran his own estate, Gross Raddow in Pomerania.

He also took a post in local government and struggled to learn some French. But he had not abandoned the hope of resuming his military career and, as there was a threat of war with Austria in 1778, he made repeated requests for reinstatement. At one point, he threatened to join the Dutch army in order to see active service, following the outbreak of civil war in Holland. Frederick the Great refused his demands to be readmitted to the army, but did subsidize improvements to his estate. Only after Frederick the Great's death in August 1786 did Blücher secure an interview with the new king, Frederick William II, and he was reinstated in his old regiment of hussars with the rank of major on 23 March 1787. His appointment was even backdated, so he was senior to the officer who had superseded him fifteen years before, and he was promoted to lieutenant-colonel in 1788 and colonel in 1790.

After fourteen years as a farmer, Blücher was a soldier again. He was forty-four, about the age at which Wellington and Napoleon fought their last battle, Waterloo. But Blücher sold his estate and threw himself wholeheartedly into his old profession. He maintained discipline, took pains to know all his soldiers and their families and set up a school for their children. But he also returned to reckless gambling and slipped deeper into alcoholism, especially with the death of his wife in June 1791 at the age of thirty-five.

The French Revolutionary Wars

In 1792, the outbreak of war with Revolutionary France gave Blücher the opportunity to see more fighting. He marched with his hussar regiment, of which he commanded a battalion, from Berlin in January 1793 and joined a Prussian corps near the border with Holland. At first, it was a frustrating time. Early in March, he watched Austrian forces attack the French near Roermond and vainly urged the young and inexperienced Prussian commander to attack from the north and cut the French line of retreat. As it was, the French were able to evacuate the town and withdraw to safety.

But over the next two years, Blücher was continually engaged in small-scale actions, ambushes, retreats and pursuits in the Austrian Netherlands and on the Maas, Saar and Rhine rivers. He was personally engaged in hand-to-hand fighting and grew in confidence, self-reliance and tactical skill. Blücher's mentality and methods during these actions as a cavalry officer were those that would distinguish him as an army commander twenty years later: he relied on personal leadership, quick decisions, independence of judgement and bluff, boldness and hard fighting rather than on detailed plans made beforehand on paper. His audacity sometimes caused him to charge impulsively into dangerous situations, but usually the decisiveness and unexpectedness of his actions enabled him to fight his way out of difficulties reasonably unscathed. He was ready to fight in a wide variety of situations, including both open and enclosed terrain, and to take full advantage of the circumstances.

The Battle of Kaiserslautern (28–30 November 1793) offers a good example of Blücher's methods. General Lazare Hoche opened an offensive from the Saar river on 18 November with the French Army of the Moselle. Opposed to him was the Prussian commander, Karl Wilhelm Ferdinand, Duke of Brunswick. Since the Duke had only 20,000 troops against Hoche's 35,000, he decided to fight a defensive battle in the mountains around Kaiserslautern and he checked the French in three days of fighting. On the third day, Hoche made a final effort to win the battle and began his onslaught with a two-hour bombardment from twenty-two guns. Blücher could see the whole attack from the heights where he stood. Towards 9 a.m., Hoche discovered that his artillery lacked enough ammunition to continue the battle and was forced to retreat. Blücher took four squadrons through a wood to attack the French left flank. He sent a request to his superior, General von Kosboth, for the support of two squadrons of cuirassiers. In front of the village of Sambach, 4 miles north-west of Kaiserslautern, Blücher found a French cavalry force, which he estimated was six times as numerous as his own command. French artillery stood on the opposite, western, bank of the Lauter river. According to his own account, Blücher realized that he could not hope to succeed against such odds, but calculated that if the French cavalry could be made to pursue him, they were likely to do so in their usual disorderly manner. He could thus draw them away from the protection of their artillery. He counted on the agility of the Polish horses of his hussars to extricate them from the pursuit and hoped that he could then defeat the French with the support of the cuirassier squadrons that he had requested.

After quickly making his decision, Blücher led the charge: 'My men laid in with the greatest determination, but the wall [of French soldiers] was too strong. We were outflanked and had to fall back. My conjectures came true: the enemy dashed behind us in a wild swarm, but our horses snatched us from their grasp.' Blücher himself had a narrow escape as he rode along a defile, pursued by a Frenchman who cocked his pistol ready to fire. He was alerted to the danger by a shout from a Prussian hussar officer and quickly turned his horse and leaped it out of the defile, while the Frenchman was killed.

By now, the two squadrons of cuirassiers had arrived, along with one of Blücher's hussar squadrons, which he had left behind in support. The leading cuirassier squadron charged straight into the French flank: 'I took advantage of this moment. I shouted to my men: "About turn!" and they immediately obeyed me with full confidence.' Blücher thus pounced on the French, completely disorganized them and pursued them through Sambach and over the Lauter river:

> Now the enemy opened an extremely heavy cannonade, which he had not been able to do until then, since I had still been fighting hand-to-hand with the cavalry. I fell back to a cannonshot's range, without suffering much from this artillery fire. In all, the loss was very low on our side ... the enemy lost very many dead and prisoners as well as a small cannon, which he had abandoned in Sambach. ... I can claim that I have hardly ever been in a more complicated fight as this one and I am all the more pleased as it turned out so splendidly in our favour.

One wonders if the action really unfolded according to a plan as Blücher claimed. It is quite possible that he simply charged prematurely as he lacked the patience to await the cuirassier squadrons and was fortunate that they arrived in time to check the French pursuit after he was repulsed.

In June 1794, Blücher was promoted to major-general. This was on the recommendation of Field Marshal Richard von Möllendorf, who pointed out that Blücher was his oldest colonel, had distinguished himself several times under his command and should be motivated even more by his promotion. Blücher had already taken acting command of his regiment in July 1793 and was confirmed in this position in March 1794. His regiment was renamed the Blücher Hussars and he wrote that he had achieved the goal of his ambition.

Despite being in his early fifties, Blücher's energy and appetite for life remained undimmed. He craved excitement and during these highly satisfying years was able to combine fighting with hunting, gambling and attending dinner parties and the theatre, sometimes on the same day. An orderly officer, Lieutenant Ludwig von Reiche, had expected to find him and his officers resting after an action near Saarbrücken, but recorded how they stayed up all night playing a game and then, in the morning, mounted their horses to carry out a reconnaissance.

'Truly, I did not do great things,' Blücher later remarked, 'but in my small sphere of responsibility I neglected nothing.' He also claimed, less modestly, that he had done more than others 'for the reputation of Prussian troops'. Thus, Blücher had a good war, but his string of local victories could not hide the fact that the overall situation was less favourable. The Allied coalition against Revolutionary France lacked shared aims, determination and coordinated effort. The Allies withdrew from the Austrian Netherlands (now Belgium) in 1794 and it was at this time that the twenty-five-year-old Arthur Wesley first saw action, as commander of the British 33rd Regiment of Foot.

Prussia made peace in April 1795 and would remain neutral for the next eleven years. Blücher remarried on 19 July after courting the twenty-two-year-old Katharina Amalia von Colomb for two months. They had a son in 1808, but he died in infancy. Blücher had two mishaps in 1795, when he lost the tip of a finger in a hunting accident and acquired a permanent limp after falling from his horse. He served in mundane peacetime roles in outlying territories near the Dutch border and in 1801 was promoted to lieutenant-general. The following year, he occupied the province of Münster, a small ecclesiastical territory near the Rhine that Prussia had annexed in agreement with France as compensation for the ceding of Prussian lands on the west bank of the river. Blücher worked with a capable civilian official, Baron Heinrich von Stein, in running Münster fairly and efficiently. The local authorities even asked the Prussian King to appoint Blücher as their governor and this was done.

Chapter 12

The Downfall of Prussia, 1806–12

The Disaster of 1806

During this time, Blücher grew increasingly alarmed as Napoleon strengthened his strategic position in central Europe, first by occupying Hanover, a possession of the British King George III, and then by crushing Austria and Russia in the Austerlitz campaign of 1805. A timely intervention by Prussia could have checked Napoleon and prevented Prussia from becoming dangerously isolated. But she remained neutral, despite Blücher's appeals to King Frederick William III to take decisive action. After Austerlitz, Napoleon was able to group his satellite states in southern and central Germany into a Confederation of the Rhine as a buffer to protect the eastern frontier of France, raise more manpower and extend French influence into central Europe. As a result, he replaced Austria as the dominant power in Germany and posed an intolerable threat to Prussia.

In August 1806, Frederick William III ordered the mobilization of the Prussian army and on 1 October issued an ultimatum to Napoleon to withdraw all French troops from Germany to the west bank of the Rhine. War was now inevitable, but Prussia had an outdated and indecisively led army and failed to seize the initiative by quickly launching a determined and sustained offensive. Also, she was nearly isolated, for Britain could offer little practical support, Austria had been defeated the year before and now remained neutral and the Russian armies were too distant to lend immediate help.

Napoleon concentrated his Grand Army and thrust north-eastwards against the Prussian capital, Berlin. As he did so, he located the Prussian armies, swept round to the west and fell on them on 14 October in the twin battles of Jena and Auerstädt. He himself crushed 48,000 Prussians at Jena with 96,000 of his men, while 12 miles to the north a detached French wing of 27,000 under Marshal Davout defeated the main Prussian army of 63,500 at Auerstädt.

Blücher experienced a bloody and frustrating day. He had command of twenty-eight squadrons of hussars and dragoons at Auerstädt, but they were unable to join him on the battlefield as a result of the chaos and congestion. The countryside was shrouded in fog, which hid Davout's numerical inferiority and increased the confusion of the Prussian high command. Blücher's commander-in-chief, the Duke of Brunswick, gave him nine squadrons of cuirassiers and dragoons, which he detached from their parent division, despite the protests of its commander. Blücher went forward, but had to leave two of the squadrons to guard a bridge at the village of Poppel. He placed the remaining seven on a hill north of Hassenhausen and advanced with twenty men to reconnoitre, but was checked by artillery fire and by a line of infantry that he had mistaken in the fog for a hedge. He sent for reinforcements, but received only three

THE 1806 CAMPAIGN

cuirassier squadrons. He now had ten squadrons to hand, but they came from different regiments and, unlike his regiment of hussars, lacked cohesion and loyalty to him.

By now, the mist had begun to lift and, unable to contain his impatience any longer, Blücher charged. But Davout had deployed his leading infantry division and Blücher had no chance of success as he came up against six battalions and ten guns to the north of Hassenhausen. Davout and his subordinates took shelter inside their infantry squares, which held their fire until the Prussian cavalry were within close range. The charge was repulsed, but Blücher rallied his men and repeated the attack three times until he lost all his adjutants and found it impossible to maintain order. When his own horse was shot beneath him, he saw his men break and flee and he escaped capture only by mounting the horse of one of his trumpeters:

> I went to the village [Spielberg] that lay behind me to halt the fleeing cavalry, snatched a standard and stood with it on the bridge in the village to check the fugitives, but in vain. They all passed me to the left and right. Everyone shouted halt, but not one did so. I shouted to the officers to look around, that the enemy was not following them, but the torrent swept everyone away with it and the cavalry continued to flee up to a wood not far from the Eckartsberg [hill].

Blücher rallied his men and then, 'with bleeding heart', informed the Prussian King that his cavalry 'had not done its duty'. During this time, further Prussian attacks, launched piecemeal, were also repelled and the coordination completely broke down when the Duke of Brunswick fell mortally wounded.

Blücher asked the King for permission to make another charge and was told that he could act as he thought best with the cavalry. He collected some more squadrons and was about to charge when a lieutenant rode up with a new order from the King to make no more attacks, 'as it would be no use'. One of Blücher's men recalled how: 'The general [Blücher] ordered us to remain halted, while he himself first spoke with the King and tried to obtain permission to attack. After some time, he returned and ordered us to move down again from the hill and cover the retreat of the army.' Blücher later wrote that for the rest of his life, he would be pained by his powerlessness at Auerstädt and that he 'had to leave the battlefield with the wretched feeling that I had not been able to have much involvement in deciding the day'.

Responsibility for the defeat lay primarily with the disorder and indecision of the Prussian high command. But Blücher had also contributed to the outcome, for, as usual, he had been too impatient. Instead of taking the time to prepare a more formidable attack in conjunction with reinforcements, he charged too soon with the troops he had to hand. He also underestimated the French, for he had not seen action for eleven years and did not realize how superior Napoleon's units were to the French Revolutionary soldiers whom he had fought in 1793–5. It was not possible to break Davout's unshaken infantry with cavalry alone, yet instead of learning from his initial repulse and awaiting Prussian infantry, Blücher reinforced failure and, by senselessly repeating his charges, caused his squadrons to disintegrate.

It was in the aftermath of Auerstädt, rather than in the actual battle, that Blücher distinguished himself. General Prince Friedrich von Hohenlohe-Ingelfingen assumed command of the surviving Prussian forces and retreated north-eastwards as Napoleon

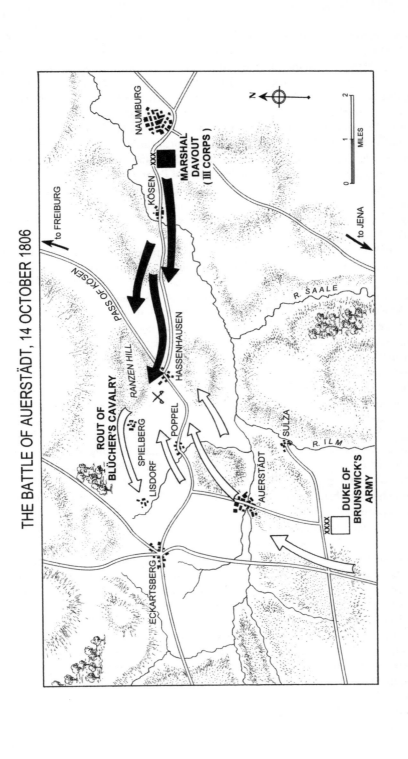

THE BATTLE OF AUERSTÄDT, 14 OCTOBER 1806

N

to FREIBURG

NAUMBURG

KÖSEN

MARSHAL DAVOUT
(III CORPS)

PASS OF KÖSEN

RANZEN HILL

HASSENHAUSEN

ROUT OF
BLÜCHER'S CAVALRY

SPIELBERG

POPPEL

LISDORF

to JENA

R. SAALE

SULZA

R. ILM

AUERSTÄDT

ECKARTSBERG

DUKE OF
BRUNSWICK'S
ARMY

0   1   2
MILES

launched a relentless pursuit. Blücher with a detached force marched sometimes with Hohenlohe's main body, sometimes by a separate route and fought several rearguard actions. After Hohenlohe surrendered at Prenzlau on 28 October, Blücher was on his own with 22,000 troops. He wanted to launch a counter-offensive, but was forced by the reality of the situation to retreat north-westwards in the hope of being evacuated by sea. He managed on 5 November to reach Lübeck, a neutral free city near the Danish border. He entered it and demanded supplies, but was attacked the next day. When the French broke into the city, he slipped away northwards with some horsemen, but had to surrender on the 7th after running out of food and ammunition. He had diverted some French forces away from East Prussia and Poland, where the Russian forces were preparing for a winter campaign, but had been unable to impose a major delay on Napoleon. His fighting retreat was more important as an encouragement for the Prussians at a time when many of their fortresses surrendered with minimal resistance in the wake of Jena.

Napoleon agreed to exchange Blücher for a captured French general and took the opportunity to interview him beforehand. Blücher reached Marienwerder, 150 miles north-west of Warsaw, but was then kept waiting for a fortnight, to his mounting impatience, before he finally met Napoleon at his headquarters at the Château of Finkenstein on 22 April 1807. Napoleon wanted to use Blücher to persuade the Prussian King to make peace, even if Russia was not yet prepared to do so. Blücher later confessed that Napoleon was so charming that he had hardly thought about his hatred of him. They talked alone, without interpreters, but managed to make themselves understood. Napoleon could speak basic German, Blücher had a little French and they also used some Latin and Polish. Napoleon held out his hand and said that he was pleased to be able to meet the bravest Prussian general, while Blücher replied that he had always wanted to see the great Emperor. Napoleon asked why Prussia had made war on him and said that he wished to make peace with the Prussian King, for he viewed conflict with Prussia like one of his hands fighting the other. Napoleon instructed Blücher to communicate everything to the King and then accompanied him to the door and gave him his hand in farewell.

Blücher's exchange took place three days later between two cavalry detachments on the Passarge river north of Liebstadt. But, instead of being given a command in Poland, where Napoleon was fighting General Levin von Bennigsen's Russian army and an attached Prussian corps, Blücher was sent with 5,000 men to join Swedish troops on the island of Rügen. The appointment made sense in that he had begun his military career there by enlisting in a regiment of Swedish hussars, and he had the prospect of seeing action in joint operations with both his Swedish allies and 10,000 British troops. He reached Stralsund in Swedish Pomerania on 30 May and organized his detachment ready to take the offensive, but was forestalled by the end of hostilities and the signing of peace at Tilsit early in July.

Napoleon was determined to prevent Prussia re-emerging to challenge his Empire and therefore reduced her to about half her size, by removing all her lands west of the Elbe river and the territory that she had acquired during the partitions of Poland at the end of the eighteenth century. Prussia was also obliged to pay an extortionate indemnity and later had to agree to limit her army to no more than 42,000 men. In the wake of the disaster, King Frederick William III had about 800 Prussian officers dismissed or imprisoned for failing to do their duty and this helped clear the way for the subsequent emergence of Blücher and other dynamic men.

Blücher was appointed Governor-General of Pomerania in August 1807 and argued bitterly with the French occupation forces, especially about their marauding. His despair at the disaster that had befallen Prussia worsened his alcoholism, which manifested itself in paranoia, delusions, emaciation and shaking hands. Hermann von Boyen, one of the leading military reformers, noted:

> He actually believed that he was pregnant with an elephant;[2] ... another time he imagined that his servants, bribed by France, had heated the floor of his room very hot so as to cause him to burn his feet. When he was sitting, therefore, he kept his feet raised from the ground, or else he would jump round on tiptoe!

When Austria began a new war with Napoleon in April 1809, Blücher urged Frederick William III to join her. The King sensibly refused to act without Russian agreement, full British support and certainty of victory, for a defeat was likely to lead to Prussia's complete partition and the end of his dynasty. Blücher was too loyal to the King to act independently, however much he wanted to see action. In contrast, another Prussian hussar, Major Ferdinand von Schill, led his regiment from Berlin on his own initiative to try and raise a revolt in Germany against the French, but was shot down by Napoleon's forces at Stralsund.

The Austrian Emperor sought peace in July after the defeat of his army at Wagram. Blücher's behaviour at this time was reminiscent of the rashness that had temporarily ended his career under Frederick the Great, three decades earlier. He requested his discharge from the army, not just out of frustration with the failure to join Austria, but also out of concern that younger men were being promoted over his head. He complained in a letter to his friend, August von Gneisenau:

> God knows with what grief I quit a state and an army in which I have been for fifty years. It breaks my heart to abandon a master for whom I would have given my life a thousand times. But all the same, by God in heaven, I will stand no more slights! I will not be treated as a superannuated commander. Younger men shall not be placed ahead of me!

Fortunately, Frederick William III's reaction was different from Frederick the Great's. He reassured Blücher of his confidence and promoted him.

In Prussia, a Military Re-organization Commission had been set up after Tilsit to reform the Prussian army and revive the defeated nation. Blücher corresponded with two of its members, Gerhard von Scharnhorst and Gneisenau, and offered advice. Unlike many conservatives, he supported reforms that he realized were essential, such as allowing non-nobles to be appointed officers. As early as 1805, even before the disaster, he had advocated the formation of a national army to replace the outdated force of professional, long-service soldiers, which was too isolated from the whole of Prussian society.

Blücher also ran a spy network, repaired fortifications and helped to train Prussian troops in secret as part of the efforts to evade Napoleon's restrictions on the size of the army. He had followed news of Wellington's exploits in the Peninsula and, on

4 October 1811, fearing that Napoleon was about to destroy Prussia altogether, he advised the Prussian King to prepare the coastal fortress of Colberg, so it could be defended in the way that Wellington had held out in Lisbon the previous winter after the French overran the rest of Portugal.

Realizing that Blücher was a dangerous enemy, the French forced Frederick William III to dismiss him from the army in November 1811. Blücher retired to an estate near Breslau given to him by the King, who also sent him money and promised to give him a new appointment as soon as possible.

Napoleon forced Prussia to support his invasion of Russia in 1812, by both helping to supply his army and providing a corps of 20,000 troops under General Hans von Yorck to protect the northern flank of his advance. But in the wake of the catastrophic retreat from Moscow that winter, Yorck signed a convention with the Russians at Tauroggen on 30 December, thereby withdrawing his corps from the war between Napoleon and Russia.

The Russian army's advance obliged Napoleon's surviving forces to fall back westwards behind the Elbe river. This freed most of Prussia, including Berlin on 4 March, from French occupation. The Prussian King had already moved to Breslau, out of Napoleon's reach. He signed an alliance with Tsar Alexander I at Kalisch on 26 February and declared war on Napoleon on 13 March.

Blücher was given command of the Prussian forces in the province of Silesia and of a Russian corps under General Ferdinand von Winzingerode. His appointment was popular, but not universally so, for some believed he was unsuited through his age, temperament and mental instability. Scharnhorst dismissed such objections and said that Blücher had to lead, even if he had 100 elephants inside him.

Blücher wrote excitedly that he was 'itching in every finger to grasp the sword'. It was only now, at the age of seventy, that he was about to make his reputation as a great general as he helped liberate central Europe from French occupation. Similarly, it was only in 1812 that Wellington fully emerged from the shadow of his brilliant elder brother, Richard. It was the relatively short period of 1812–15 that made them famous.

Chapter 13

The Army of Silesia, 1813–14

Spring 1813

For the spring 1813 campaign, the Allies fielded a main Russian army under Field Marshal Prince Mikhail Kutusov, flanked by General Ludwig von Wittgenstein's Russo-Prussian army in the north and Blücher's Army of Silesia in the south. Blücher thrust westwards, entering Saxony on 23 March and swiftly reaching its capital, Dresden. But Kutusov, who was cautious and in poor health, moved more slowly. Following his death on 28 April, he was replaced by Wittgenstein as the Allied commander-in-chief.

After assembling a new army to replace the one destroyed in Russia, Napoleon returned from Paris and launched a counter-offensive eastwards on Leipzig. Wittgenstein concentrated the Allied armies south of his line of advance and on 2 May attacked his flank near the town of Lützen. But the Allies failed to exploit this initial superiority of numbers and committed their units piecemeal instead of launching an all-out attack at the start of the battle. This enabled Napoleon to concentrate his units on the battlefield until by the evening he outnumbered the Allies and was pressing them from three sides.

Blücher's Army of Silesia spearheaded the initial Allied assaults. An officer of his staff described how

> Blücher mostly remained in the greatest silence in more or less dangerous positions, ceaselessly smoking his pipe. When it was finished, he held it out behind him and shouted 'Schmidt', whereupon his orderly gave him another, full, one and the old man continued leisurely smoking. We remained for a long time very close to a Russian battery. A shell fell nearby and right in front of us. 'Your Excellency, a shell', everyone shouted.
>
> 'Well then, leave the devilish thing be', said Blücher quite calmly. He watched until it burst and only then made his way to another position.

Later that afternoon, Blücher charged with his cavalry, but received a flesh wound when a musketball cut across his back. He also suffered two more minor injuries and had his horse shot beneath him. He hurriedly had his wound dressed and returned to the fray.

In the evening, Napoleon finally drove the Allies back with a powerful attack in the centre. Colonel Baron Ludwig Wolzogen, who was serving as a Russian staff officer, recalled how an Allied council of war decided on retreat:

> As this decision was made, I suddenly heard an old Prussian general, who had his arm in a bandage, get very worked up about it. 'What,' he exclaimed, 'should all the blood have been shed here for nothing? Never, never, will I

retreat. Instead, I will cut down the French this very night, so that those people will be ashamed who uttered the word retreat.'

In the darkness, I was unable to recognize the man, who spoke these words loudly enough for the monarchs to hear them clearly. I therefore inquired who he was and received the answer: 'Blücher!'

Accordingly, Blücher made a last charge. Despite the exhaustion of the horses and a hollow way that he encountered in the darkness, he caused considerable alarm and penetrated up to about 200 paces of Napoleon himself before being checked by French infantry squares.

Next morning, the Allies retreated in good order and without being pressed, partly because the French were too tired after their exertions during the battle and the tense night that had followed Blücher's charge. The Allied troops did not consider themselves beaten, as Jäger Wilhelm Alberti of the East Prussian Cuirassier Regiment revealed in a letter to his parents: 'The result of the whole battle is that we held the battlefield but are now sitting down here on the Elbe – God knows why. A huge number on both sides have fallen and the bravery of the Prussians has been unbelievably great.'

Blücher shared such feelings and wrote to his wife: 'Apart from the fact that I received three balls at once and also had a horse shot dead, all is well and I am, and remain, fully active. I have satisfaction enough in having attacked Mr Napoleon twice [during the battle] and in having thrown him back both times.'

The Allies retreated 100 miles to the east and offered battle again at Bautzen. Wittgenstein insisted on fighting on the defensive in a strong, entrenched position behind the Spree river, although Blücher thought that this was over-cautious and wanted to play a more active role. During the two-day battle (20–1 May), Napoleon fought his way across the Spree to pin down the Allies frontally while he sent Marshal Ney to fall on their northern wing. Blücher could contain his impatience no longer and demanded his horse, so he could lead a charge, and was with difficulty prevented from doing so. Ney failed to press home his attack and the Allies were able to withdraw in good order, but Blücher was visibly depressed at this new defeat. 'It was a truly melancholy sight,' recalled a staff officer, Captain Ludwig von Reiche, 'as we found Blücher, dismounted and sitting despondently on a rock.'

On 26 May, during the retreat, Blücher's forces ambushed Napoleon's advanced guard at Haynau and seized eighteen guns. Blücher left the details of the attack to his staff and did not personally command the action, but the victory helped restore Allied confidence and spread Blücher's fame.

An armistice was signed at Pleischwitz on 4 June, for both sides were exhausted and needed to regroup, and it was later extended with an agreement that hostilities would not recommence until 17 August.

The Autumn 1813 Campaign

When fighting began again in August, Napoleon faced a more complex and adverse strategic situation. Austria declared war on him on 12 August and Swedish troops also took the field under their Crown Prince. The Allies therefore enjoyed superior numbers and could place three armies in a semi-circle around Napoleon in central

Europe. These were Prince Karl von Schwarzenberg's Army of Bohemia to the south; Blücher's Army of Silesia to the east; and the Crown Prince of Sweden's Army of the North. Schwarzenberg was also the Allied commander-in-chief, but was hindered by interference from the Allied monarchs, who personally accompanied his army.

During the spring campaign, the Army of Silesia had fought at Lützen and Bautzen only as a contingent of the united Allied army and had been constrained by the caution and indecision of the Allied high command. This now changed and in the autumn the three Allied armies often operated at more than 100 miles from each other. Blücher became an independent army commander and was able to exert a greater influence on the course of the campaign by taking the initiative. His Army of Silesia contained 95,000 men, but was of mixed quality and included poorly equipped and trained Prussian militia as well as Russian and Prussian regulars.

On 14 August, Blücher began hostilities by entering the neutralized ground, three days earlier than was allowed under the terms of the armistice. The violation was excused on the basis that the French had already broken the terms, especially by surprising and smashing a formation of Prussian irregulars, Lützow's Freicorps, near Leipzig on 17 June.

The Allies planned to avoid a battle with Napoleon himself except on favourable odds. Any army targeted by him was to retire while the others attacked his detached forces and menaced his lines of communication. As a result, the Allies hoped to deny him a decisive victory and force him to march back and forth to meet each successive threat. Thus, when Napoleon advanced against the Army of Silesia on 21 August, he merely chased it back eastwards in disorder. Despite his keenness to attack, Blücher appreciated the wisdom of avoiding battle on this occasion. 'I am well in health,' he wrote, 'and very happy to have played a trick on the great man. He ought to be furious at not having been able to make me accept battle.'

Nonetheless, the Army of Silesia's retreat undermined its morale and it was fortunate for Blücher that Napoleon had to return to save his main base, the city of Dresden, from Schwarzenberg's Army of Bohemia, which had advanced northwards through the mountains into Saxony. To contain Blücher, Napoleon left behind a covering force, the Army of the Bober under Marshal Jacques Macdonald, a mediocre commander unequal to an independent command.

Blücher naturally resumed the offensive and on 26 August his army and the Army of the Bober blundered into each other near the Katzbach river. Macdonald's advance was disjointed and heavy rain prevented the flintlock muskets of either side from firing, which enabled Blücher to exploit his superior numbers of cavalry. In fact, as his Chief of the General Staff, Gneisenau, noted, it was like a battle of antiquity, when battles were decided not by firearms but by cold steel. Blücher launched a decisive attack with 55,000 of his Prussians and Russians against 27,000 of Macdonald's men, some of whom were still climbing to the plateau above the Katzbach in considerable confusion. 'Now my children, I have enough French over here,' he told his troops. 'Now at them!'

They drove the French back down the slopes to the raging Neisse river, a tributary of the Katzbach, where many drowned. 'Today was the day that I have longed for so dearly,' Blücher wrote to his wife that evening. 'We have completely beaten the enemy and taken many guns and prisoners.'

Blücher pursued Macdonald vigorously during the days that followed, ignoring objections from subordinates that he was pressing his troops too hard. He inflicted heavy casualties, took at least 14,000 prisoners and caused thousands more to desert. He also captured two eagle standards and much of Macdonald's artillery. This timely success was the Army of Silesia's first important battlefield victory (Haynau on 26 May had been a small action) and gave it a priceless self-confidence. It was never as efficient, cohesive or formidable as Wellington's army was in the final years of the Peninsular War, but under Blücher's leadership it steadily built on its initial success. One of the members of Blücher's staff noted the confidence that reigned in his headquarters after the Battle of the Katzbach, and wrote that doubts and concerns rarely surfaced there-after. The Katzbach was also Prussia's first major, decisive victory for over fifty years, for her successes during her two-year involvement in the French Revolutionary Wars (1793–5) had been limited in both scale and significance.

At this time, Blücher was in good shape physically and morally. His adjutant, Captain August von Nostitz, noted: '[Blücher's] health left nothing to be desired. His strong and vigorous body bore with ease all the fatigues of war and, although he was seventy, his spirit had retained an almost youthful cheerfulness.'

Blücher bought an English greyhound, which became devoted and would outlive him by only a few months. It travelled in his waggon, slept on his bed and had to be looked for nearly every day during the marches.

Early in September, Blücher again withdrew and avoided battle as Napoleon personally moved against him. The cautious Schwarzenberg wanted the additional security of having the Army of Silesia reinforce him, but Blücher and his staff insisted on a more ambitious role. They wanted to march north, join the Crown Prince of Sweden and boldly cross to the west bank of the Elbe river to threaten Napoleon's rear. Blücher was allowed to have his way and Schwarzenberg was instead reinforced by another Allied force, Bennigsen's newly arrived Army of Poland. Gneisenau wrote on 26 September:

> Since the others do not want to do so, we will open the show and assume the leading role. . . . In the main army [under Schwarzenberg], they always draw up new plans and never execute them, while the Crown Prince of Sweden hangs around between the Nuthe and Elbe rivers even after winning two victories.

Tsar Alexander I later remarked that the Allies would still be stuck in the mud of Bohemia if Blücher had not drawn them out of it by crossing the Elbe.

Operations now shifted 50 miles to the west and focused on the city of Leipzig, which became Napoleon's new base. To the north of the city, Blücher fought his way over the Elbe river at Wartenburg on 3 October, reluctantly followed by the Crown Prince of Sweden, his nominal superior. Napoleon headed north to counter-attack, but instead of tamely retiring back across the Elbe, Blücher and the Crown Prince un-expectedly evaded Napoleon's blow by going westwards.

Napoleon, having failed to catch Blücher, returned southwards to Leipzig. All four Allied armies gradually closed in around the city and between 16 and 19 October attacked Napoleon on three sides with superior numbers. Blücher in the north was exasperated by the reluctance of the Crown Prince of Sweden to become seriously

THE LEIPZIG CAMPAIGN, AUTUMN 1813

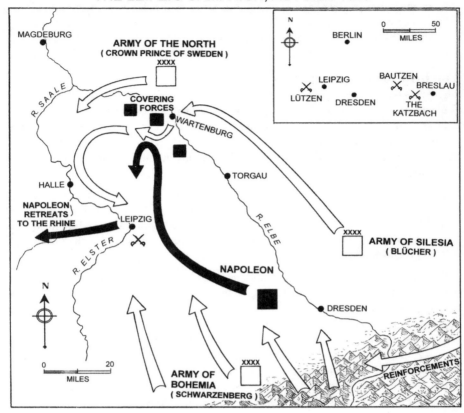

engaged; it did not help matters that the Crown Prince, formerly one of Napoleon's marshals, Jean-Baptiste Bernadotte, had been one of Blücher's opponents in 1806. Blücher secured a promise of cooperation only by agreeing to lend him 30,000 of his troops.

On the 18th, Napoleon began to retreat and the next day, the Allies attacked his rearguard holding Leipzig itself. Blücher wanted to be the first into the city and yelled his usual battle cry 'Vorwärts! Vorwärts!' His Russian soldiers eventually realized what he was shouting and promptly nicknamed him 'Marshal Forwards!' At last the fighting was over, completing a disastrous defeat for Napoleon. Blücher greeted the Emperor of Austria, the Tsar of Russia and the King of Prussia inside the city and was made Field Marshal. He informed his wife on 25 October: 'I no longer know what to do with the decorations, for I am laden like an old coach horse. But the thought that makes it all worthwhile for me is that I was the one who humiliated the arrogant tyrant.'

The victorious Allies pressed westwards up to the Rhine, the eastern frontier of France. Blücher wrote to his wife on 3 November:

> The great undertaking is now finished, the French are completely thrown
> over the Rhine. For successive days I have always advanced my headquarters

in the evening to where Napoleon had previously left and I have always slept on the same spot. He has lost most of his army, especially his artillery, and if we had not made great mistakes, he himself would have been lost with all his army. But he will not be moving back into Germany soon, for what he saved is in a miserable condition.

The Invasion of France: 1814

The Allies now prepared to invade eastern France with Blücher's Army of Silesia and Schwarzenberg's Army of Bohemia, while additional forces operated in support in Belgium, northern Italy and south-western France. Blücher crossed the Rhine in the north at Kaub, Mannheim and Coblenz on 1 January 1814, just over a week after Schwarzenberg had crossed in the south. He lost only 300 men in doing so and wrote to his wife:

> The early New Year's morning was a joyous one for me, seeing that I crossed the proud Rhine. The banks rang with the cries of joy, and my brave troops were enthusiastic in their reception of me. The enemy offered but little opposition. . . . My brave comrades are making such a noise that I shall have to go and hide myself in order that quiet may be restored.

Blücher and Schwarzenberg outnumbered Napoleon by more than two to one, but would take three months to reach Paris. Some Allied leaders, fearful of heavy casualties, hoped to use limited military operations to put pressure on Napoleon for a negotiated settlement. The Austrians, for example, did not necessarily want to see Napoleon toppled, for a weak France could become a Russian satellite. Blücher took on a significance out of proportion to the numbers under his command as he was exceptional in having a clear military aim and an unshakeable resolve to achieve it. 'We must go to Paris,' he demanded. 'Napoleon has paid his visits to all the capitals of Europe; should we be less polite?' Only in Paris could the Allies secure a lasting peace and security for Europe.

But Blücher's determination could become recklessness. Schwarzenberg complained on 29 January:

> Blücher, and even more so Gneisenau, to whom the good old man must lend his name, thrust on Paris with such a great and quite childish rage and they trample on all the rules of war. They run madly to Brienne without covering the highroad from Châlons to Nancy with a considerable corps. Without worrying about their rear and flanks, they make plans only for fine parties in the Palais Royal [in Paris], which is ridiculous at such an important moment.

It was equally true that Schwarzenberg was over-cautious. He saw his own Army of Bohemia as the main Allied force, with Blücher's role being merely to cover its northern flank.

After raising more conscripts, Napoleon reached the front and counter-attacked the Allies towards the end of January. His initial target was Blücher's Army of Silesia, which he attacked on 29 January at Brienne-le-Château, 90 miles east of Paris. After the failure of the initial French attacks, the fighting died down and Blücher returned to his headquarters in the town's château. But the action flared up again later that evening and Blücher and Gneisenau narrowly escaped when the château was captured by French infantry.

Blücher ordered a counter-attack and by midnight had regained most of the town, but not the château, where the French were too well established. He then fell back 4 miles to La Rothière, where with the support of Schwarzenberg's army he attacked and defeated Napoleon in another battle on 1 February. Next day, he wrote to his wife:

> The great action has taken place. Yesterday, I clashed with the Emperor Napoleon. The Tsar of Russia and our King came as the battle began; both monarchs entrusted everything to me and remained spectators of the fight. At 1 p.m., I attacked the enemy and the battle lasted until night and not until 10 p.m. did I drive the Emperor Napoleon from all his positions and his defeat was complete. Sixty guns and more than 3,000 prisoners have fallen into my hands. The number of dead is very high, for the fighting raged with the utmost bitterness. You can imagine how many thanks I received from the monarchs. [Tsar] Alexander clasped my hand and said: 'Blücher, today you have put the crown on all your victories; mankind will bless you.'

Blücher has been criticized for the way he fought the battle and particularly for making repeated frontal attacks on the village of La Rothière instead of concentrating more pressure against Napoleon's flanks. But visibility was limited by falling snow and time was short, for dusk fell early in February. Attempts at major outflanking moves would have been hindered by poor quality roads and ran the risk that Napoleon might retreat without a battle or else defeat Blücher's weakened centre. Blücher was also constrained by Schwarzenberg, who lent him some corps from the Army of Bohemia but did not give him full freedom in how to use them.

After the battle, Blücher moved his headquarters back to the Château of Brienne. He found that the room where he had previously slept had been occupied by Napoleon. It was usual for quartermasters to write in chalk the names of the occupants or units on the doors of billets. On the doors of the Château of Brienne were written 'Feldmarschall Blücher' at the top, then 'Sa Majesté l'Empereur' and then again, at the bottom, 'Feldmarschall Blücher'.

Blücher was elated at the result of La Rothière, for it was his first personal victory over Napoleon. (At Leipzig, Blücher had been only one of several Allied commanders.) Lady Burghersh, the twenty-two-year-old wife of the British military attaché at Schwarzenberg's headquarters, wrote to her mother: 'I wish you could see that delightful, fine old Blücher. At seventy-two years old he tires out all his young aides-de-camp and officers, and is equally alert in mind and body. He calls Burghersh the "lord of the *schöne Frau*", i.e. the pretty wife!'

But Blücher was now dangerously over-confident. He and Schwarzenberg advanced on Paris, but along parallel routes 30 miles apart. They thereby eased congestion and the difficulties of supplying large numbers of troops in winter, but made it harder for them to support each other. Blücher also allowed his army to become strung out over a distance of more than 45 miles as it pursued a French detached force under Marshal Macdonald and tried to intercept it. Misled by information from Schwarzenberg, Blücher believed as late as 9 February that Napoleon was still in the south opposite the Army of Bohemia. Furthermore, an Allied detachment linking the two armies had been withdrawn to join Schwarzenberg, leaving Blücher's flank exposed. Unaware of this, he wrote to his wife on the 10th:

> We now have 15 [German] miles left to Paris.[3] We are sure to arrive before his capital in eight days. In all probability, Napoleon will lose his crown. . . . We are still in the grip of winter here; today it is mild and rainy. At my current location is produced the best Champagne in the whole of France and it is drunk by generals and common soldiers alike. It also agrees with me fairly well. . . . Now we set off for Paris and I do not believe that Napoleon will fight another battle.

But that is exactly what Napoleon did. He thrust northwards into Blücher's exposed southern flank, crushing one of his Russian corps at Champaubert on 10 February and cutting the Army of Silesia in two. He then turned on the two corps to the west and defeated them at Montmirail and Château-Thierry (11 and 12 February). Yet Blücher's spirits were hardly affected by these defeats, partly as information from a French prisoner suggested that Napoleon was now withdrawing on Paris. He wrote to his wife on the 13th:

> I have had three unpleasant days. Napoleon attacked me three times in three days with all his strength and all his Guards, but he did not achieve his aim and is today retreating on Paris. I will follow him tomorrow, then our armies will unite and everything will be decided by a big battle before Paris. Do not fear that we will be beaten, for that is not possible, unless an unheard-of mistake happens.

In fact, Napoleon had not finished his attacks and on the 14th he struck at Blücher himself and the two rearmost corps of the Army of Silesia at Vauchamps. Blücher beat a fighting retreat, during which he was knocked over and nearly captured or trampled underfoot. His adjutant, August von Nostitz, noted that Blücher was keenly aware of the danger that threatened his army and the outcome of the campaign, but was too caught up in the confusion to provide his usual leadership:

> Had it been a matter of capturing a village or storming a battery, he would have shown the way with the flag in his hand and exerted the whole force of his heroic strength to tip the balance. But on this day, although he was always in personal danger, he was able to exercise his usual influence neither on the course of the battle nor on the morale of his troops.

The Army of Silesia had lost at least 16,000 men, or a third of its strength, in less than a week. Blücher retreated to regroup, but was now reinforced by two corps, transferred from the Army of the North, which had been operating against French forces in Belgium. These corps amounted to 47,000 men and more than compensated for his recent losses. Blücher therefore again marched on Paris, intending to collect these men on the way. When Napoleon pursued him, he hurriedly abandoned his advance and fell back northwards to cross the Aisne river and unite with his reinforcements.

Blücher occupied the Chemin des Dames ridge near the village of Craonne and gave battle on 7 March. He planned to check Napoleon with a defensive action across the top of the ridge while sending a mass of cavalry to outflank him to the north. But the

BLÜCHER IN 1814

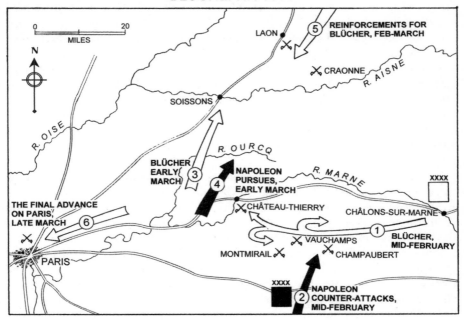

coordination of the plan miscarried and Blücher had to order a retreat after a bloody and indecisive battle.

Blücher withdrew 9 miles to the north, to a strong defensive position based on the hilltop city of Laon. Here, on 9 March, he again offered battle. By now, he outnumbered Napoleon by 90,000 men to 36,500 and easily checked all his attacks before routing his detached right wing under Marshal Marmont on the eastern side of the city that evening.

But Blücher's health had been undermined by the physical and mental strain. He was feverish and had to command from a chair at the top of the hill of Laon, where he was nearly injured when a cannonball smashed through a mill and wounded several of his retinue with flying splinters of wood. That night, he completely collapsed and had to have his inflamed eyes bandaged against the light. Confined to his bed and deprived of exercise, he lapsed into depression, constantly fretted at the thought of death and complained about his suffering. According to Nostitz: 'The Field Marshal's one idea was to resign his command and quit the army. Every announcement, every report, no matter from whom or about what, was disgusting and loathsome to him.'

While Blücher was incapacitated, Gneisenau, his Chief of the General Staff, cautiously cancelled plans for an ambitious move to encircle Napoleon from the east. This allowed Napoleon to break contact and withdraw on the 10th and the disappointment worsened existing friction within the Army of Silesia. The Russians, for example, believed that they, rather than the Prussians, were having to bear the brunt of the fighting, while a Prussian corps commander, General Hans von Yorck became so exasperated that he left in his coach and had to be summoned back by Blücher scribbling a note, with his hand guided by Nostitz: 'Old comrade, history should not have to relate such things of us! Be sensible and come back!' These incidents showed that Blücher was indispensable as the leader of his army. It is hardly surprising that one of his subordinates, General Count Louis de Langeron, is said to have exclaimed: 'Let us bring this lifeless corpse along with us!'

Napoleon now made a fatal blunder. After moving southwards against Schwarzenberg and being checked by his superior numbers at the Battle of Arcis-sur-Aube (20–1 March), he marched eastwards against his lines of communication, calculating that this would cause him to retreat. Instead, the Allies ignored the threat to their rear and advanced with both their armies on Paris. Blücher recovered his spirits, but could still barely ride a horse and instead lay in a carriage and shaded his eyes with a lady's green silk hat.

In Napoleon's absence, the weak French forces available to defend Paris were no match for Blücher and Schwarzenberg's combined strength of about 100,000. The French held the hills north and east of the city, but were driven back in a bloody battle on 30 March. Blücher spent most of the day in his carriage, which was parked close to his reserves, but in the middle of the afternoon, as the Allied offensive became more general, he mounted a horse and personally ordered an assault on the suburb of La Chapelle just outside the city walls. An armistice soon halted the fighting, for the marshals in charge of the defence recognized the unfeasibility of further resistance. They agreed to evacuate the city and the Allies entered it the next day. Despite his illness, Blücher dearly wanted to take part in this triumphant entry, but was talked out of it by his staff.

Napoleon, who had hurriedly marched back westwards with his army, was too late to save his capital and was forced to abdicate on 6 April. Blücher had played a vital role in securing his downfall. 'The amazing old fellow always attacked me with the same fury,' Napoleon remarked a month later. 'Hardly had I defeated him than he again stood ready for battle before me.'

Blücher now resigned command of the Army of Silesia, which he had led from the banks of the Oder river to the walls of Paris. 'I have to thank this army for the happiest and brightest moments of my life,' he wrote to the King. 'I regard the army as if it were my family.'

The feeling was a mutual one. One of his corps commanders, General Count de Langeron, wrote: 'This army had the fortune to contribute more to the conclusion of the war than the other armies and to make its brave, old leader immortal.'

Lady Burghersh saw Blücher at a dinner on 20 April: 'I was quite shocked at the alteration in him since his illness. He is quite broken, and I do not think he will live long.'

But he confounded expectations by completely recovering within a month. He was made Prince of Wahlstadt on 3 June, after a village near the Katzbach river, the site of one of his greatest victories. At this time, he was inundated with British admirers who came to see him in France and he explained how he had to shake each of them by the hand and how they were the craziest people he knew. He wrote to his wife from Paris on 6 May: 'More than 100 English people have come here, just to see me and make my acquaintance. Yesterday, the famous Lord Wellington came here and I am invited to spend three days with him, but I must be very careful not to drink too much.'

In June, Blücher visited Britain with the King of Prussia and Tsar Alexander I. On his arrival at Dover, the people wildly cheered 'Blücher for ever!' and demanded locks of his hair as souvenirs. Later, when he returned to Prussia, he had a rapturous reception in all the towns and villages through which he passed and then retired to his estate at Krieblowitz in Silesia.

Blücher was proud of his role in defeating Napoleon, but grew disillusioned with the European settlement that began to emerge from the Congress of Vienna. He believed that France had not been sufficiently punished, or Prussia rewarded for her sacrifices. He decided to resign altogether from the Prussian army, but his request was still being considered when news came of Napoleon's escape from exile. Blücher was delighted at the prospect of renewed war: 'It is the greatest piece of good luck that could have happened to Prussia! Now the war will begin again, and the armies will make good all the faults committed in Vienna!'

Blücher was appointed to command the Prussian Army of the Lower Rhine, with Gneisenau once again as his Chief of the General Staff.

Part Four

The Waterloo Campaign, 1815

Chapter 14

The First Battles

After regaining power in March 1815, Napoleon faced the prospect of an Allied invasion of France that summer. Characteristically, he decided to seize the initiative and strike a pre-emptive blow by invading the United Netherlands, an amalgamated Belgium and Holland. Success would enable him to increase his strength with Belgian manpower and possibly even cause the fall of the British government, making it easier to secure an advantageous peace settlement.

For Britain, the United Netherlands were a key strategic region, above all as her security would be at risk if the French controlled the powerful naval base of Antwerp. Wellington reached Brussels on 4 April and began to build an army, for his experienced and disciplined forces of the Peninsular War had been disbanded the previous year. By mid-June, he could field 93,000 men in his Army of the Low Countries, but they were of mixed quality. Only one-third of them were British and even they included large numbers of inexperienced troops. The other two-thirds came from the United Netherlands and the German states of Hanover, Brunswick and Nassau and were often young and untried. 'I have got an infamous army,' Wellington complained on 8 May, 'very weak and ill-equipped, and a very inexperienced staff.'[4] But he exaggerated, in order to press for more resources, and the situation improved by the start of hostilities. Historians have tended to be over-critical of Wellington's foreign troops and to ignore units that distinguished themselves, such as the Dutch–Belgian infantry brigade and artillery battery that played a leading role in the defeat of Napoleon's Imperial Guard at the climax of Waterloo. They have also focused too much on a few mistakes by one of Wellington's corps commanders, the twenty-two-year-old Prince of Orange, and not enough on the ability of the vast majority of his senior officers. Wellington was certainly better served by his key subordinates at the Battle of Waterloo than Napoleon was by his.

Blücher, too, commanded a poorer quality army than before and in fact, if any army deserved to be called infamous, it was his more than Wellington's. His Army of the Lower Rhine of 117,000 men had to be hastily assembled after eleven months of peace and in the middle of a major reorganization of the Prussian army. Its troops ranged from disciplined regulars to *Landwehr*, or militia, and included men from areas, such as Westphalia, Berg and the Rhineland, that had recently been annexed to Prussia after twenty years of French occupation. Soldiers from these provinces may have resented their exploitation by France, but also had little liking for the Prussians and would not always fight with much spirit. A contingent from Saxony even had to be disbanded after elements mutinied on 2 May and attacked Blücher's headquarters. Furthermore, Blücher had no Guards or other elite regiments with his army and his cavalry was especially weak, being badly equipped, trained and mounted and poorly led. Nor did he have any reserves under his direct control, since all the units were assigned to his four corps. His corps commanders were capable rather than outstanding, but he did have the important advantage of an experienced and professionally trained General Staff.

Against Wellington and Blücher's combined strength of 210,000, Napoleon could bring only the 124,000 men of the Army of the North, for he had to deploy other troops to guard the frontiers and interior of France. He generally had more experienced troops than either Wellington or Blücher, but lacked enough time for his units to develop cohesion or for all his men to be fully equipped. The political upheavals of the past year made the troops doubt the loyalty of many of their senior officers, who had often willingly served the Bourbon monarchy. Morale was therefore brittle and this would have serious consequences in the event of a defeat.

Since he was so outnumbered, Napoleon needed to surprise and defeat Wellington and Blücher piecemeal before they could concentrate from their cantonments covering 100 miles of frontier. He planned to strike between their two armies and then attack each of them in turn. Five years after the campaign, Wellington told a friend of his admiration for Napoleon's careful preparations for the surprise attack that opened hostilities: 'Bonaparte's march upon Belgium was the finest thing ever done – so rapid and so well combined.'

Napoleon's Onslaught

The attack began in the early hours of 15 June. Officers read Napoleon's order of the day to their troops immediately before they marched. In it, he reminded them that it was the anniversary of two of their most famous victories, Marengo (1800) and Friedland (1807), which had both been fought on 14 June. He told them that a coalition of European princes now threatened the independence of France and that the French army was marching to repel this aggression:

> Soldiers! We shall have to make some forced marches, fight some battles, run some risks, but with constancy victory will be ours. The rights, the honour and the happiness of the country will be reconquered. For every Frenchman who has courage, the moment has come to conquer or die!

Despite some delays, the French invasion initially went well. Napoleon drove in the Prussian outposts and seized the crossings over the Sambre river at Charleroi, 30 miles south of Wellington's headquarters at Brussels. Napoleon then pushed the left wing of his army along the Brussels road against Wellington and the right wing towards Fleurus in the north–east against Blücher. He would use his reserve to reinforce either wing as was required.

At 1 p.m., Blücher wrote to his wife from his headquarters at Namur, 20 miles east of Charleroi: 'At this moment, I learn that Bonaparte has attacked all my outposts. I immediately break off and move against my opponent. I will give battle with pleasure and will write immediately to you of the outcome.' He began to concentrate his army in a previously selected position around the village of Ligny, 10 miles north–east of Charleroi. The concentration was covered by the Prussian I Corps under General Hans von Ziethen, which made a fighting retreat in the face of Napoleon's advance. Blücher reached Ligny towards the end of the day and, as his adjutant, Major August von Nostitz, recorded: 'The Prince [Blücher] thanked General Ziethen with a sincere handshake. Then he rode to nearly all the various formations, praised and encouraged them and was welcomed everywhere with hearty cheers.'

It was not until late that afternoon that Wellington learnt of the start of hostilities. He was reluctant to concentrate his army until he was sure of the true axis of the French offensive: he suspected that the reported attack was merely a diversion and that Napoleon would make his real offensive further west, near Mons. 'I have always avoided a false move,' he observed later. 'I preferred being late in my movement to having to alter it.' For similar reasons, he had been slow to react to Marshal Soult's offensive over the Pyrenees in July 1813, as he had not been convinced at first that it was aimed at Pamplona rather than San Sebastian.

Initially, therefore, Wellington simply took the precautionary step of concentrating his divisions at assembly points across western Belgium. These orders, issued at 7 p.m., kept the Mons area covered. But Wellington did not yet know that the Prussians were concentrating at Ligny and that they had uncovered the road running due north from Charleroi to Brussels. Since his own orders omitted to cover this road, a dangerous gap would open between himself and Blücher.

The left wing of Napoleon's army was already advancing along the Brussels road under Marshal Ney. Fortunately, two of Wellington's Dutch generals, Jean-Victor de Constant-Rebecque and Henri-Georges de Perponcher, would disregard Wellington's orders to concentrate the 2nd Dutch–Belgian Division at Nivelles and would instead do so further east, at the crossroads of Quatre Bras, thus blocking the Brussels road and protecting Blücher's western flank at Ligny.

Wellington then received further reports, including the news that Blücher was concentrating at Ligny. At 10 p.m., he issued a set of After Orders, which began to shift his army towards his eastern flank to support Blücher. That night, Wellington attended a ball given by a British resident of Brussels, the Duchess of Richmond, which was dramatically interrupted by news that the French had penetrated almost as far as Quatre Bras. The ball broke up as officers returned to their units and prepared to march at first light. Wellington took a few hours' sleep and was woken at 5 a.m. on 16 June to be reassured that Mons had not been attacked.

Wellington rode south and reached Quatre Bras towards 10 a.m. He found the bulk of the 2nd Dutch–Belgian Division at the crossroads, but could see little sign of any French activity, for Ney had not yet brought up his rearmost units. He therefore took the opportunity to ride over to Ligny, 6 miles to the south-east, to confer with Blücher. Lieutenant-Colonel Ludwig von Reiche, the chief-of-staff of the Prussian I Corps, described how Wellington arrived soon after 1 p.m.:

> He wore a simple blue overcoat without decorations, an ordinary three-cornered hat with three cockades next to each other, one black and two (Spanish and Portuguese) red, with a bush of red over white feathers hanging down between the two brims of the hat, as was the English way at that time. Otherwise, he was dressed very inconspicuously and so none of our troops realized who or what he was. As I knew him from the review at Grammont, I was able to tell them and naturally everyone who was standing nearby turned to look at the famous war hero. ...
> The horse that Wellington rode on this occasion drew our attention just as

much. Behind the saddle was strapped a small valise, which an officer of his retinue said contained a change of clothes. Also, a portfolio together with a pen and ink was fastened in place of the pistol holster. These indicated how English industry can be compendious and practical.

At one moment, Wellington and Blücher could clearly see Napoleon and his staff making a reconnaissance on the opposite side of the battlefield. The Prussians had now concentrated three of their four corps at Ligny, ready to offer battle against Napoleon and the bulk of the French army. They wanted support from Wellington and received an overly optimistic impression of when they would receive it. This remains one of the most controversial aspects of the campaign and it has been suggested that Wellington deliberately deceived the Prussians into accepting battle in order to cover the concentration of his army. But Wellington was often over-confident and the apparent French inactivity at Quatre Bras that morning had hardly indicated to him that he would encounter much opposition. He also seems to have been misled by the miscalculations of his staff into thinking that he would soon have a powerful force united at Quatre Bras ready to take the offensive.

The Battle of Quatre Bras
When Wellington returned to Quatre Bras towards 2.30 p.m., he found the French preparing a general attack against the Dutch–Belgian troops holding the position. He later recalled:

> The straggling fire there had continued from morning ... I was informed that the [French] army was collecting in a wood in front. I rode forward and reconnoitred or examined their position according to my usual practice.
>
> I saw clearly a very large body of men assembled, and a [marshal] reviewing them, according to their usual practice, preparatory to an attack.
>
> I heard distinctly the usual cries: 'En avant! en avant! L'Empereur récompensera celui qui s'avancera!' [Forwards! Forwards! The Emperor will reward whoever advances!]
>
> Before I quitted the Prince of Orange [to ride forward], some of the officers standing about had doubted whether we should be attacked at this point.
>
> I sent to the Prince of Orange from the ground on which I was standing, to tell him that he might rely upon it that we should be attacked in five minutes, and that he had better order the retreat towards the main position of the light troops and guns which were in front, and which could make no resistance to the fierce attack about to be made upon us.
>
> These were accordingly withdrawn, and in less than five minutes we were attacked by the whole French army under Maréchal Ney. There was in fact no delay or cessation from attack from that time till night.

The Battle of Quatre Bras was a confused and desperately fought action. The 1st Regiment of Foot Guards, for example, lost more men in the final two hours of the fighting than it did in the whole Battle of Waterloo. Ensign Edward Macready of the 30th (or the Cambridgeshire) Regiment of Foot vividly described how his company

Napoleon: detail from his statue at Montereau, where he defeated the Austrians and Württembergers on 18 February 1814.

Wellington in the famous portrait by Sir Thomas Lawrence.

Blücher, sketched during his visit to England in June 1814.

Napoleon on the bridge at Arcole, 15 November 1796.

Napoleon as First
Consul, 1803.

Napoleon crossing
the Alps, May 1800.

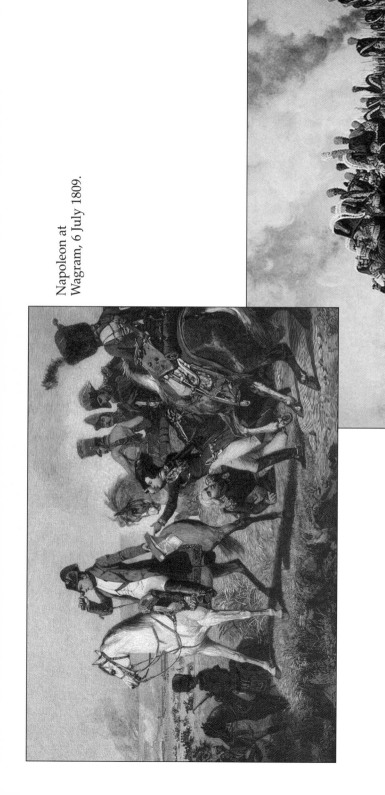

Napoleon at
Wagram, 6 July 1809.

Napoleon and his
staff at Borodino,
7 September 1812.

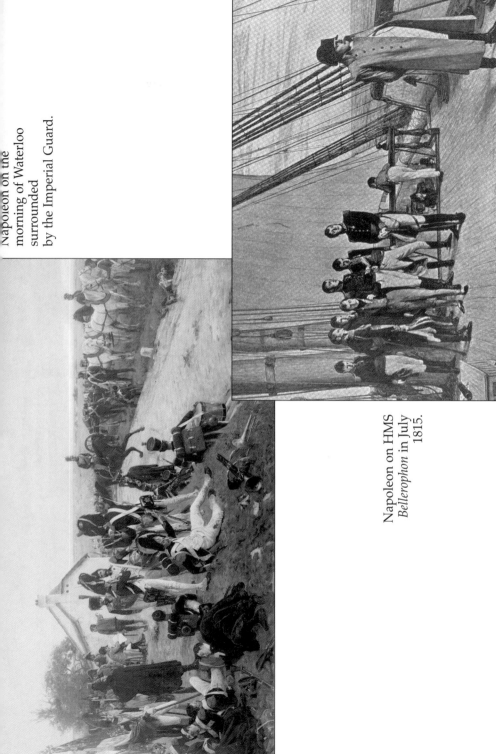

Napoleon on the
morning of Waterloo
surrounded
by the Imperial Guard.

Napoleon on HMS
Bellerophon in July
1815.

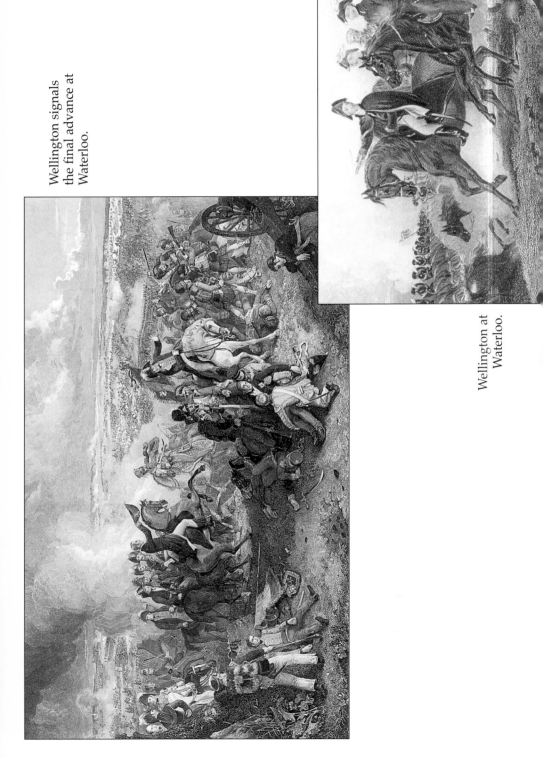

Wellington signals
the final advance at
Waterloo.

Wellington at
Waterloo.

Major-General the Hon Sir Arthur Wellesley in 1804.

Field Marshal the Duke of Wellington.

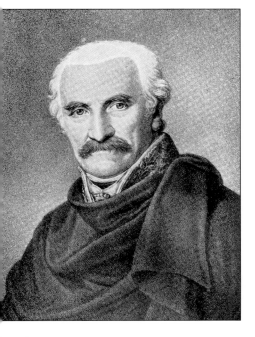

Blücher.

Gneisenau.

The grim reality of Napoleonic warfare: the Battle of Leipzig, 19 October 1813. French infantry (left) fight Prussian *Landwehr* or militia.

THE BATTLES OF QUATRE BRAS AND LIGNY, 16 JUNE 1815

THE WATERLOO CAMPAIGN

N

0 10
MILES

BRUSSELS

BLÜCHER

WATERLOO • WAVRE

MT ST JEAN

NIVELLES

QUATRE BRAS

MONS

WELLINGTON

LIGNY

NAMUR

R. MEUSE

CHARLEROI

FRONTIER

R. SAMBRE

NAPOLEON INVADES

BLÜCHER

SOMBREFFE

TONGRINNE

BALÂTRE

BRYE

BUSSY MILL

LIGNY

BOIGNÉE

NAPOLEON

ST AMAND

NAVEAU MILL

LA HAYE

FLEURUS

MARBAIS

TILLY

THYLE

MELLET

VILLERS-PERWIN

QUATRE BRAS

WELLINGTON

BOIS DE BOSSU

MARSHAL NEY

FRASNES

FRENCH I CORPS SPENDS DAY MARCHING BETWEEN THE BATTLEFIELDS

N

LIBERCHIES

to BRUSSELS

WELLINGTON'S REINFORCEMENTS

0 2
MILES

reached the battlefield and was splashed with mud and dirt as several cannonballs flew over a wood and landed nearby:

> This was what they called 'our baptism'. We soon reached Quatre Bras, and on turning the end of the wood found ourselves bodily in the battle. The roaring of great guns and musketry, the bursting of shells, and shouts of the combatants raised an infernal din, while the squares and lines, the galloping of horses mounted and riderless, the mingled crowds of wounded and fugitives (foreigners), the volumes of smoke and flashing of fire, struck out a scene which accorded admirably with the music. As we passed a spot where the 44th, old chums of ours in Spain, had suffered considerably, the poor wounded fellows raised themselves up and welcomed us with faint shouts, 'Push on old three tens – pay 'em off for the 44th – you're much wanted, boys – success to you, my darlings.' Here we met our old Colonel riding out of the field, shot through the leg; he pointed to it and cried, 'They've tickled me again, my boys – now one leg can't laugh at the other.' ...
>
> I don't know what might have been my sensations on entering this field coolly, but I was so fagged and choked with running and was crammed so suddenly into the very thick of the business, that I can't recollect anything at all, except that the poor Highlanders (over whom I stumbled or had to jump almost every step) were most provokingly distributed.

Despite its ferocity, Quatre Bras was only a secondary action, for the key battle that day was between Napoleon and Blücher at Ligny. The outcome at Quatre Bras mattered only in so far as it affected the outcome at Ligny and for both Wellington and Ney, this meant controlling the vital crossroads. As a result, Quatre Bras was an encounter battle in which Wellington was unable to defend a strong position of his own choosing.

It is often said that Wellington was outnumbered until the evening, by which time he had built up his strength as reinforcements reached the crossroads from both Brussels in the north and his cantonments to the west. In fact, he had slightly more troops in action than Ney from as early as 4 p.m. and a clear superiority by 6 p.m. But he remained outgunned until the final two hours of the battle, which exposed him to heavy casualties. He also had hardly any cavalry during the whole action and this, more than anything, was what seriously delayed and constrained him. Ney never had more than 2,600 cavalry engaged at any one time, but because of his clear-cut superiority in this arm he was able to dominate the small battlefield with them. This was particularly true as the crops grew as high as 6 feet and sometimes prevented Wellington's infantry from seeing an incoming French cavalry charge until it was too late. At one point, Wellington himself had to gallop to safety from French cavalry and leap his horse over the bayonets of the 92nd (Highland) Regiment of Foot as it crouched down in a ditch at the edge of a road.

Wellington should have been defeated. Ney had 45,000 troops available, but used no more than 21,000. Even at the end of the battle, Wellington had only 36,000 men in action and the intervention of the 20,000 troops of Ney's I Corps under General Jean-Baptiste Drouet, Count d'Erlon would have restored the balance. But Napoleon had summoned d'Erlon to fall on Blücher's western flank at Ligny and, because of poor staff work and a breakdown in communications, Ney was not informed of this move. When he found out, he assumed that d'Erlon had marched off without orders and furiously recalled him, with the result that he intervened at neither Ligny nor Quatre Bras.

Wellington was fortunate to face Ney, who was a less subtle and dangerous opponent than some of his other Peninsular adversaries, such as the wily Marshal Massena. Ney failed not only to concentrate enough forces on the battlefield, but to coordinate his attacks, as his own subordinates noted. General Maximilien Foy, an experienced divisional commander who had fought Wellington in the Peninsula, noted that the attack 'was rushed and senseless; you do not proceed like that against the English'. Another of Ney's men, Major Jean-Baptiste Jolyet of the 1st Regiment of Light Infantry, complained: 'We did not know who was in command and after arriving on the battlefield, we did not see a single general. ... Our regiments fought well, there were some brilliant actions and guns were taken from the enemy, but there was no coherence, no leadership. We seemed to be abandoned.'

Such comments are confirmed by the casualty figures for French officers, which show clearly that some units were far more heavily engaged than others. The 1st Regiment of Line Infantry, for example, lost twenty-seven officers, but the 3rd Regiment of Light Infantry none. Ney launched his attacks at Quatre Bras haphazardly and without making full use of the resources at his disposal. One of Napoleon's ADCs, General Count Flahaut de la Billarderie, wrote: 'I was close to Ney throughout the Quatre Bras engagement. Nobody could have shown greater courage, I might even say greater contempt for death, than he did. But here my praise of him must end, for the affair resolved itself into a series of spasmodic attacks delivered without any semblance of a plan.'

Ney never fully understood that Napoleon intended Ligny rather than Quatre Bras to be the key battle and appears to have acted for much of the day in a blind rage. At one point, he was seen in the thick of the action, shouting: 'What, will there not be a musketball or a cannonshot for me?'

Like Blücher, Ney was a fighting general, adored by his troops, but too impatient and courageous and too prone to acting on the spur of the moment. Not surprisingly, he, too, had begun his military career as a hussar.

In contrast, Wellington kept tight control of the battle. He commanded for most of the day from the crossroads at the centre of his position, where he had a good view from relatively high ground and where he could direct his reinforcements as they arrived along the roads from both the north and west. Unfortunately, this post was also kept under heavy French artillery fire, as a British officer explained:

> This heavy fire was maintained against us in consequence of the Duke and his staff being only two or three metres in front of the 92nd, perfectly seen by the French, and because all the reinforcements passed along the road in which we were. Here I had a remarkable opportunity of witnessing the sang-froid of the Duke, who, unconcerned at the shot, stood watching the enemy and giving orders with as much composed calmness as if he were at a review.

In the evening, a brigade of French cuirassiers made a desperate charge along the Brussels road, riding down the 69th (or the South Lincolnshire) Regiment of Foot and causing another British battalion to flee for safety to the Wood of Bossu. Some of the cuirassiers continued up to the crossroads, where Wellington was waiting with the 92nd Regiment. He had dismounted and was standing behind the centre of the regiment. 'Ninety-second, don't fire until I tell you,' he called. Coolly, he waited until the cuirassiers were only twenty to thirty paces away and then gave the order, which brought down scores of men and horses and caused the survivors to flee. He later recalled laughingly that those cuirassiers who were unhorsed, but not killed, were so encumbered by their metal cuirasses and heavy jackboots that they could not stand up again, but lay sprawling and kicking like so many overturned turtles.

By the evening, Wellington had been sufficiently reinforced to switch to the offensive. He first sent the 92nd to drive back two columns of French infantry and retake a house 300 yards south of the crossroads. This enabled him to deploy for a general advance and by the close of the battle at dusk, towards 8.30 p.m., he had regained nearly all the ground held by his troops that morning. But he had not been able to support Blücher except indirectly, by covering his western flank and containing Ney.

The Battle of Ligny

Meanwhile, Napoleon had won an important, but indecisive victory over Blücher at Ligny. The battle began towards 3 p.m. with French infantry attacks on the villages along the Ligny brook, supported by heavy artillery fire. Ferocious fighting raged in the streets and houses, with some soldiers throttling their opponents with their bare hands and even the wounded trying to kill each other with sidearms or bayonets. A Frenchman, Captain Putigny of the 33rd Regiment of Line Infantry, vividly wrote of the attack on the village of St Amand:

> I emerged from a gully at the head of my company. An artillery salvo bellowed out its song of death and threw me flat on the ground. I wanted to get up and dash forward, but my shoulder was smarting and I fell heavily again. My arm was not bleeding much, but could not do anything. It wasn't easy to stand up again without support. My right hand dropped my sword. Then I was on my feet. I picked up the sword and rebuffed my lieutenant, who urged me to go and have my wound dressed. Only a madman would miss such a day!

On the other side of the battlefield, many of Blücher's troops were equally keen to join the fight. Franz Lieber of the Prussian 9th (Colberg) Infantry Regiment explained:

> Our destiny was first a trying reserve; the enemy's brass [artillery] played hard upon us; shell shots fell around us and took several men out of our column. We were commanded to lie down; I piqued myself on not making any motion when balls or shells were flying over us. Behind us stood some cavalry; one of their officers had been a near neighbour to us in Berlin. He rode up to me and asked me to write home should he fall; he would do as much for me should I be shot down. He soon after fell. We longed most heartily to be led into the fire, when our officer, a well-tried soldier, ... spoke these few words: 'My friends, it is easier to fight than to stand inactive

exposed to fire; you are tried at once by the severest test, show then that you can be calm as the oldest soldiers. My honour depends upon your conduct. Look at me, and I promise you, you shall not find yourselves mistaken.'

Napoleon watched the fighting develop from his observation post, the Naveau mill at the town of Fleurus on the southern edge of the battlefield. His servant, the Mameluke Ali, noticed a group of young staff officers standing nearby:

> In this group they roared with laughter and joked noisily about the different scenes occurring some distance in front between some Prussians and French. The Emperor, who heard the noise these officers were making, cast glances towards them from time to time to show his tedium and displeasure. At last, irritated and bothered by so much light-heartedness, he said, looking severely at the one who was laughing and chattering most: 'Monsieur! You must neither laugh nor joke when so many brave men are killing each other before our eyes.'

The battle gradually absorbed and wore down Blücher's units, leaving them vulnerable to a final attack by Napoleon's reserves, the crack Imperial Guard and Reserve Cavalry. The attack was postponed when d'Erlon's I Corps, summoned from Ney's wing, inclined too far to the south and emerged behind Napoleon's far left wing and caused some alarm. It took time to identify his column, which was then recalled by Ney.

Despite this delay, Napoleon's final attack seized the village of Ligny and broke into the heart of the Prussian position, but was checked by increasing resistance as night fell. Just as he had done at Lützen in 1813, Blücher personally led a cavalry charge to try and check the French advance. His adjutant, Major von Nostitz, revealed how Blücher was too impatient to organize this counter-attack properly and how it quickly fell apart:

> The Prince mounted his horse and soon clearly saw the hostile column emerging from Ligny. He asked me to estimate its strength and I replied that I would make certain of it, if he was willing to promise not to leave the height until I returned, so I could be sure to find him again. The Prince gave me the assurance I wanted and I quickly rode on the left side of the column, as far as I needed to make a good estimate. I counted sixteen squadrons of cavalry, but was not able to judge whether even more troops followed the column.
>
> I hastened back to [Blücher]. He had awaited me with the greatest impatience and had already sent the order to General Röder to counter the enemy with the cavalry of the I Corps. Once I had reported and estimated the strength of the enemy cavalry at about sixteen squadrons, the Prince said:
>
> 'Come now, we want to take our cavalry and really knock the enemy about with it.'

Blücher prepared to charge with three regiments under Major von Lützow. Nostitz pointed out that part of General von Treskow's brigade was also at hand and recommended using it to assail the flank of the French cavalry, to increase the chances of success of Lützow's frontal attack. But Blücher rejected this idea as unnecessary.

Nostitz learned that Lützow did not even know what he was facing and therefore told him about the sixteen squadrons and advised him not to make an isolated attack with his leading regiment, the 6th Uhlans. But Lützow seemed to pay little attention to the warning and, in any case, allowed the direction of his advance to veer away from the French cavalry, so that he came up against the Imperial Guard infantry. Lützow himself was taken prisoner and his uhlans were routed.

The whole charge then collapsed as the other two Prussian cavalry regiments followed the same line of advance, became demoralized by the rout of the uhlans and noticed too late that they had already passed to the side of the French cavalry. Nostitz described how:

> The Prince [Blücher], who had personally been at the head of the cavalry, had to follow the withdrawal. He rode a very beautiful white English horse, which the Prince Regent had given him the previous year during his visit to London. I, too, rode a white horse ... Both these horses were struck by musketballs almost at the same time: that of the Prince in the left side next to the saddle-strap and mine in the neck.
>
> I soon saw that the Prince's horse had been mortally wounded and that this had placed us in danger and I urged him to gain more ground as quickly as possible. The Prince responded to my entreaty, but soon felt, from the convulsive movement of his horse, that it was about to collapse. He just had time to say, 'Nostitz, I am done for now!' as his horse fell dead in full career.

Nostitz jumped from his horse and prepared, with a pistol in his hand, to share Blücher's fate. He watched silently as French cuirassiers approached in pursuit of the Prussian horsemen. The French passed so close to the two men that they jostled Nostitz's horse, but they failed to recognize Blücher in the gathering dusk. These cuirassiers were only an advance detachment of their main column and were driven back when the Prussian cavalry rallied. Major von Bursche of the Elbe Landwehr Cavalry collected some men from various units, who rescued Blücher from under his dead horse and placed him in the saddle of an NCO of the 6th Uhlans. Bursche also ensured that Blücher and Nostitz then headed to the right, towards Sombreffe, instead of to the left, as Blücher wanted, where they would again have run into danger of being captured. Blücher had been rescued just in time, for Nostitz saw the main body of the French cavalry already advancing towards them.

Rumours that Blücher had actually been captured soon spread. Captain Fritz __,[5] who was serving in the 1st Westphalian Landwehr Cavalry, recalled:

> Towards evening [on 16 June], a wounded Uhlan officer who somehow was dispersed to us, suddenly brought the news that Field Marshal Blücher, who in his favourite manner had personally attacked at the head of the cavalry, had fallen with his horse and then been captured by the French. I was almost paralysed with horror as I heard this terrible news, which appeared not to be in doubt.
>
> I immediately sent a reliable and agile Landwehr cavalryman to the height of Brye, where I knew Blücher's headquarters were situated, to bring me the news as quickly as possible, regardless of the circumstances. The time that

passed until the soldier could return was the most painful of my whole life. Eventually, he rode back on a sweat-drenched horse and informed me that the Field Marshal had indeed fallen with his shot charger and had been somewhat crushed, but otherwise was with us again, safe and well. Rarely have I thanked God more whole-heartedly as at this news, while my Landwehr cavalrymen, with whom I immediately shared it, broke out into loud shouts of joy.

The Allies Retreat: 17 June

The Battle of Ligny cost Blücher's army 20–25,000 men, including 8–10,000 deserters. His men were ordered to fall back 13 miles to the north and rally around the town of Wavre, where they were joined by the fresh and newly arrived IV Corps under General Friedrich von Bülow.

Captain Fritz __ described the retreat on the morning of 17 June:

> The cheerfulness and vigour of our ... Field Marshal [Blücher] was essential in sustaining the firm morale of the army. He had had his bruised limbs bathed with brandy and then after being bandaged he had had a stiff drink. Now, although riding must have caused him considerable aching, he mounted his horse and thus rode alongside the troops, exchanging jokes and banter, which spread like wildfire, with many individual soldiers. ... I my-self only saw the old hero riding quickly past me, although I would gladly have told him of my heartfelt joy at his lucky escape.

Nostitz confirmed the depth of this feeling:

> The army had learnt how the Prince had narrowly escaped being taken prisoner. The urge to thank me for rescuing the beloved commander that day seemed to be as widespread as the devotion and reverence for him. Who-ever saw me shook my hand, regardless of whether they were friend or stranger. I would not have exchanged these heartfelt handshakes for any-thing in the world, for they were the most wonderful reward that I could have had and 16 June 1815 was the best day of my life.

Wellington learned on the morning of 17 June of Blücher's defeat at Ligny. He calmly turned to Captain George Bowles of the Coldstream Guards and told him: 'Old Blucher has had a d—d good licking and gone back to Wavre ... As he has gone back we must go too. I suppose in England they will say we have been licked. I can't help it; as they are gone back, we must go too.'

Lieutenant James Hope of the 92nd Regiment recalled how Wellington after giving orders for his army's retreat walked about for an hour, deep in thought:

> Now and then his meditations were interrupted by a courier with a note, who, the moment he had delivered it, retired to some distance to wait his Grace's will. The Field-Marshal had a small switch in his right hand, the one end of which he frequently put to his mouth, apparently unconscious that he was doing so. His left hand was thrown carelessly behind his back, and he walked at the rate of three and a half to four miles in the hour. He was

dressed in white pantaloons, with half-boots, a military vest, white neck-cloth, blue surtout, and cocked hat.

Wellington knew that the Prussian defeat at Ligny had left him exposed at Quatre Bras, for Napoleon would be able to move against his eastern flank. He therefore withdrew 8 miles to a more secure position, the ridge of Mont St Jean near the village of Waterloo.

After detaching 32,000 men under Marshal Emmanuel de Grouchy to pursue Blücher, Napoleon brought the rest of his army to link up with Ney at Quatre Bras in the afternoon. His furious pursuit of Wellington's cavalry rearguard up the Brussels road was too late to inflict significant casualties and became bogged down in the mud when a thunderstorm unleashed torrents of rain.

Despite the initial setback in the campaign, the Allied commanders-in-chief remained confident of victory. Blücher had promised to march to Wellington's support with at least two of his corps and wrote to his wife from Wavre:

> The action [at Ligny] lasted until the night. Both armies have lost many men. I have drawn closer to Lord Wellington today and in a few days there will probably be another battle. Everyone is full of courage and after Napoleon has had some more battles like the last one, he and his army will be finished. ...
>
> I went missing in the affair when they shot dead my beautiful English white horse. The same thing happened to Gneisenau and from our falls with our horses, we both had something taken out of us. ...
>
> You may share this letter in Berlin and also say that they should soon hear more, for we will fight now and then until we are in Paris once more. My troops have fought like lions [at Ligny], but we were too weak as I did not have [one] of my corps with me. I have now concentrated all my men.

Nostitz explained that after reaching Wavre, Blücher spent the rest of the day lying fully clothed on a sofa, physically still and in pain, but with his mind cheerful and constantly active:

> The entire army was on the march, reports came in from all troops and orders were issued for the new objectives. This necessitated many, diverse discussions with Gneisenau and Grolman and a number of others. The Prince's doctor, Dr Bieske, did everything possible to relieve the pain caused by such a violent shock. His whole right side was black and blue.

Blücher said that, regardless of the state of his health, he would rather be tied on his horse than forgo the pleasure of leading the army:

> The desire to take bloody revenge had mastered all his thoughts and intentions and was still further increased in him by the reports of the great losses that we had suffered on that fatal day [at Ligny] and by the death or serious injury of so many of his well-known and respected companions-in-arms.

That night, Blücher slept well, despite many interruptions. As Nostitz noted: 'The pains had not gone, but appeared less noticeable, because the time for deciding the fate of the whole campaign moved ever nearer.'

Chapter 15

The Battle of Waterloo

All three armies spent a miserable night in their bivouacs, as the rain stopped only in the morning of 18 June. Napoleon had to delay the start of his attacks on Wellington's position, for he would not be able to collect his rearmost units and deploy his army until late in the morning. Even then, the soaked ground would reduce the effect of his artillery bombardment by muffling the shell bursts and preventing many of the cannonballs from ricocheting along the ground.

Preparations for Battle

Wellington left his headquarters in the village of Waterloo at 6 a.m. and rode south to inspect his army before the battle. Although less pronounced than the often-mountainous positions he had defended in the Peninsula, his ridge did conceal his troops and to a considerable extent protect them from artillery fire. A track ran along the ridge crest, while behind the army, two paved highroads, diverging from the village of Mont St Jean, eased access to all parts of the position for guns, reinforcements and supplies.

Out in front, fortified farms anchored the position on either flank and strengthened the centre: Hougoumont in the west, La Haie Sainte in the centre and a collection of two minor farms, a village and a château (Papelotte, La Haye, Smohain and Frischermont) in the east. Wellington could hold the position in strength, as he had about 70,000 troops to cover a front of 4 miles, or an average of 17,500 per mile. As the battle developed, he would be able to concentrate his army still further by drawing troops from his unengaged western wing to reinforce his centre, thus reducing his front line to just 2.25 miles. In contrast, he had had only 5,700 men for each mile of his 9-mile position at Busaco, and 6,300 for each of the 6 miles at Fuentes de Oñoro. This greater concentration of troops was one of the reasons why Waterloo was such a bloody battle.

Wellington personally adjusted the details of his dispositions that morning and later claimed that 'I never gave myself so much trouble, as I did that day to place the Troops.' The narrow front of his army made it easier for him to exercise command and control. He delegated authority to three sector commanders, Sir Thomas Picton in the east; the Prince of Orange in the centre; and Sir Rowland Hill in the west, while Lord Uxbridge commanded the cavalry. This freed Wellington to move along his position throughout the day and thus keep a grip on the battle as a whole and to intervene personally wherever he was most needed. He had the freedom to transcend all boundaries: he could go anywhere and intervene at any place, at any time. The relevant sector commanders and their divisional and other subordinates, plus the cavalry and artillery officers, would make the right local moves as they became necessary. But by riding around the battlefield, Wellington was the one man who could gain a picture of developments along his entire line and he could react immediately by issuing orders

THE BATTLE OF WATERLOO, 18 JUNE 1815

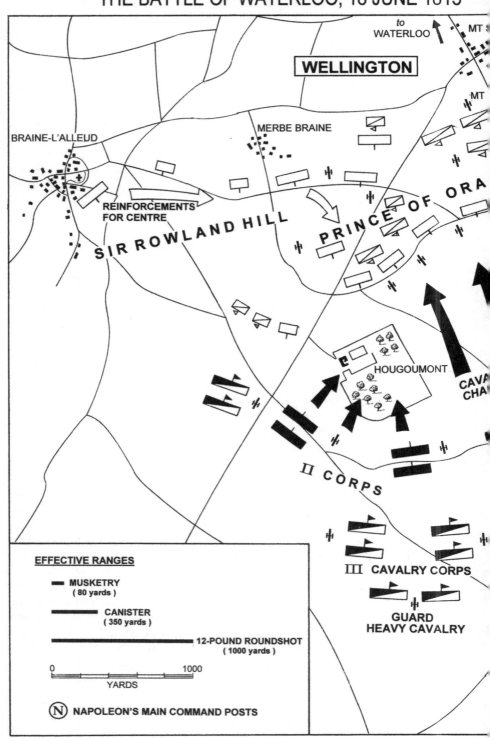

to
WATERLOO

MT S

WELLINGTON

MT

MERBE BRAINE

BRAINE-L'ALLEUD

PRINCE OF ORA

REINFORCEMENTS
FOR CENTRE

SIR ROWLAND HILL

HOUGOUMONT

CAVA
CHA

II CORPS

III CAVALRY CORPS

GUARD
HEAVY CAVALRY

EFFECTIVE RANGES

■■ **MUSKETRY**
(80 yards)

CANISTER
(350 yards)

12-POUND ROUNDSHOT
(1000 yards)

0   1000
        YARDS

Ⓝ **NAPOLEON'S MAIN COMMAND POSTS**

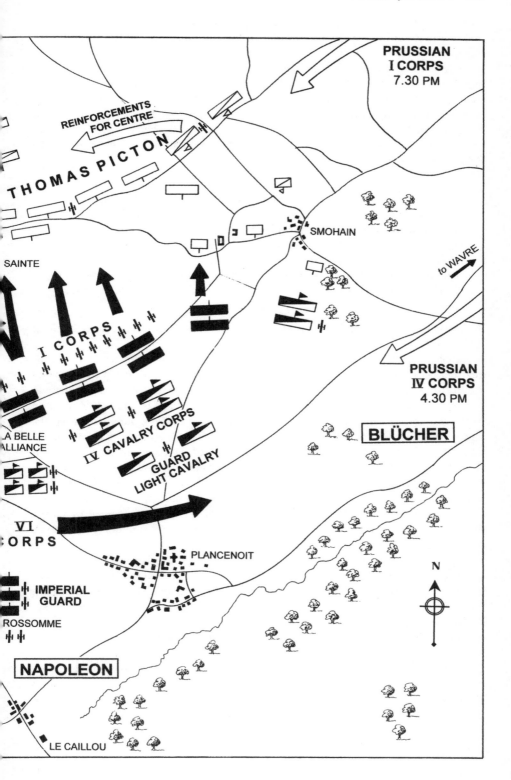

PRUSSIAN
I CORPS
7.30 PM

REINFORCEMENTS
FOR CENTRE

THOMAS PICTON

SMOHAIN

SAINTE

to WAVRE

I CORPS

PRUSSIAN
IV CORPS
4.30 PM

LA BELLE
ALLIANCE

IV CAVALRY CORPS

GUARD
LIGHT CAVALRY

BLÜCHER

VI
CORPS

PLANCENOIT

N

IMPERIAL
GUARD

ROSSOMME

NAPOLEON

LE CAILLOU

directly to any unit in any sector. For example, the 3rd Dutch-Belgian Division was told to wait in reserve to the west for orders from either Sir Rowland Hill, who was the sector commander, or from Wellington himself.[6]

At Wavre, the Prussian IV Corps, which was to lead Blücher's advance, was already marching towards Wellington. Gneisenau was conscious of the dangers of the move, using unpaved roads across difficult and water-logged terrain, for if Wellington was defeated, the Prussians would be left exposed to the full weight of Napoleon's army, including Marshal Grouchy's detachment to its rear. But Blücher's determination was unshakeable. At 9.30 a.m., he sent a message to General Baron Carl von Müffling, the Prussian liaison officer at Wellington's headquarters:

> I request you will say to the Duke of Wellington, in my name, that even ill as I am, I shall, nevertheless, put myself at the head of my troops, for the purpose of immediately attacking the enemy's right flank, should Napoleon undertake anything against the Duke. If, however, the day should pass over without a hostile attack, it is my opinion that we ought tomorrow, with our combined forces, to attack the French army. I commission you to communicate this as the result of my inward conviction, and to represent to him that I consider this proposal to be the best and most suitable in our present position.

Still anxious, Gneisenau had a postscript added, asking Müffling to ascertain if Wellington was firmly resolved to defend his position.

Napoleon held a breakfast conference with his senior subordinates at his head-quarters at Le Caillou towards 8 a.m. Some of them had fought against Wellington and the British in the Peninsular War and feared that it would be difficult to defeat them in a frontal attack. But Napoleon rightly judged that any attempt to outflank Wellington would take too long and be too complex given the state of the ground, as indeed the difficulties of Blücher's march to the battlefield showed. Whereas a frontal attack would fix and grind down Wellington's army, as had happened to the Russians at Borodino, an outflanking move would merely cause him to retreat without a decisive battle. At this stage, Napoleon had no reliable evidence that Blücher was in a position to intervene that day and, without Prussian support, Wellington would certainly have been driven from his position, even by a frontal attack. Napoleon planned to make a diversion against Hougoumont in the west and then punch through Wellington's eastern wing with his main attack after a massive bombardment.

Napoleon's denigration of Wellington at this conference has become notorious, but was merely an attempt to boost the morale of his generals. He had followed Wellington's career in the Peninsula and was aware of his abilities and determination, but in public he had to dismiss his subordinates' ideas that Wellington was an invincible commander: 'Because you have been beaten by Wellington, you think him a great general. I tell you that Wellington is a bad general, that the English are bad troops and that this will be a picnic.'

At 10 a.m., the French army deployed for battle in a show of strength. 'The very earth seemed proud to bear so many proud men,' Napoleon later remarked. 'I passed along the ranks; it would be difficult to express the enthusiasm which animated all the soldiers ... Victory seemed certain.'

A French staff officer, Colonel Auguste Pétiet, recalled how:

> The Emperor rode up and down the lines of the army and was received as always with cheering. He dismounted and took up a position on a quite high mound near La Belle Alliance, from where it was possible to see the battlefield and the two armies ready to come to blows. Napoleon had spread a map on his little table and while examining it, he seemed to be absorbed by profound strategic plans. I was stationed at the foot of this mound; my eyes could not leave this extraordinary man whom Victory had for so long showered with her gifts. His stoutness, his dull, white face, his heavy walk made him seem very different from the General Bonaparte I had seen at the beginning of my career during the campaign of 1800 in Italy.

The Battle Begins

Napoleon opened the battle at 11.30 a.m. and launched a series of assaults northwards across the valley against Wellington's ridge. The battle began with an attack on the farm of Hougoumont in the west, which drew in more and more French infantry, whereas Wellington carefully fed in only the minimum of troops needed to hold the place. Even in the afternoon, when Napoleon had the buildings bombarded by a battery of howitzers and set on fire, the garrison of British Foot Guards and German troops held out and inflicted heavy casualties on the French. Wellington later recalled:

> I remember seeing a large French column entering the wood behind Hougoumont, and another about as large going out on another side. I said: This is the oddest manoeuvre I ever saw; but on looking more closely I found that the last column consisted only of wounded. There were thousands limping off from the field.

Napoleon watched the progress of the battle from a couple of viewpoints on the French side of the valley and, as an ADC, Major Lemonnier-Delafosse, recorded:

> Never did one meet a greater or more perfect calm than that of Napoleon on the day of this battle, as he looked down over his army which for two hours already had attacked and pushed back the enemy on the whole line. Satisfaction could be seen written on his face, all was going well and there is no doubt that at this moment he thought his battle was won. I admired him for a long time, my eyes were unable to leave him. He was the genius of war.

But Napoleon's battle plan unravelled early in the afternoon with the repulse of his main attack. It began with a massive artillery bombardment, followed by an assault on Wellington's eastern wing by the 16,000 infantrymen of the French I Corps formed in heavy columns. The brunt of the attack was borne by two brigades of British and Scottish infantry under Lieutenant-General Sir Thomas Picton, but they were heavily outnumbered. Wellington described how he intervened during these tense moments:

> A column of French was firing across the road at one of our regiments. Our people could not get at them to charge them, because they would have been disordered by crossing the road. It was a nervous moment. One of the two forces must go about in a few minutes – it was impossible to say which it

might be. I saw about two hundred men of the 79th [Regiment], who seemed to have had more than they liked of it. I formed them myself about twenty yards from the flash of the French column, and ordered them to fire; and, in a few minutes, the French column turned about.

At the height of this action, two brigades of British heavy cavalry rode forward from reserve and made a decisive charge, riding down and completely repulsing the French infantry columns. But in the excitement of the moment, some of the horsemen charged too far, right across the valley, and suffered heavily when counter-attacked by fresh cavalry.

'Never did I see such a pounding match'

The battle was taking shape as a straightforward battle of attrition, even though Wellington and Napoleon were both masters of manoeuvre. Indeed, Wellington had expected Napoleon to try and outflank him to the west. 'Never did I see such a pounding match,' he wrote a month later. 'Both were what the boxers call gluttons. Napoleon did not manoeuvre at all. He just moved forward in the old style, in columns, and was driven off in the old style.'

Napoleon had to reconsider how to defeat Wellington, but now knew from a Prussian prisoner that Blücher was marching against his eastern flank. He had been forced to detach the VI Corps to contain him, thus depleting his reserves.

Towards 4 p.m., Ney began to lead massed French cavalry forward against Wellington, apparently under the mistaken impression that he had started to retreat. These cavalry charges eventually involved as many as 9,000 horsemen, but, since they lacked close support from infantry and artillery, failed to break the defensive square formations of Wellington's infantry. Ney has often been criticized for these unsupported charges, but by now the French had little infantry left, apart from their ultimate reserve, the Imperial Guard. Ensign Rees Gronow of the 1st Regiment of Foot Guards described the awesome experience of having to face one of the charges:

> The charge of the French cavalry was gallantly executed; but our well-directed fire brought men and horses down, and ere long the utmost confusion arose in their ranks. The officers were exceedingly brave, and by their gestures and fearless bearing did all in their power to encourage their men to form again and renew the attack. ... The horses of the first rank of cuirassiers, in spite of all the efforts of their riders, came to a stand-still, shaking and covered with foam, at about twenty yards' distance from our squares, and generally resisted all attempts to force them to charge the line of serried steel.

By now, it was clear to Wellington that Napoleon would not try to outflank him and that his western sector under Hill would not be attacked. Consequently, as casualties mounted in the centre during the afternoon, he ordered Hill to feed his units into the Prince of Orange's central sector as reinforcements, in the same way that he had drawn in units from quiet areas of his line to repel Massena's attacks at Busaco. Hill himself arrived in this sector and his presence bolstered Wellington's command and control, as the casualties locally were heavy among the senior officers. Besides the Prince of

Orange, both divisional commanders (Major-General George Cooke of 1st Division and Lieutenant-General Sir Charles Alten of 3rd Division) and two brigade commanders (Colonel Christian von Ompteda and Major-General Sir Colin Halkett) were out of action. Hill's presence from the late afternoon onwards helped to offset the effect of these casualties.

Wellington himself stayed in the central sector for most of the battle; he was so often at the crossroads where the Brussels highroad crossed the ridge crest that an elm tree here became famous as the 'Wellington Tree' and bits of it were much prized by souvenir hunters after the battle. Since the brunt of the French attacks fell in the centre, it was of course the most important area and Wellington, like Hill, could by his presence help the decimated group of local senior officers. At first, Wellington conscientiously issued orders through the Prince of Orange while in his sector, but as the action heated up, he often gave them directly to the divisional commanders.[7]

Although he still maintained his position, Wellington suffered heavy casualties, particularly from French artillery fire from the other side of the valley in between the French cavalry charges. He reinforced his front line with reserves and personally encouraged his men by sharing their danger. 'Standfast,' he urged them. 'We must not be beat – what will they say in England?'

Elsewhere, it was: 'Hard pounding, this, gentlemen; try who can pound the longest.'

Alternatively he told them: 'Wait a little longer, my lads, you shall have at them presently.'

His first question on riding up to a regiment tended to be: 'Who commands here?' He would then question the commander about the local situation; reassure and advise him; warn him of any impending attack; and, above all, emphasize his determination to hold on to the bitter end. For example, he asked one brigade commander: 'Well, Halkett, how do you get on?'

The reply was: 'My Lord, we are dreadfully cut up; can you not relieve us for a little while?'

Wellington told him bluntly that was impossible. Halkett understood: 'Very well, my Lord, we'll stand till the last man falls.'

A battalion commander was later asked whether he had been anxious about how the battle would end, but replied: 'Oh, no, except for the Duke. We had a notion that while he was there nothing could go wrong.'

The Prussian Intervention

Blücher had also been exhorting his men, as they struggled along muddy tracks towards the battlefield: 'Forwards, children! I hear it said that it can not be done, but it must be done. I have promised my brother Wellington and surely you don't want me to break my word.' A *Landwehr* soldier clapped Blücher on the knee and exclaimed: 'Good luck today, Father Blücher!' By 4.30 p.m., Blücher had collected the head of General von Bülow's IV Corps in the Wood of Paris on the eastern edge of the battlefield. Nostitz recalled how:

> The Prince with his eagle eyes surveyed the whole battlefield, clearly recognized the course of the fight and in particular gave the greatest attention to the employment of the English batteries. ...

It must have been between 4 and 5 p.m. when the Prince, who had always observed the battle line with the greatest attention, believed he noticed an English battery had stopped firing and had prepared to depart. This seemed to him a sign that the English army was starting to retreat and made him decide not to postpone his intervention in the great battle a moment longer.

Blücher sent Nostitz to Bülow with the order to advance out of the wood and begin the attack. Bülow explained that so far he had available only his cavalry and two of his four infantry brigades and asked if Blücher was aware of this. Nostitz said no and immediately returned to inform him. But Blücher's response was uncompromising: 'And even if only one brigade is ready, the attack must begin.'

When Blücher insisted on joining the advance, Nostitz told him that he risked a repeat of his near-capture at Ligny. Blücher merely laughed, shook Nostitz's hand and said it was in his nature as a hussar.

Napoleon had deployed his VI Corps to contain the Prussians and protect his flank. Blücher concentrated his assaults on the village of Plancenoit in the south-eastern corner of the battlefield, as it lay less than 0.75 miles from the Brussels road, and thus threatened Napoleon's line of retreat. 'If only we had the damned village,' Blücher exclaimed.

Plancenoit repeatedly changed hands. Blücher was still being reinforced by troops as they arrived from Wavre and by 8 p.m., he had 40,000 men in hand. He prepared another assault against the village, with supporting attacks on the French units in the open countryside further north. Already, he had saved Wellington from defeat by distracting Napoleon's attention and tying down nearly 13,000 of his reserves, including part of the Imperial Guard.

Napoleon's Command System

Napoleon remained on the French side of the valley and left his battle captain, Marshal Ney, to lead the attacks against Wellington's ridge. But the contrast with Wellington's highly personal command style has sometimes been exaggerated. Wellington had to command from his front line, as it was only from there, on the crest of the ridge, that he could see the battle. Napoleon could not have commanded effectively from the thick of the battle by advancing into the valley and would have increased his risk of becoming a casualty for no good reason. In many ways, it was better for a general to operate from one or two fixed command positions, the locations of which were made known to all subordinates and staff officers, than to move around the battlefield and expect them to find him. Nor does a commander necessarily have to share the dangers of the battlefield, or even maintain a visible presence, in order to be a strong and successful leader, as Air Marshal Sir Arthur Harris, the head of Bomber Command, demonstrated during the Second World War.

Napoleon's command system had worked effectively just two days earlier at Ligny, where he remained at the fixed point of the Naveau mill and only moved forward for the final attack. Wellington also adopted a similar command style at some of his offensive battles. He directed most of the Battle of Orthez (1814) from the viewpoint of a Roman camp in the rear of his army and at Toulouse later that year had to delegate the command of his main attack to the east of the city to Marshal Beresford because the battlefield was so extended. Just as Napoleon's subordinates escalated their attacks at Waterloo, Wellington at Toulouse was unable to prevent Sir Thomas Picton from launching bloody and unsuccessful assaults on the north-western side of the city instead of merely demonstrating.

Wellington did not manage to keep an infallible grip at Waterloo. His second most important strongpoint, the farm of La Haie Sainte, fell because of a shortage of rifle ammunition. Wellington later lamented the loss of the farm and blamed it on the sector commander, 'who was the Prince of Orange'. But he immediately added: 'No in fact it was my fault, for I ought to have looked into it myself.' Nor was the command and control of his cavalry satisfactory. Lord Uxbridge had intended to group the seven British and King's German Legion cavalry brigades into divisions, but had been prevented from doing so by Napoleon's sudden invasion. Thus the brigades generally acted independently, except for the combined charge of the two heavy brigades against Napoleon's main attack early in the afternoon. Uxbridge had to coordinate this charge himself and personally led it. But if he could have left this task to a divisional commander, he himself would have been free to bring up light cavalry to cover the subsequent retreat of the heavy dragoons and limit their losses when they were counter-attacked.

Note, too, that Wellington's mobility became more restricted as the battle progressed. By the late afternoon, he remained mostly in his central sector, a front of only 0.75 miles. The French cavalry charges often forced him to take shelter, as Lieutenant Archibald Hamilton of the Scots Greys pointed out: 'At this time the action was evidently all against us ... the Duke of Wellington was shut up occasionally in squares, all his staff disabled, being either killed, wounded or dismounted; there was therefore no one to report anything that occurred in the centre of the army.' [8]

The impact of Ney's cavalry charges on Wellington's command and control has usually been overlooked. If Napoleon or Ney had been able to support their cavalry with large numbers of infantry and artillery, they might have shattered much of Wellington's front line, for with the cavalry hovering around his squares he would have found it difficult to move to critical spots, to send orders, receive messages or coordinate a major counter-attack.

Nor did Napoleon's position to the rear mean that he remained inactive. He often intervened, even in tactical matters. He sent the VI Corps to contain the Prussians. He ordered a battery of howitzers to be formed to bombard Hougoumont. He ordered a cuirassier brigade to counter-attack the British heavy cavalry when it charged too far. He ordered Ney to seize the farm of La Haie Sainte in the centre of the battlefield. He sent the Young Guard to counter-attack the Prussians at Plancenoit. He ordered the III Cavalry Corps to reinforce Ney's cavalry charges. He ordered Ney, again, to seize La Haie Sainte, this time, at about 6 p.m., successfully.

Napoleon's mistake was not his position on the battlefield, or the fact that he delegated authority, but his failure to supervise his subordinates sufficiently. In Italy in 1796, he had insisted on unity of command: 'One bad general is better than two good ones.' But at Waterloo, he let a fatal command gap open between himself and Ney in particular. He allowed the diversionary attack on Hougoumont to escalate into a full-blooded and costly assault and the battle plan to degenerate into a series of furious and disjointed attacks which wasted time and troops, as Ney repeated the mistakes of Quatre Bras and squandered his opportunities.

The main reason for Napoleon's lack of grip was not illness, the unconvincing excuse that French historians have traditionally offered, but his distraction by the Prussian threat to his eastern flank. Blücher had, in fact, inflicted on Napoleon one of his own favourite strategies, by falling on his flank and threatening to sever his line of retreat, and its impact on Napoleon's command and control at Waterloo is the ultimate testimony to its effectiveness.

The Final Attacks

After the fall of La Haie Sainte, Ney finally mounted a combined-arms attack by pushing forward a limited amount of infantry and artillery. But by now his cavalry was largely spent and he needed a large, fresh force of infantry to achieve a success. Yet Napoleon dared not release his Imperial Guard until he had contained the Prussians at Plancenoit. 'Troops!' he snapped in response to a request from Ney for reinforcements. 'Where does he expect me to get them? Does he expect me to make them?'

This was undoubtedly the most favourable moment for sending the Imperial Guard against Wellington, before he could shore up his crumbling centre with his final reserves. But a breakthrough would still have been uncertain. In any case, the Imperial Guard could not immediately attack, for its battalions had been redeployed along the Brussels road to face the Prussians. It would take time to concentrate these 9,000 men amid the confusion of a crowded battlefield and prepare them for an assault.

It was only in the evening, after temporarily checking the Prussians at Plancenoit with two Old Guard battalions, that Napoleon again turned his full attention to Wellington and released his Imperial Guard infantry. Even then, only five battalions actually attacked, for a second wave was still being organized in the valley. Colonel Octave Levavasseur, ADC to Marshal Ney, saw Napoleon lead the battalions into the valley before handing command to Ney for the assault on the ridge crest:

> I saw the Emperor, followed by his staff, pass by close to me. When he arrived opposite his Guard, which was drawn up on the other side of the road, he said: 'Let everyone follow me!' He rode forward along the road which was swept by one hundred enemy guns.
>
> One hundred and fifty bandsmen now marched down at the head of the Guard, playing the triumphant marches of the Carrousel. Soon the road was covered by the Guard marching by platoons in the Emperor's wake. The cannonballs and canister which struck them left the road strewn with dead and wounded.

The Imperial Guard battalions reached the crest of Wellington's ridge in succession and struck a 500-yard section of his centre. He took personal charge of the 1st Regiment of Foot Guards to defeat part of the attack. Captain Harry Weyland Powell later wrote that men who saw the clash from a distance and more to the side later told him that the effect of his regiment's fire seemed to drive the head of the French column bodily back.

Other battalions were defeated by German and Dutch–Belgian units, while a final advance was broken by Lieutenant-Colonel Sir John Colborne, who on his own

The end at Waterloo: Napoleon and his army flee the battlefield.

initiative took the 52nd (or the Oxfordshire) Regiment of Foot (Light Infantry) out of its position in the front line and wheeled it round to fire into the vulnerable flank of the French column. This decisive move completed the Imperial Guard's defeat and threw it back into the valley.

The repulse of the Guard, and the arrival of the Prussian I Corps at the eastern end of Wellington's line, appalled Napoleon's exhausted army. Horrified shouts of 'The Guard falls back!' echoed round the battlefield. As the French units began to dis-integrate, Wellington realized that it was time to complete the victory by ordering a general advance and he dismissed concerns from those who advised caution: 'Oh, damn it,' he exclaimed. 'In for a penny, in for a pound!'

He waved his hat three times in the direction of the French and in response, his army swept forwards into the valley and precipitated a rout. 'In a few moments,' wrote a French general, 'our magnificent army was no more than a rabble of fugitives.'

Lieutenant John Kincaid of the 95th Regiment vividly remembered the moment of victory:

> Presently a cheer, which we knew to be British, commenced far to the right, and made every one prick up his ears; – it was Lord Wellington's long-wished-for orders to advance; it gradually approached, growing louder as it grew near; – we took it up by instinct, charged through the hedge down upon the old knoll, sending our adversaries flying at the point of the bayonet. Lord Wellington galloped up to us at the instant, and our men began to cheer him; but he called out, 'No cheering, my lads, but forward, and com-plete your victory!'
>
> This movement had carried us clear of the smoke; and, to people who had been for so many hours enveloped in darkness, in the midst of destruction, and naturally anxious about the result of the day, the scene which now met

the eye conveyed a feeling of more exquisite gratification than can be conceived. It was a fine summer's evening, just before sunset. The French were flying in one confused mass. British lines were seen in close pursuit, and in admirable order, as far as the eye could reach to the right, while the plain to the left was filled with Prussians.

Wellington advanced with his army right across the battlefield, praising and encouraging his men as he did so: 'Well done, Colborne! Well done!' he told the commander of the 52nd Regiment. 'Go on. Never mind, *go* on, *go* on. Don't give them time to rally. They won't stand.'

When some of his staff expressed concern for his safety during these closing stages, he replied: 'Never mind, let them fire away. The battle is gained; my life's of no consequence now.' After night fell, he rode back northwards and met Blücher by chance near the inn of La Belle Alliance. Lieutenant Basil Jackson of the Royal Staff Corps recalled how, just before Wellington reached the inn,

> the outlines of a numerous party on horseback, surrounded by crowds of infantry, could be made out, though it was dark, approaching the road from the direction of Papelotte and La Haye. When first observed, the party was about fifty yards from the road, and, on seeing it, the Duke, aware, perhaps, that it was Marshal Blücher and his Staff, turned aside to meet the brave old Prussian. I was very close to the two heroes during their short conference, which may have lasted about ten minutes; but it was too dark for me to distinguish old Blücher's features. It is a remarkable circumstance that this meeting should have taken place within two or three hundred yards of La Belle Alliance; and most probably Blücher did express a wish for the battle to bear that name ['the fine alliance'], as we have been told. It must have been quite half-past-nine when these distinguished men shook hands and parted.

Wellington later recalled that Blücher embraced and kissed him on horseback, exclaimed 'Mein lieber Kamerad!' (my dear comrade) and then, slipping into French, added, 'Quelle affaire!' (what a business).

Wellington lost 15,000 men in the battle and Blücher 7,000. The number of Napoleon's casualties will never be known, but was probably about 30,000, not including prisoners and deserters. One of Wellington's soldiers recorded that after most battles, officers would visit neighbouring units and ask who had been hit, but after Waterloo they asked, 'Who's alive?'

Wellington agreed to leave the pursuit that night to the Prussians and then rode back to his headquarters in the village of Waterloo. All his most senior subordinates had been put out of action at least temporarily: Sir Thomas Picton was killed; Lord Uxbridge and the Prince of Orange grievously wounded; Sir Rowland Hill concussed. His own escape from death or injury was near miraculous, for at least five officers were seriously wounded in his immediate vicinity. He and his staff undoubtedly attracted the attention of the French gunners. Captain William Verner of the 7th Hussars recalled how Wellington passed back and forth in front of his regiment: 'It was observable that whenever his party came in a line with us, the shots, which were directed on him, poured upon us in quick succession.'

At the start of the battle, Wellington had to tell his retinue: 'Gentlemen, we are rather too close together: better divide a little.' But he knew that danger was unavoidable if he was to exercise effective command and control. 'The finger of Providence was upon me,' he wrote afterwards, 'and I escaped unhurt.'

One of his ADCs, Lieutenant-Colonel the Hon. Sir Alexander Gordon, died in his headquarters in the early hours of 19 June. Wellington's surgeon, Dr John Hume, deliberated whether to disturb him immediately with the news:

> I decided to see if he was awake; and ... I tapped gently at the door, when he told me to come in. He had, as usual, taken off all his clothes, but had not washed himself; and as I entered the room he sat up in his bed, his face covered with the dust and sweat of the previous day, and extended his hand to me which I took and held in mine whilst I told him of Gordon's death, and related such of the casualties as had come to my knowledge. He was much affected. I felt his tears dropping fast upon my hands, and looking towards him, saw them chasing one another in furrows over his dusty cheeks. He brushed them suddenly away with his left hand, and said to me, in a voice tremulous with emotion, 'Well, thank God! I don't know what it is to lose a battle, but certainly nothing can be more painful than to gain one with the loss of so many of one's friends.'

Later that morning, Wellington rode to Brussels, where he told his friend Thomas Creevey: 'It has been a damned serious business. Blücher and I have lost 30,000 men. It has been a damned nice thing – the nearest run thing you ever saw in your life.' Then he added: 'By God! I don't think it would have done if I had not been there!'

In his dispatch, Wellington attributed the victory to the cordial and timely assistance that he had received from Blücher and wrote of his own men:

> It gives me the greatest satisfaction to assure your Lordship that the army never, upon any occasion, conducted itself better. The division of Guards, under Lieut. General Cooke, who is severely wounded, Major General Maitland, and Major General Byng, set an example which was followed by all; and there is no officer nor description of troops that did not behave well.

He was more effusive in private and wrote to his brother William:

> It was the most desperate business I ever was in. I never took so much trouble about any battle, & never was so near being beat.
>
> Our loss is immense particularly in that best of all Instruments, British Infantry. I never saw the Infantry behave so well.

As for Blücher, he wrote exuberantly to his wife:

> What I have promised, I have kept. On 16 June, I was forced to retreat by weight of numbers, but on the 18th, in conjunction with my friend Wellington, I did Napoleon in. No one knows where he has gone. His army is totally routed and his artillery is in our hands. His decorations, which he himself wore, have just been brought to me ...

Part Five

Aftermath, 1815–52

Chapter 16
Aftermath

Wellington was appalled by the carnage of Waterloo and a month later told a friend, Lady Shelley:

> I hope to God that I have fought my last battle. It is a bad thing to be always fighting. While in the thick of it I am too much occupied to feel anything; but it is wretched just after. It is quite impossible to think of glory. Both mind and feelings are exhausted. I am wretched even at the moment of victory, and I always say that, next to a battle lost, the greatest misery is a battle gained.

He and Blücher began a joint advance on Paris on the day after the battle, to exploit their victory and bring the war to a quick end.

Blücher had brought three-quarters of his army to Waterloo, leaving General Johann von Thielemann's III Corps at Wavre as a rearguard. Thielemann contained Napoleon's detached right wing under Marshal Grouchy during 18 and 19 June despite being outnumbered. After learning of Napoleon's defeat, Grouchy skilfully retreated to France, fighting a rearguard action at the city of Namur as he did so.

Paris
Napoleon returned to Paris on 21 June, abdicated for the second and final time the next day and retired to the Château of Malmaison outside the city, leaving power in the hands of a provisional government. He offered his services as a general to fight the Allied invasion, but was refused.

Wellington and Blücher breached the triple line of fortresses guarding the French frontier and arrived before Paris at the end of June. Characteristically, Blücher moved faster than Wellington, but his army inflicted considerable looting and destruction during its advance, whereas Wellington preserved the discipline of his forces.

Blücher wanted Napoleon surrendered so the Allies could execute him, but Wellington considered this unworthy of them and refused to be involved. Napoleon left Malmaison as the Prussian army approached and reached the port of Rochefort on the Atlantic coast on 3 July.

Blücher moved round to the unfortified southern side of Paris, while Wellington remained to the north. Their combined strength was about 120,000, while the French had around 60,000 regulars, supported by second-line troops, available to defend the capital. Blücher's troops were involved in a series of clashes with the French, during which two Prussian hussar regiments were trapped and smashed at Versailles on 1 July. Blücher suffered heavily in these actions and, like Wellington, was tired of the bloodshed. He wrote to his wife on 3 July: 'I have lost almost 3,000 men yesterday and again today. I hope to God that they will be the last in this war, for I am weary and fed up with the slaughter.' The French provisional government signed a convention that same day, under which its army evacuated Paris and retired south of the Loire river, where it was subsequently disbanded. Wellington and Blücher occupied the city on the 7th and King Louis XVIII was restored to his throne the next day.

After reaching Rochefort, Napoleon vainly hoped to sail to the United States, but was foiled by adverse winds, a blockade by the Royal Navy and the refusal of the British government to grant a safe conduct. On 15 July, he surrendered to Captain Maitland of HMS *Bellerophon*, after placing himself under the protection of the Prince Regent. His hopes of spending the rest of his life in England were dashed, for he was too dangerous to be allowed to remain in Europe. Instead, he was transferred to HMS *Northumberland* and taken to the remote South Atlantic island of St Helena.

The victory of Waterloo gave Wellington and the British a leading role in reinstating the Bourbon monarchy and securing peace, which was concluded by the signing of the Treaty of Paris on 20 November. Wellington's moderation and common sense contributed to the fact that peace prevailed between the great European powers until the Crimean War (1854–6). But his task was hindered by the French Ultras, or radical royalists, who launched a 'White Terror' and hunted down prominent Bonapartists. Marshal Ney, the most prominent victim, was shot by a firing squad on 7 December. Wellington's refusal to intervene and ask Louis XVIII for clemency was controversial, but he regarded Ney's fate as an internal issue for the French government. Ney had not only deserted the Bourbons on Napoleon's return from Elba, but had led troops over to him and an example had to be made.

Blücher

Blücher was bitterly disappointed by the apparent leniency of the Allied statesmen, who seemed to him to disregard the sacrifices that Prussia had made in toppling Napoleon. Nor did he distinguish sufficiently, as Wellington did, between Napoleon and the French people. He vainly demanded massive financial reparations and tried to blow up the Pont de Jena, the bridge that commemorated Napoleon's victory over Prussia in 1806. When he encountered opposition from Louis XVIII's Foreign Minister, Charles-Maurice de Talleyrand, Blücher wrote bluntly that the bridge would be blown up and that he could not conceal the pleasure Talleyrand would give him if he previously stationed himself upon it. In the event, the Prussian engineers bungled the task in July 1815 and the bridge remained intact, but was renamed the Pont des Invalides.

Blücher again suffered from delusions and gambled heavily while in Paris, as Ensign Rees Gronow of the British Foot Guards noted:

> His manner of playing was anything but gentlemanlike, and when he lost, he used to swear in German at everything that was French, looking daggers at the croupiers. He generally managed to lose all he had about him, also all the money his servant, who was waiting in the ante-chamber, carried. ...
> [When] the croupier stated that the table was not responsible for more than ten thousand francs, Blücher would roar like a lion, and rap out oaths in his native language which would doubtless have met with great success at Billingsgate, if duly translated: fortunately, they were not heeded, as they were not understood by the lookers-on.

Blücher also insisted on taking part in a horse race, but was thrown violently from his horse and dislocated his shoulder. He left Paris in the autumn and reached Breslau early in 1816. He divided his time between Berlin and Krieblowitz in Silesia, where he improved his estate and bred horses, but his last years were clouded by sadness about the mental illness of his son, Franz. He fell sick and took to his bed in September 1819 and, after a last visit from the Prussian King, died on the 12th at the age of seventy-six.

Napoleon

Napoleon reached St Helena in mid–October 1815 and spent the remaining five and a half years of his life there. In his youth, he had compiled a list of British global possessions and had noted: 'St Helena: a small island.' It had few landing places, was guarded by British ships and a garrison and lay 600 miles from the nearest island (Ascension) and twice that distance from Africa.

While in exile, Napoleon dictated his memoirs to his followers and sought to portray himself as a champion of liberalism and nationalism, a man of peace forced into war by his opponents and a benevolent ruler who had planned to unite rather than subjugate Europe. Embellished by supporters, this Napoleonic Legend proved a potent myth, not least for the liberal and nationalist movements opposed in the decades after Waterloo to the autocratic regimes like Austria and Russia that had helped defeat him. The myth was exploited by Napoleon's nephew, Louis Napoleon, who posed as Napoleon's heir in seizing power and establishing the Second Empire (1852–70). Napoleon also sought to explain away his defeat at Waterloo by blaming it on his subordinates, especially Ney and Grouchy. He also criticized the way Wellington and Blücher had fought the campaign, even though they had beaten him. Part of his resentment was due to his incorrect belief that Wellington had been personally responsible for exiling him to St Helena.

Napoleon quarrelled with the British governor of the island, Lieutenant-General Sir Hudson Lowe, whose anxiety to prevent any escape or rescue attempt made him rigid in supervising his detention. He was aggrieved that Lowe insisted on calling him 'General Bonaparte' on the grounds that the British government had never recognized him as Emperor of the French. He suffered from boredom and declining health and became more reclusive, rarely leaving his residence of Longwood. He died on 5 May 1821, aged fifty-one. The cause, either stomach cancer or poisoning on the orders of the Bourbon monarchy, remains controversial.

Napoleon was initially buried on St Helena, but his remains were repatriated to France in 1840 and placed in the Invalides in Paris. His first wife, Josephine, had died in 1814, while his second, Marie-Louise, had returned to Austria after his first abdication and later married her ADC and lover, General Count Adam von Neipperg. Napoleon's son, the King of Rome, was given a new title, the Duke of Reichstadt, brought up as a Habsburg prince and died from tuberculosis in 1832, aged just twenty-one.

Wellington

'Now I may say I am the most successful general alive,' Wellington commented on hearing of Napoleon's death. But his views of Napoleon gradually changed after Waterloo.[9] In public, he scorned him as a systematic liar and fraudster, but praised him as a general. In 1831, for example, he was asked whether Napoleon was really so superior to all his marshals: 'Oh yes – there was nothing like him. He suited a French army so exactly! Depend upon it, at the head of a French army there never was anything like him. In short, I used to say of him that his presence on the field made the difference of forty thousand men.' To have denigrated Napoleon's generalship publicly would, of course, have undermined his own reputation as the man who had helped defeat him. But he became scathing about his military record in private memoranda and conversations, particularly after learning that Napoleon had left 10,000 francs in his will to André Cantillon, a Frenchman who had tried to assassinate Wellington in Paris in 1818.

For the first three years after the peace settlement of 1815, Wellington commanded a multi-national Army of Occupation in north-eastern France. When the occupation ended, Wellington was a national hero and still only forty-nine years old and for the next three decades, he served with fluctuating fortunes as a statesman. He joined the Cabinet in December 1818 as Master-General of the Ordnance, but the government was faced with unrest and economic problems following the end of a brief post-war boom. In 1820, Wellington was nearly unhorsed by a mob championing King George IV's estranged wife, Queen Caroline of Brunswick, and the turmoil of these years undermined his determination to remain a public servant aloof from party politics. He grew convinced of the need to exclude the Whigs and Radicals from power in order to uphold the pillars of the establishment – the monarchy, aristocracy and Church of England – and prevent the country from sliding into revolution.

Wellington undertook several diplomatic missions, for he had a European reputation as a result of his military victories. After the death of the Duke of York in 1827, he served for two brief periods as commander-in-chief of the British army. Then, in 1828, he formed a government and was more successful as prime minister than is generally realized. It was during his period in office that his Home Secretary, Robert Peel, created a modern police force through the Metropolitan Police Act of 1829. A year later, Wellington helped secure an armistice between Belgium and Holland and arrange for an international conference in London to prevent France from establishing control over the newly independent Belgium.

Wellington also ensured the repeal of the Test and Corporation Acts, which for over a century had theoretically barred all but practising members of the Church of England from public office, and in April 1829 he pragmatically forced through the Catholic Emancipation Act against bitter opposition when it became clear that it was the only way to avoid bloodshed. In doing so, he fought a duel with Lord Winchilsea to quash allegations that he had acted deceitfully. The question of Catholic Emancipation had been outstanding since the union of Ireland with Great Britain in 1800 and the passing of the Act was the high point of Wellington's premiership, even though it contributed to his subsequent downfall by both encouraging further change and increasing the divisions in the Tory party.

Renewed economic problems led to a wave of violence and widespread support for Parliamentary Reform. But Wellington was out of touch with the mood of the country and blinded by fear that Reform would be unstoppable and would result in a repetition of the horrors of the French Revolution. He resigned on 16 November 1830, after a defeat on a minor issue, and his fall marked the end of two decades of Tory rule.

Wellington remained active in politics for another sixteen years. In 1831–2, he led opposition in the House of Lords to Reform bills introduced by the new Whig prime minister, Lord Grey, and became so unpopular that he had to fix iron shutters to protect the windows of his London home, Apsley House, from stone-throwing mobs. It was during these months that Wellington lost his wife, Kitty, on 24 April 1831. The political crisis ended after a Reform bill was passed in June 1832, Wellington having pragmatically refrained from further opposition on the grounds that it would be counter-productive.

He acted as a caretaker prime minister for three weeks in 1834, before serving in Sir Robert Peel's administration, which lasted four months. During the next six years, Wellington led the opposition in the House of Lords and helped Peel develop the Conservative Party to replace the old and irretrievably split Tories.

After the General Election of 1841, Peel formed a Conservative government. Wellington held a cabinet seat without office and was able to resume his former, unique position as a statesman aloof from party politics and dedicated to the service of Crown and Country. He acted as a trusted confidant to the young Queen Victoria and returned to his former post of commander-in-chief of the British army in August 1842. He regained his former popularity, but was now in his seventies and suffered increasingly from ill-health. He had been deaf in the left ear following a botched cure for earache in 1826 and had suffered strokes in 1839–40.

After the Conservatives lost office in 1846, Wellington withdrew from active politics, but remained as commander-in-chief for the final six years of his life. Sweeping reforms of the army and its administration had become necessary, but were prevented by financial constraints and complacency. The results of this neglect would be painfully obvious in the army's chaotic administration, logistics and medical services during the Crimean War (1854–6). Wellington's own conservatism and declining health contributed to the problem, but should not be exaggerated: despite being unenthusiastic about new weapons, he approved the introduction of the percussion cap and of the Minié rifled musket. He also urged a significant increase in the country's defences, only to find that this was politically impossible, despite the potential threat from France. He complained in 1838: 'The state of our military force is very distressing. The Government will not – they dare not – look our difficulties in the face, and provide for them. I don't believe that any Government that could be formed in these days would have the power.' Wellington's greatest legacy to the British army was an example of duty and steadfastness that would stand it well in the decades to come, not least on the battlefields of the Crimea.

Despite his decline, Wellington helped prevent riots during the Chartist unrest of April 1848 by skilfully organizing the defence of London. He continued to collect honours and appointments, including those of Colonel-in-Chief of the Rifle Brigade and Lord Lieutenant of Hampshire (1820), Constable of the Tower of London (1826), Colonel of the Grenadier Guards (1827), Lord Warden of the Cinque Ports (1829), Chancellor of Oxford University (1834), and Ranger of Hyde Park and St James's Park (1850).

He delighted in writing dry, acerbic replies to a flood of letters and requests. For instance:

The Duke of Wellington presents his compliments to Mr. Cruttwell, and has received his letter.

The Duke begs Mr. Cruttwell to publish upon the currency if he pleases, and to speak upon the subject to whom he pleases.

The Duke desires to have nothing to say to it; and he entreats Mr. Cruttwell not to give himself the trouble of writing to him again.

He complained in 1839 about the mass of correspondence he had to answer: 'Rest! Every other animal – even a donkey – a costermonker's donkey – is allowed some rest, but the Duke of Wellington never! There is no help for it. As long as I am able to go on, they will put the saddle on my back and make me go.' In fact, he liked to work and took pride in his steadfast public service. 'I am the servant of the Crown and People,' he explained. 'I have been paid and rewarded, and I consider myself retained.'

By the end of his life Wellington was a national institution, known simply as 'the Duke', just as Napoleon had been 'the Emperor' and Blücher had been referred to in Prussia as the 'Father of the Fatherland'. He had come to embody the British ideal of a selfless, devoted and incorruptible public servant. A friend, Lord Mahon, wrote in 1842:

I have been painfully struck at remarking how much the Duke's sources of enjoyment and relaxation are yearly declining. When first I knew him, who so fond of hunting and shooting? The latter he had more than eight years, the former more than two, relinquished. Riding he still uses as a means of health, but seems much less to delight in. Country visits were once very agreeable to him; from these he now wholly abstains. But what strikes me most of late is his loss of taste for music. . . . Thus one by one all his pleasures have dropped from him like leaves from a tree in winter. Only one remains – public or private business – which ... he transacts with undiminished alacrity and readiness. His zeal for the public service – his determination to fill his part and do his duty – will never, I am persuaded, end but with his life.

Wellington's prestige and popularity were confirmed by his reception during visits to the Great Exhibition in London in 1851. He died aged eighty-three at Walmer Castle on the afternoon of 14 September 1852. One and a half million people watched his funeral procession in London on 18 November, from the Horse Guards to St Paul's Cathedral, where he was buried. Among the mourners was Count von Nostitz, the Prussian representative, who had formerly been Blücher's adjutant and had accompanied him on his visit to England four decades earlier, in 1814.

Part Six

Assessment

Chapter 17

Personalities

Napoleon

'Fear nothing, my friends,' declared Napoleon at Montereau in 1814, 'the cannonball that is to kill me has not yet been made.' It was this sense of destiny that sustained him through his tumultuous career, for few men have undergone such dramatic and sudden reversals of fortune. From poverty and a week and a half under arrest as a young officer, he rose to become Emperor of the French and master of Continental Europe, before dying in exile as a prisoner of the British, his most inveterate foes. He was single-minded in pursuit of his ambitions. 'I can do things other than war,' he informed Josephine in 1807, 'but duty comes first. All my life, I have sacrificed everything, peace, self-interest, happiness, to my destiny.'

Contrary to myth, Napoleon was not a self-made man, for, like both Wellington and Blücher, he was noble by birth and, unlike them, benefited from a privileged education at some of the best schools in France. He also made full use of influential connections. Nor was Napoleon shorter than average for his time, although his feet and hands were small. His height is often given as 5 feet 2½ inches, but this was a French measurement and corresponded to an English height of 5 feet 6. He had a broad chest and shoulders and put on weight after gaining power. His magnetism lay largely in his restless and intensely focused energy and in his large and piercing eyes, which intimidated even hardened soldiers. 'I could not look at him,' admitted an Imperial Guardsman, Jean-Roch Coignet. 'He would have frightened me; I only saw his horse.'

Napoleon had fine, dark brown hair and wore it long when young, as was fashionable at the time, but had it cut short in his early thirties, partly to disguise incipient baldness, and was nicknamed 'le Tondu' (the shorn one) by his men. Like Wellington, he was scrupulous about personal hygiene and being clean-shaven.

He could be charming when he wanted, but used cynical bribery and calculated displays of anger to overcome resistance. After a fit of rage, he told the Abbé de Pradt: 'You think you have really seen me angry? Don't fool yourself: with me, the anger never goes beyond there.' As he spoke, he drew his hand across his neck, to show that his emotion never affected his head.

He habitually kept those around him in a state of nervous anticipation through his sudden demands and fits of temper, to ensure instant obedience. He was always in a hurry. 'I am in a rage with everyone at Milan,' he complained in July 1796: 'Nothing gets here, no artillery, no officers, no gunners. I am sending you an aide-de-camp to stir things up. In the present situation days equal centuries.' It was his relentless, driving energy, not just his genius, that made Napoleon so dynamic and feared a commander. 'Rapidity! Activity! Activity! All lies with you!' he added to an order to Marshal Massena in April 1809.

He has been criticized for his horsemanship, for he did not sit properly in the saddle and had several falls. But, like Wellington, he was a tireless and energetic rider, able to cover long distances quickly. In January 1809, he rode 75 miles across northern Spain from Valladolid to Burgos in just five hours. He also had a travelling coach, equipped so he could eat, work and sleep while on the move.

Despite popular belief, Napoleon did not thrive on lack of sleep, except for limited periods. One of his most important aides, General Armand de Caulaincourt, stated: 'The Emperor needed much sleep, but he slept when he wanted, during the day as well as at night.' Napoleon even slept in the shade of some stacked drums at the height of the Battle of Wagram (1809) and for over an hour at Bautzen (1813). In total, Napoleon slept about seven hours in every twenty-four, in several phases. After a few hours' sleep in the evening, he tended to get up at about 11 p.m., in time to receive the first reports from his corps commanders. He would then spend two or three hours, or more, in considering the intelligence and his maps and in giving his orders, which would reach his subordinates in time to be executed at dawn.

It has been estimated that Napoleon produced a total of 50,000 to 70,000 letters during the fifteen years that he governed France, or an average of ten to twelve letters every day. He dictated rather than wrote, for his handwriting was poor and could not keep pace with his thoughts. Sometimes, he dictated several letters to different secretaries at the same time. He compartmentalized his mind, focusing ruthlessly on one subject at a time until he exhausted it: 'Different subjects and different affairs are arranged in my head as in a cupboard. When I wish to interrupt one train of thought, I shut that drawer and open another. Do I wish to sleep? I simply close all the drawers and there I am – asleep.'

Napoleon was a master of the use of propaganda to portray himself and his regime favourably, discourage opposition and strengthen support. 'Scarcely once has he ever tripped into truth!' remarked Wellington sarcastically. In the bulletins that he used to describe the exploits of his army, Napoleon blatantly manipulated the casualty figures and often quoted heroic speeches supposedly made by dying officers, like Captain Auzouy of the Grenadiers à cheval of the Imperial Guard, who told his comrades to leave him lying on the field of honour at Eylau: 'Tell the Emperor that I have but one regret, which is that in a few moments I shall be no longer able to do any thing for his service, and the glory of our fine France ... to her my last breath.'[10] Napoleon had the official account of the Battle of Marengo rewritten, to conceal how close he had come to defeat, to attribute the victory to his skill and to play down the role of his subordinates and the timely arrival of one of them, General Desaix.

He systematically exaggerated the strength of his own army and minimized that of his enemy, as he knew that battles were won as much, if not more, by morale and mental impressions as by the actual balance of forces. He explained in 1809 that it was a natural instinct for men to overestimate an enemy's strength and that even experienced soldiers had difficulty forming an accurate idea of opposing numbers. By constantly exaggerating his forces, he encouraged his own troops and intimidated opponents.

While on campaign, Napoleon usually wore the dark green undress coat of a colonel of the Chasseurs à cheval of the Imperial Guard, with the addition of his famous grey overcoat and black cocked hat. Occasionally, especially on Sundays and for reviews, such as that on the Battlefield of Ligny on the morning of 17 June 1815, he wore the

Napoleon on the morning of Wagram, 6 July 1809.

dark blue coat of a colonel of the Grenadiers à pied of the Guard. He thus identified with his soldiers and stood out from his glittering retinue. Pierre Louis Mayer, a conscript in the 35th Regiment of Line Infantry, recalled how he saw Napoleon pass before him:

> After waiting half an hour, we heard a confused murmur of 'Long live the Emperor!' at the same time perceiving in the distance a cloud of dust such as I have never seen before. The noise rapidly drew nearer and all the soldiers, raising their shakos on the points of their bayonets, shouted 'Long live the Emperor!' We saw the whole Imperial staff arrive, a number of at least eighty, all on horseback, each one more beautiful than the last and all covered with gold. [My] lieutenant had only time to say to me 'There he is!' ... He wore his green coat of a chasseur of the guard, with a little star and his cross of honour on his breast. There we have the way in which this extraordinary man distinguished himself by his simplicity.

Wellington

Wellington's style was calmer and more informal. He discouraged overt displays of enthusiasm and told a friend after Waterloo: 'I hate that cheering. If once you allow soldiers to express an opinion, they may on some other occasion hiss instead of cheer.' To Ensign Rees Gronow of the 1st Regiment of Foot Guards, Wellington and his staff on the morning of Waterloo 'all seemed as gay and unconcerned as if they were riding to meet the hounds in some quiet English county'.

Wellington usually wore a mixture of civilian and military clothes: a blue or grey frock coat, with a white waistcoat, white or grey pantaloons, black boots and a low cocked hat. In winter, or bad weather, he also wore a blue or white cloak, or a greatcoat.

One of his commissaries in the Peninsula, August Schaumann, noted: 'In him there is nothing of the bombastic pomp of the Commander-in-Chief surrounded by his glittering staff. He wears no befeathered hat, no gold lace, no stars, no orders – simply a plain low hat, a white collar, a grey overcoat, and a light sword.' He was comfortable and recognizable by his men and did not draw enemy fire by being ostentatious. He rarely wore full-dress uniform and claimed that 'there is no subject which I understand so little.' But he looked informal and efficient rather than untidy and was nicknamed 'The Beau' for his care over his appearance. His Judge Advocate-General, Francis Larpent, had many opportunities of observing him at his headquarters and commented in February 1814:

> In one instance Lord Wellington is not like Frederick the Great. He is remarkably neat, and most particular in his dress, considering his situation. He is well made, knows it, and is willing to set off to the best what nature has bestowed. In short, like every great man, present or past, almost without exception, he is vain. He cuts the skirts of his own coats shorter, to make them look smarter: and only a short time since I found him discussing the cut of his half-boots, and suggesting alterations to his servant, when I went in upon business.

Eyewitnesses recorded fascinating glimpses of Wellington in informal moments. Larpent, for example, recorded seeing him in July 1813 wearing a silk handkerchief over his head against the rain while he directed efforts to extinguish a fire that had broken out in the chimney of his quarters. Similarly, Napoleon sometimes cut a less heroic figure than that portrayed in famous paintings. The artist Jacques–Louis David depicted him crossing the Alps in 1800 mounted on a rearing charger, with the names of his predecessors, Hannibal and Charlemagne, engraved on the rocks beneath him. In reality, he rode a mule and made part of the descent from the St Bernard pass by sliding on his backside.

Wellington tended to be reserved on first acquaintance, but relaxed with friends, who grew used to his unrestrained whoops of laughter. Captain George Elers, who knew him in India, recalled:

> At this time [1796] he was all life and spirits. In height he was about 5 feet 7 inches [actually 9 inches], with a long, pale face, a remarkably large aquiline nose, a clear blue eye, and the blackest beard I ever saw. He was remarkably clean in his person, and I have known him shave twice in one day, which I believe was his constant practice. ... He spoke at this time remarkably quickly, with, I think a very, very slight lisp. He had very narrow jaw-bones, and there was a great peculiarity in his ear, which I have never observed but in one other person, the late Lord Byron – the lobe of the ear uniting to the cheek. He had a particular way, when pleased, of pursing up his mouth. I have often observed it when he has been thinking abstractedly.

Baron Jean-Baptiste de Crossard, who was attached to Wellington's headquarters during the Talavera campaign of 1809 as a representative of the Austrian Emperor, recorded his impressions:

In addition to his noble and imposing appearance, he has a polished manner. Always free of awkwardness, he has the knack of putting everyone at his ease. His face indicates a mind that is actively thinking. Quite fond of pleasure, he can be merry outside of business. Women are not without influence on his feelings, but I believe he can resist their attractions when duty demands.

Wellington kept himself physically fit and regularly hunted foxes for both exercise and diversion. Occasionally, he showed small signs of his inner tension, for example during the Battle of Waterloo when he nervously played with his expandable telescope and repeatedly looked at his watch. But he usually looked calm and that and his reputation inspired confidence among his troops. Lieutenant John Kincaid of the 95th Regiment remarked:

> From the moment that I joined the army [in the Peninsula in 1810], so intense was my desire to get a look at this illustrious chief, that I never should have forgiven the Frenchman that had killed me before I effected it. My curiosity did not remain long ungratified; for, as our post was next the enemy, I found, when any thing was to be done, that it was his also. He was just such a man as I had figured in my mind's eye, and I thought that the stranger would betray a grievous want of penetration who could not select the Duke of Wellington from amid five-hundred in the same uniform. ... We would rather see his long nose in the fight than a reinforcement of ten-thousand men any day. Indeed, there was a charm not only about himself but all connected with him, for which no odds could compensate.

Wellington's self-confidence enabled him to sleep at will, for as he told Lady Salisbury in 1835: 'No, I don't like lying awake – it does no good. I make it a point never to lie awake.' He tended to sleep for six hours a night and made a habit of doing 'the business of the day in the day' and then relaxing in the knowledge that he had done all that was possible: 'When I throw off my clothes, I throw off my cares, and when I turn in my bed it is time to turn out.' The Reverend Spencer Maddan, tutor to the family of the Duke and Duchess of Richmond, noticed the results of this ability to relax completely when he wrote from Brussels in June 1815:

> The Duke of Wellington seems to unite those two extremes of character which Shakespeare gives to Henry V – the hero and the trifler. You may conceive him at one moment commanding the allied armies in Spain or presiding at the conference at Vienna, and at another time sprawling on his back or on all fours upon the carpet playing with the children.

Like Napoleon, Wellington corresponded in detail on a wide variety of military, political and diplomatic subjects. His experience and self-confidence made him decisive and his Judge Advocate-General, Francis Larpent, noted his ability to do a mass of business: 'I like [him] much in business affairs. He is very ready, and decisive, and civil, though some complain a little of him at times, and are much afraid of him. Going up with my charges and papers for instructions I feel something like a boy going to school.'

He notably disliked officers who had to refer to written notes when reporting to him, because they lacked the self-confidence to rely on their memory. He claimed that he once reduced his Adjutant-General, Major-General the Hon. Charles Stewart, to tears during an argument, but his explosions of temper, though terrifying, were short-lived and were often followed by an invitation to dinner. Captain John Stepney Cowell, an officer of the Coldstream Guards, described how at the end of 1810:

> This winter I frequently dined with Lord Wellington, and, on the first occasion of doing so, my attention was naturally fixed on observing the manners and conversation of our chief; they seemed perfectly natural, straightforward and open. He conversed with liveliness on most subjects. There was at this period a light-heartedness of manner about him, which betokened more of self-confidence than anxiety or care, and which gave an agreeable tone to the society around him. Although upon his acts depended the fate of nations, few, from observation, could discover that he felt himself to be in a more responsible position than the youngest subaltern of his army. He seemed to enjoy the boyish tricks of those about him; weighty affairs did not appear to have impaired his zest for the playfulness or jokes of his followers. At table he seldom spoke of military matters, and never of passing events in Portugal; the news of the day from England, the amusements, or social state of Lisbon, or allusions to foreign countries, most frequently formed the topics of his conversation.

Blücher

Blücher, too, had a powerful presence. He was a tall and physically impressive man, with a resolute expression, prominent nose, strong chin and grey moustache. He often had a pipe in his mouth and had been left with a permanent limp from a riding accident in 1795. Even in old age, he retained the wild and youthful spirits of a subaltern of hussars and had less concern than Napoleon or Wellington for his personal prestige or dignity. A British captain who saw him in Paris after Waterloo wrote that 'he is an uncouth-looking old man and was spitting over a bridge when I saw him.'

Captain Fritz __[11] had known Blücher earlier in his career and visited him again at his headquarters in 1813:

> The general, or Marshal 'Forwards' as he was soon called, was still just the same as I had known him earlier. Rank, fame and years had not had the slightest effect on him. He laughed and joked and also cursed like a real hussar officer, and he had ready for everyone, noble or commoner, general or corporal, an earthy jest, a suitable joke and also, if it seemed necessary to him, a firm rebuke. It was precisely this unforced joviality, which nothing could distract, that was of inestimable worth for the Army of Silesia and contributed considerably to raising it and making it capable of great deeds.

Just as Napoleon believed in his destiny, Blücher drew strength from his religious faith. He prayed for guidance before going into battle and, according to his surgeon, Dr Carl Bieske:

He also firmly believed in predestination, and that he and every other man, even to the end of his life, was under the protection of a higher power. He asserted that, in the midst of the greatest peril, he never had an idea of being shot dead, and thought that, if he had not felt certain of it, he would have lost his head as many others, for every man in a greater or less degree, previous to a battle and when going into it, has an instinctive dread in his bosom; and he who knows how best to overcome it is the bravest after all.

Blücher's confidence also came from his physical strength. Baron Carl von Müffling, who served at his headquarters in 1813–14, noted how he had often fought hand-to-hand early in his career: 'In this way he had gradually convinced himself that there was no military predicament from which one could not ultimately extricate oneself by fighting, man to man.' Even as an army commander, Blücher often fought personally. During the Battle of Vauchamps (1814), some French cavalrymen rode up close as he and his staff were retreating with a weak escort. 'I will give it the fellows,' he exclaimed, before dashing at one of the horsemen and making him flee. It is hardly surprising that he had so many narrow escapes: he was wounded at Lützen (1813), nearly captured at Brienne (1814) and Ligny (1815) and almost trampled underfoot at Vauchamps.

As a straightforward, fighting general, Blücher was too ready to rely on bravery alone and to discount the advantages of intelligence and spies, in stark contrast to both Wellington and Napoleon. During his final advance on Paris in March 1814, Blücher reached the town of Meaux, 25 miles east of Paris, and was told that a Frenchman was stationed at an open window, noting the numbers of the troops. He merely laughed: 'Let him be quiet; if he can keep count, and not lose his patience, so much the better; I hope he will reach Paris before we do, and take his news there.' Similarly, when a French divisional commander, General Louis Bourmont, Count de Ghaisne, deserted to the Prussians at the start of the Waterloo campaign, Blücher reacted with contempt for his treason rather than delight at the prospect of obtaining useful information. Referring to the white Bourbon cockade worn by Bourmont, he exclaimed: 'It makes no difference what people pin on themselves as an emblem! A dirty scoundrel will never change!'

Blücher saw the world in black and white and this is what made him intensely loyal. As Müffling advised Wellington in 1815: 'You may depend upon this: when the Prince has agreed to any operation in common, he will keep his word, should even the whole Prussian army be annihilated in the act.' But his unsophisticated outlook also made Blücher ruthless. He had few qualms in occupying and extorting supplies from the neutral free city of Lübeck in 1806, or violating the armistice in August 1813, for to him the end justified the means. In his twenties, he was even involved in dubious transactions involving stolen horses.

Despite his keenness for action, he grew tired of war in his final years. On the day after the Battle of La Rothière (1814), he rode over the battlefield with the Allied monarchs and told the Prussian King's young son that in an unjust war, each drop of spilt blood was like boiling oil on the conscience of the ruler.

Chapter 18

Styles of Leadership

It would be difficult to find three more outstanding leaders. Each carefully maintained the morale of his army, in his own unique style and in a way that suited the character of his army.

Napoleon

Napoleon realized that French troops, especially after the Revolution, could not be led as if they were machines. Instead, he appealed to their honour, enthusiasm and love of distinction. During the siege of Toulon (1793), he found volunteers to serve in a particularly dangerous post by erecting a sign that read, 'Battery of men without fear'. Even the humblest soldier could expect rewards for deeds of valour: the cross of the Legion of Honour, or a precious sabre engraved with the name of the action for which it was awarded, or admission to Napoleon's elite reserve and bodyguard, the Imperial Guard.

Many such rewards had an attached financial benefit. In the case of his most senior subordinates, such as the marshals, the rewards were lavish and included gifts of land with incomes of thousands of francs. Such enormous riches were given only to a privileged few, but their scale mesmerized Napoleon's army and he played on the notion, however illusory, that every soldier potentially had a marshal's baton in his knapsack. General Desaix noted in Italy in 1797:

> General Buonaparte's extraordinarily effective method of encouragement consisted firstly of considerable promotions for officers, especially young men whom he placed, as far as he could, in high-ranking posts. He retired the old or mediocre. Above all, he fired up the spirit of emulation by giving much praise in his reports to the brave men who had distinguished themselves. He has never seen a demi-brigade [regiment] without persuading it that he considered it the foremost in the army.

Napoleon had flags made for each of his demi-brigades in the Army of Italy. They bore the names of their battle honours and those actions in which they had most distinguished themselves were inscribed in larger letters. Words of praise from Napoleon were added, such as 'Brave 18th, I know you: the enemy will not stand before you', or 'I was calm, the 32nd was there.'

Napoleon consciously played on rivalries between his units. At the Battle of Saint-Georges on 15 September 1796, he told the 32nd Demi-brigade: 'The 4th must not enter Saint-Georges before you do.' The soldiers replied: 'Let us through, we'll soon do it.'

Napoleon knew that men fought better if they knew why they were fighting and one of his soldiers, Captain Elzéar Blaze, noted:

In general, after a battle, an order of the day acquainted us with what we had done; for we often achieved great things without knowing it. In his proclamations to the army ... he told us that he was satisfied with us, that we had surpassed his expectations, that we had flown with the rapidity of the eagle; he then detailed our exploits, the number of soldiers, cannon, and carriages that we had taken; it was exaggerated, but it was high-sounding and had an excellent effect.

For example, on the day after Austerlitz (1805), the order of the day read:

Soldiers, I am pleased with you! In the Battle of Austerlitz you have accomplished all I expected of your valour; you have crowned your eagles with immortal glory. An army of 100,000 men commanded by the Emperors of Russia and of Austria had been dispersed or captured in less than four hours. What escaped your arms was drowned in the lakes. Forty flags, the standards of the Russian Imperial Guard, 120 guns, twenty generals, more than 30,000 prisoners are the result of this eternally glorious battle. This famous infantry, that outnumbered you, was unable to resist your attack, and henceforth you have no rivals to fear.

Soldiers! When we have completed all that is necessary to secure the happiness and prosperity of our country, I will lead you back to France; there you will be the constant objects of my loving care. My people will hail your return with you, and you will have but to say, 'I was at the battle of Austerlitz', to hear the reply, 'He is one of the brave!'

But men are not led by praise alone and Napoleon's rebukes were scathing. In November 1796, he assembled the officers and NCOs of the 39th and 85th Demibrigades. 'Soldiers! I am no longer proud of you!' he began. 'You have shown no discipline, no steadiness, no courage; you have abandoned every position. Men of the 39th and of the 85th, you are no longer French soldiers. Chief-of-staff, put on their flags: 'They are no longer of the Army of Italy.' The men looked crestfallen, but Napoleon then reminded them of their earlier deeds of valour, re-inspired them and made them promise to perform prodigies.

Similarly, Napoleon skilfully harangued the 4th Regiment of Line Infantry for losing an eagle standard at Austerlitz:[12]

Where is your eagle? [A moment of silence.]

You are the only regiment of the French army to which I can put this question! I would rather I had lost my left arm than an eagle! It will be carried in triumph at St Petersburg and in 100 years' time the Russians will still proudly display it. The forty flags that we have of theirs are not worth your eagle! So have you forgotten how to defend yourselves against cavalry? Who commanded the regiment? What steps did he take when he saw himself charged by the cavalry? Where were your officers, your grenadiers? Should you not all have died before losing your eagle? I have just seen many regiments that have barely any more officers or soldiers in the ranks, but they have preserved their flag and their honour. As for you, I see your strong, large companies and yet I do not find my eagle again in your ranks!

What will you do to make up for this shame, to silence your old comrades of the army who will say when they see you: 'There's the regiment that lost its eagle'? [Silence.]

At the first opportunity, your regiment must bring me four enemy flags and then I will see if I should give it back an eagle.

A lieutenant who heard the speech noted that it was made loudly and with the greatest vehemence: 'It had, on those who heard it, an indescribable effect. I know that it gave me gooseflesh. I felt covered in a cold sweat and, at times, my eyes brimmed with tears. If it had been necessary a moment later to lead this same regiment into action, it would certainly have done marvels.'

Napoleon's punishments were imaginative and, like his praise, directed at a man's honour. In Egypt in January 1799, he discovered that a surgeon had been too cowardly to help some wounded men whom he suspected were infected with bubonic plague. Napoleon ordered him to be dressed in women's clothes and paraded through the streets on a donkey, while wearing a board on his back inscribed with the words: 'Unworthy of being a French citizen – he fears death.'

Napoleon led when necessary by personal example. He received a bayonet or pike wound at Toulon (1793) and was badly bruised by a spent ball on his heel at Ratisbon (1809). He personally sited the guns at Lodi, led an attack on the bridge at Arcole (1796) and rallied his men at Marengo (1800). On the eve of the battle of Jena (1806), he extricated an artillery column that had become stuck in a ravine. At Lützen (1813) he exposed himself to fire to an unusual degree, as he needed to steady his young conscript soldiers by his example. Similarly, at Arcis-sur-Aube (1814) he rode his horse over a live shell when he noticed that his men were terrified by it: the explosion disembowelled his horse, but left him unharmed. But most of the time, Napoleon could leave the tactical details of a battle to his subordinates and concentrate on its overall coordination. Too many personal interventions would have reduced their impact; it was often sufficient for his troops to know that he was present on the battlefield and that they would be fighting under his eyes.

Napoleon took care to be seen sharing dangers and discomforts with his men. Jean-Roch Coignet described how Napoleon spent the night before the Battle of Eylau (1807) with his Imperial Guardsmen:

He had us make him a fire, so we brought wood and bales of straw. He asked for a potato from each mess and we brought him twenty potatoes. He sat on a bale of straw in the midst of his old grumblers, with a stick in his hand and we saw him turning his potatoes in the fire and sharing them with his ADCs.

Particularly in the early years, Napoleon reviewed his troops regularly, showed himself to them, received petitions for advancement or complaints about conditions and spoke to them man-to-man. But Wellington scorned Napoleon's theatrical gestures and oratory and dismissed stories of how he had a phenomenal memory and ability to recognize old soldiers at reviews. He claimed that Napoleon simply had a list made beforehand by his subordinates, so he could call individual soldiers out of the ranks and pretend that he had remembered them and their services.

Moreover, the degree to which Napoleon genuinely cared for the lives of his soldiers is debatable. In Egypt, he readily abandoned an army that he had led to disaster and especially in later years he tended to use brutal frontal assaults regardless of heavy casualties. During the retreat from Moscow, he made a point of being seen walking with a stick through the snow with his men two or three times a day, but actually spent most of his time in his carriage and ate well every day, even as his army starved.

Wellington

Wellington's more sober and austere leadership style reflected the nature of his troops as much as his own personality. His remark that his common soldiers were 'the very scum of the earth', has since become notorious as an indication of his supposed coldness and ingratitude, but was in fact simply a statement of the obvious. Whereas French armies were raised by conscription, the British army relied on recruitment and few men volunteered for such unattractive prospects if they had an alternative. Many enlisted to escape justice or after fathering illegitimate children or simply to obtain alcohol. Wellington added that 'it really is wonderful that we should have made them the fine fellows that they are' and he did so partly by enforcing strict discipline and by not hesitating to flog or execute wrongdoers.

It is small wonder that Wellington had the respect of his troops rather than the adoration enjoyed by Napoleon and Blücher, or that he was later referred to as 'that inflated god almighty' by Commissary August Schaumann. Napoleon led by a semi-deified aura of mystique and Blücher by close personal contact with his troops, by his image as a father figure and by his reputation as a fighting general. Owing to the nature of their leadership, they retained the confidence of their men and junior officers, even if not all their senior subordinates, despite disasters or repeated defeats.

In contrast, Wellington led by trust and personal example. His soldiers trusted him to win and knew the care he took to keep casualties to a minimum. Sergeant William Wheeler of the 51st (or the 2nd Yorkshire West Riding) Regiment of Foot (Light Infantry) wrote in 1816:

> If England should require her army again, and I should be with it, let me have 'Old Nosey' to command. Our interests would be sure to be looked into, we should never have occasion to fear an enemy. There are two things we should be certain of. First, we should always be as well supplied with rations as the nature of the service would admit. The second is that we should be sure to give the enemy a d—d good thrashing. What can a soldier desire more?

Wellington suffered setbacks such as the failure to take Burgos (1812), but never the defeats that are the toughest test of a commander's leadership. This was partly because he usually recognized the limits to what was possible and, with a few exceptions such as the Talavera campaign (1809), did not undertake over-ambitious or recklessly bold ventures like Napoleon's invasion of Russia (1812) or Blücher's headlong advance on Paris (1814).

Like Napoleon, Wellington usually remained aloof from personally taking part in combat, at least after his service as a young officer in the Low Countries and also in India, where, for example, he led a cavalry charge at Conaghull (1800). The historian

Wellington at Waterloo.

John Keegan has called Wellington's leadership style 'anti-heroic', for he eschewed theatrical displays of gallantry. In fact, he never drew his sword from its scabbard during the whole day at Waterloo. He told his friend, Lady Shelley: 'I never expose myself except when it is necessary. It is very wrong in a commander to expose himself unnecessarily.' But often it was necessary, in order to see for himself, maintain his grip on the battle and encourage his men by setting a personal example of courage. He had an instinct for being at the most critical spot and sometimes took temporary command of a battalion in order to restore the situation: 'When I come myself, the soldiers think what they have to do the most important as I am there, and that all will depend on their exertions; of course, these are increased in proportion, and they will do for me what perhaps no one else can make them do.'

It is unfortunate that we do not know more about how Wellington's subordinates viewed some of his personal interventions. We know that Vice-Admiral Horatio Nelson's famous signal at the Battle of Trafalgar in 1805, 'England expects every man will do his duty', provoked Vice-Admiral Cuthbert Collingwood to exclaim that he wished Nelson would stop signalling, as they knew well enough what to do. Similarly, at Waterloo we know that some Nassau infantrymen bad-temperedly fired a few shots in Wellington's direction when he tried to rally them near Hougoumont. But how, for example, did Major-General Peregrine Maitland regard Wellington's personal assumption of command of his brigade of Foot Guards at the climax of the battle? Wellington's famous written order to the garrison commander at Hougoumont, in which he instructed him to keep his men in those parts of the buildings not on fire, certainly conveyed the importance of holding the farm and would have countered any feelings of isolation. But equally, it might have seemed over-fussy to such a hard-pressed officer, in the way it detailed obvious measures that undoubtedly were already being taken.

It seems surprising that, at least according to the traditional account, Wellington did not go into equal detail when Lord Uxbridge asked him on the eve of Waterloo about his plans. Uxbridge rightly thought that he ought to know what his commander intended to do, in case Wellington became a casualty. Wellington asked who would attack first: himself or Bonaparte. Then he pointed out: 'Well, Bonaparte has not given me any idea of his projects; and as my plans will depend upon his, how can you expect me to tell you what mine are?'

He then added reassuringly: 'There is one thing certain, Uxbridge, that is, that, whatever happens, you and I will do our duty.' In fact, Wellington may have said more. According to hearsay evidence, he told Uxbridge to 'keep Hougoumont',[13] and so perhaps he did discuss how he expected the battle to unfold. We simply do not know for sure.

Wellington's personal command style entailed considerable risk, but he was remarkably fortunate. 'I escaped as usual unhurt,' he informed his brother William after the First Battle of Sorauren (28 July 1813), 'and I begin to believe that the finger of God is upon me.' He was, in fact, slightly wounded at Orthez (1814) and struck by spent musketballs on other occasions. Baron de Crossard, the Austrian representative at his headquarters, described one such incident at the Battle of Talavera (1809):

> It is at the most difficult moments that his presence of mind and imperturbable calm seem to increase. He is always to be found at the point of danger, in a position where he can be seen and heard by the whole line and his face and voice can always bolster the most hesitant. A ball hit him and pierced his uniform. We heard the blow and all ran to him in dread. Sir Arthur alone didn't even bat an eyelid: placing his hand on the spot where he had been hit, he coolly said: 'It's nothing.'

Wellington narrowly escaped capture before the Battles of Talavera, Salamanca (1812) and Sorauren and during a French cavalry charge at Quatre Bras (1815), while Napoleon was nearly killed or captured by Cossacks both at Malojaroslavets (1812) and shortly before the Battle of Brienne (1814).

Wellington is often said to have been notoriously sparing of praise, but this is an oversimplification. Some of his remarks could be as sweeping in their praise as others were in their criticism. He once said that the Austrian general, Archduke Charles, knew more about warfare than either himself or Napoleon: 'We are none of us worthy to fasten the latchets of his shoes, if I am to judge from his book and his plans of campaign.' This was certainly an exaggeration, for despite his victory over Napoleon at Aspern-Essling (1809), Archduke Charles was a cautious and methodical commander.

After a battle, Wellington would issue a general order to thank his army and also write an official dispatch to inform the British government of the details, just as Napoleon would produce both a proclamation to his army and a bulletin to notify the French people. Some of Wellington's dispatches, especially the one for Waterloo, have been criticized for their terseness, but it would have been impossible to mention all deserving officers by name given the limitations of time and space, or even to identify them so soon after the battle. It is interesting that Napoleon's bulletins, as distinct from his proclamations, were often no more profuse in their praise than were Wellington's dispatches. They also caused resentment because of their favouritism, for example when they mentioned Napoleon's ADCs and ignored other deserving men, or praised the privileged Imperial Guard more than the rest of the army. General Armand de Caulaincourt wrote:

In general, [Napoleon] had little respect for mankind. He rarely gave praise, even to those who had done the most, unless it was at a time when he needed them to do still more. But in addition, and doubtless in a sort of spirit of fairness, he reprimanded little, or not at all, those who did badly, when it wasn't for very serious matters.

Sometimes, as with his independent-minded brother Louis, whom he had made King of Holland, Napoleon not only withheld praise from subordinates, but criticized them relentlessly in order to keep them in a state of nervous subservience.

Wellington did sometimes mention individual officers in his dispatches. On 1 August 1813, he stated that it was 'impossible to describe the enthusiastic bravery of the 4th division' in the recent fighting in the Pyrenees and he particularly noted the conduct of two officers of Portuguese regiments, Lieutenant-Colonel O'Toole and Captain Joachim Telles Jurdão. He added that a dispatch did not give scope to record all the details but that the Prince of Orange, who would carry it to England, would be able to give more information verbally.

Note, too, that Wellington published, for his troops, the often fulsome replies that he received to his dispatches, for example from the Prince Regent, the Secretary of State for War, the Houses of Parliament and the Commander-in-Chief of the British army.

As for his general orders in which he personally thanked his army, some were actually similar in style to Napoleon's proclamations. For example, he issued one on 12 May 1809 after crossing the Douro river at Oporto:

> The Commander of the Forces congratulates the troops upon the success which has attended their operations for the last four days, during which they have traversed above eighty miles of most difficult country, in which they have carried some formidable positions; have beaten the enemy repeatedly; and have ended by forcing the passage of the Douro, and defending the position so boldly taken up with a number far inferior to those by which they were attacked. In the course of this short expedition the Commander of the Forces has had repeated opportunities of witnessing and applauding the gallantry of the Officers and troops, &c. &c.

Similarly, on 2 October 1811, he drew the army's attention to the units that had distinguished themselves in the recent action at El Bodon: 'The Commander of the Forces has been particular in stating the details of this action in the General Orders, as, in his opinion, it affords a memorable example of what can be effected by steadiness, discipline, and confidence.' He also made a point of praising the gallantry and steadiness of his newly reformed Portuguese troops after their first major battle under his command at Busaco (1810).

It is true that he was less effusive on other occasions. After Waterloo, he simply noted in his general order of 20 June 1815:

> The Field Marshal takes this opportunity of returning to the army his thanks for their conduct in the glorious action fought on the 18th inst.; and he will not fail to report his sense of their conduct, in the terms which it deserves, to their several Sovereigns.

After Salamanca, his general order of 23 July 1812 read more like a rebuke: 'He trusts that the events of yesterday have impressed all with a conviction that military success depends upon troops obeying the orders which they receive, and preserving the order of their formation in action; that upon no occasion must they allow themselves to depart from it one moment.'

But Wellington also showed his appreciation of his troops in other ways. For example, on 16 March 1811, he asked the commanding officers of the 43rd, 52nd and 95th Regiments to name a sergeant of each regiment to be recommended for promotion to Ensign, to show his approval of these units. In a general order of 30 September 1810, he pardoned four men of the 45th (or the Nottinghamshire) Regiment of Foot for robbing some Portuguese civilians, in recognition of the regiment's gallantry at Busaco. Commissary Schaumann explained that Wellington was often merciful to regiments of which he was fond and described an incident involving the 1st Hussars of the King's German Legion, which had a reputation for efficiency. Wellington was talking to the officers of the regiment in 1813, when one of their men rode up with a stolen, bleating sheep. To their relief, Wellington merely smiled, turned his back and pretended not to notice.

One of Wellington's problems was that he was loath to change a published dispatch if it transpired that he had made an unfair criticism, for example when he blamed the 13th Regiment of (Light) Dragoons for allowing the French to escape at the action of Campo Maior (25 March 1811). This fostered resentment and accusations of favouritism, as did his sometimes over-hasty and blanket condemnations of an entire corps for the failings of a few of its members. After Waterloo, for example, he complained about the Royal Artillery in a letter to the Master-General of the Ordnance:

> To tell you the truth, I was not very pleased with the Artillery in the battle of Waterloo. . . . I had a right to expect that the officers and men of the Artillery would do as I did, that is, to take shelter in the squares of infantry till the French cavalry should be driven off. But they did no such thing; they ran off the field entirely, taking with them limbers, ammunition and everything: and when, in a few minutes, we had driven off the French cavalry, and had regained our ground and our guns, and could make good use of our artillery, we had no artillerymen to fire them; and in point of fact, I should have had no artillery during the action if I had not kept a reserve in the commencement.

But, whatever the reticence and lack of balance of his written dispatches, Wellington made a point of encouraging his men verbally in battle. At Busaco, he exclaimed to the commander of the 88th (or the Connaught Rangers) Regiment of Foot: 'Upon my honour, Wallace, I never witnessed a more gallant charge than that just now made by your regiment.' Similarly, Sergeant Duncan Robertson of the 92nd (Highland) Regiment of Foot recorded that during the advance on Paris after Waterloo: 'The Duke of Wellington in person came up and thanked us for the manner in which we had conducted ourselves during the engagement, and lavished the highest eulogiums upon us.'

Whereas Napoleon as a head of state was able to issue decorations and financial rewards to his soldiers as he wished, Wellington did not have the authority to do so.

Yet claims that he neglected such incentives are untrue, for it was on his recommendation that the Waterloo Medal was issued, as the British army's first campaign medal to be awarded without distinction of rank to every officer, NCO and soldier. It should also be remembered that Napoleon's more lavish use of rewards failed to secure the loyalty or continued enthusiasm of all his high-ranking subordinates. By 1814, many of his marshals and generals had grown tired of war and wanted to enjoy in peace the status and riches that they had obtained.

Wellington was more concerned with his troops' fighting efficiency than their appearance on the parade ground. William Grattan of the 88th Regiment commented that he 'was a most indulgent commander; he never harassed us with reviews, or petty annoyances, which so far from promoting discipline, or doing good in any way, have a contrary effect'.

He could also be surprisingly supportive of subordinates and remarked after Brigadier-General Robert Craufurd narrowly escaped a mauling on the Coa river in July 1810: 'If I am to be hanged for it, I cannot accuse a man who I believe has meant well, and whose error was one of judgement, not of intention.'

Indeed, Wellington's reputation as a cold and aloof commander has been exaggerated. General Sir George Napier, who served under him as a subaltern, saw the other side of his character: 'He has a short manner of speaking and a stern look, which people mistake for want of heart; but I have witnessed his kindness to others, and felt it myself in so many instances and so strongly, that I cannot bear to hear him accused of wanting what I know he possesses.' Napier described what happened after one of Wellington's ADCs, Captain the Earl of March, was seriously wounded at the Battle of Orthez (1814). Dr Hare gave orders that anyone entering March's room should be as quiet as possible and refrain from speaking:

> About the middle of the night, as Dr. Hare was sitting dozing in a chair opposite Lord March's bed, who had fallen asleep, the door of the room gently opened and a figure in a white cloak and military hat walked up to the bed, drew the curtains quietly aside, looked steadily for a few seconds on the pale countenance before him, then leaned over, stooped his head, and pressed his lips on the forehead of Lord March, heaved a deep sigh, and turned to leave the room, when the doctor, who had anxiously watched every movement, beheld the countenance of *Wellington!* his cheeks wet with tears.

Blücher

Blücher's style of leadership was more informal than Wellington's. His Prussian troops were often young, inexperienced and poorly trained and equipped and they responded well to his jovial and infectious self-confidence. As a result of his age, Blücher was seen as a father figure: he addressed his troops as his 'children' and was known by them as 'Papa Blücher'. He therefore enjoyed a natural authority and this made possible a degree of familiarity with his men that Wellington avoided and that could have undermined the position of a younger and less forceful commander.

Blücher was genuinely interested in his staff, asked after their families and regularly wrote about them in his letters to his wife. After some of them repeatedly turned up late at the assembly point of his headquarters, he gave them a dressing down: 'Gentlemen, lateness is a sister of idleness.' But after he had spoken his mind, he returned to his usual, friendly self.

Although poorly educated, Blücher was thoroughly experienced in human nature and a shrewd leader of men. If his army was short of food, he would allow only boiled potatoes to be served at his table, in contrast to Napoleon during the retreat from Moscow. When he met stragglers during a march, he might dismount and walk behind them to encourage them to catch up with their units. Or he might shame them by making them put straw in their shakos, so they would be men of straw. In contrast, when he passed a battalion that he esteemed for its bravery, he would ride with his staff along one side of the road rather than disturb its march.

Once, during an action at Löwenberg in 1813, he saw a battalion of *Landwehr*, or militia, withdrawing, apparently without orders, and so he addressed it harshly. But a staff officer explained that the battalion had actually been ordered back to collect more ammunition and that it had fought as well as a battalion of grenadiers, despite being in action for the first time. Blücher had the humility to accept that he had made a mistake, promised to put it right and again spoke to the battalion, this time in friendly terms.

Blücher's surgeon, Dr Bieske, wrote:

> In every battle he exposed himself more than once to be killed, for wherever the hardest fighting occurred he was certain to be present, in order to see to every necessary disposition and, by being on the spot, to profit by every opportunity. It is beyond all doubt that his presence had the greatest influence, for when he said to the soldiers, 'Now boys, you must not let the French take that village, or that wood, or some other important position,' they would certainly turn again and capture it when it was within the bounds of possibility.

The Army of Silesia contained both Russian and Prussian contingents and it was primarily Blücher who smoothed the friction between the two. He often made a point of asking his Russian soldiers for some brandy or a light for his pipe in order to persuade the Prussians to see them as comrades and the Russian officers to treat their own men less harshly. Captain Fritz __ recorded:

> It was often very touching to see how sincerely these bearded [Russian] soldiers shouted for joy when the old man suddenly appeared among them. It was precisely this love for him that inspired the Russian troops to their greatest efforts and during the 1813 and 1814 campaigns I never saw them advance more vigorously than when they knew the Field Marshal was near them. I was endlessly asked by Russian troops who had just returned from a bloody fight, what Field Marshal 'Paschol' [Forwards] would say of their deeds. Some Russian generals were even somewhat jealous now and then of the boundless veneration that their troops always showed for General Blücher.

Blücher's men instinctively felt that he was one of them. The Cossacks even convinced themselves that he had been born by the Don river and that only later had he happened to come to Prussia.

Blücher excelled at handling difficult subordinates. His Russian corps commanders in the Army of Silesia were sometimes reluctant to obey Prussian orders and one of them in particular, General Count Louis de Langeron, was notoriously lacking in fire and determination. Blücher had as much, if not more, trouble from one of his Prussian generals, the touchy and temperamental Hans von Yorck. He once remarked: 'Yorck is a poisonous fellow. He does nothing but argue, but when he does start, he gets his teeth in like no one else.' Blücher handled him with the right mixture of firmness and flattery. At the Battle of Laon (1814), for example, he exclaimed to a messenger from Yorck: 'By God, you old Yorckists are brave and trustworthy fellows! If we could no longer rely on you, the sky would fall in.' Captain Fritz __ thought that no one else could have coped with three such difficult corps commanders as Yorck, Langeron and General Fabian von der Osten-Sacken.

Blücher could also be adept at handling allies, particularly the challenging Crown Prince of Sweden in 1813, but was sometimes openly critical when he felt frustrated by them in pursuit of his objective. He was undiplomatic when prevented from crossing the Rhine into France immediately after he reached the river in 1813 and his attitude in Paris after Waterloo was unhelpful to Wellington and other Allied statesmen as they tried to secure a lasting peace.

Blücher was eloquent and loved making speeches. Henrik Steffens, who served at his headquarters in 1813–14, wrote:

> His speech was bold, like a rough, uncultivated soldier, yet sometimes it rose to such a pitch of eloquence as had been heard from no military hero of modern times; he obeyed the impulse of the moment, but the impulse was deep as it was quick; his perception was so vivid that he would see every difficulty in an instant and be dashed into despair; a few more instants and he would grasp the means of action, and fasten on his object with redoubled energy. That object was Napoleon's downfall.

'He always knew,' recorded his surgeon, 'at the proper moment how to work upon the soldiers' feelings, and only a few comforting words were necessary, and at once toil, hunger and thirst, and all the hardships of war were forgotten.'

Many in Blücher's army thought that its retreat after the Battle of Lützen (1813) was an unnecessary disgrace. Blücher heard of this and decided to address the troops. Steffens recalled:

> This was my first opportunity of admiring his astonishing eloquence. ... 'You are right,' I heard him say, 'you are not beaten – you kept the field, and the enemy withdrew; their loss was greater than yours'; and he then explained to them all his motives for not pushing on the battle, as well as those for retiring. I heard him repeat the same to various divisions as they came up; and while I praise the facility and noble simplicity of his expression, as well as the power of giving the same meaning in so many various forms, as often as he had to repeat it, I must confess that there was something besides the words which gave such effect to the address, and that much was owing to the appearance and manner of the aged but powerful-looking man.

Some of Blücher's written proclamations to his army may have been produced by Gneisenau, or other members of his staff, but this would have happened only after the intended contents had been discussed with him. Interestingly, the proclamation issued after Blücher's victory at the Katzbach echoed Napoleon's style and tone in the way it informed the men how much they had achieved, praised them and then urged them on to further efforts. It also had a pious touch, which perhaps came from Blücher's schooldays at Rostock, or from the influence of Belling, under whom he had served as a young hussar:

> Silesia is cleared of the enemy. Brave soldiers, of the Russian and Prussian army under my command, it is to your vigorous exertions and resolution, to your patience in supporting fatigues and privations, that I owe the good fortune of having wrested this fine province out of the hands of a greedy and rapacious enemy. The implacable foe, with haughty defiance, met you on the Katzbach. You issued with the rapidity of lightning, from behind the heights. You disdained to attack him with the distant fire of musketry, but advanced upon him without pausing. Your bayonets, and the nervous strength of your arm, drove him down the steeps of the raging Neisse and the Katzbach. You have since waded through torrents and rivers; you have passed the nights in storms, without shelter, short of provisions, and struggling with every want; but you murmured not, you pursued with promptitude and energy the flying enemy. I return you thanks for your exalted, praiseworthy conduct. He alone is a true soldier that possesses such qualities.
>
> One hundred and three pieces of cannon, 250 tumbrils, the camp-hospital of the enemy, his provisions, a general of division, two generals of brigade, a great number of colonels, staff and other officers, 18,000 prisoners, two eagles, and other trophies, have fallen into your hands. The remainder of those who opposed you on the Katzbach, terrified at the sight of your bayonets, have taken to flight. The roads and the fields between the Katzbach and the Bober bear the unequivocal marks of the confusion and dismay of the enemy. Let us sing praises to the Lord of Hosts, by whose help you have overthrown your enemies, and return him thanks, in the hour of prayer, for the victory he has given into our hands. Three volleys shall be fired in honour of the day, and terminate your devotions. And then, once more, seek the enemy in the field.

Chapter 19

Methods of Command and Control

Napoleon

Napoleon was a unique commander and organized his headquarters as an extension of himself, to serve him alone rather than provide a model for future generations. He stated in 1808: 'In war, men are nothing; it is one man who counts. ... When, at the dead of night, a good idea flashes through my brain, the order is given in a quarter of an hour, and in half an hour it is being carried out by the outposts.'

Napoleon was really his own chief-of-staff. Marshal Louis Berthier, who nominally held that position until 1814, lamented: 'I am nothing in the army. I receive, in the Emperor's name, the reports of the marshals, and I sign these orders for him, but I am personally null.' Berthier's complaint is confirmed by a letter to him from Napoleon on 14 February 1806: 'Adhere strictly to the orders that I give you. Carry out your instructions punctually; keep everyone alert and at his post. I alone know what must be done.' Napoleon insisted on supervising everything in detail and informed his brother Joseph in 1806 that he took more pleasure in going through the monthly returns of his troops than a young girl had in reading a novel.

At the centre of Napoleon's headquarters, or *Grand Quartier-Général*, was his household, or *Maison*, which included his personal staff, his ADCs and orderly officers and his Cabinet. The Cabinet contained an intelligence office, a secretariat and a topographical office under General Louis Bacler d'Albe, who helped Napoleon plan his operations.

Besides the *Maison*, the *Grand Quartier-Général* included two other major elements: the *Grand Etat-Major Général*, or army staff, under Marshal Berthier and the *Intendance* under Pierre Daru, which was reponsible for logistics, medical arrangements and financial records. Other, secondary, staffs were attached to the *Grand Quartier-Général*, such as those of the provost and the postal service.

The size of Napoleon's *Grand Quartier-Général* reflected his dual role as both head of state and army commander and in December 1806, his *Maison* alone contained about 800 people. But not all of the headquarters accompanied him during a campaign: on a battlefield he would have a *Petit Quartier-Général*, a little, or tactical, headquarters of key personnel, and an escort of Imperial Guard cavalry, while the main headquarters was further to the rear, sometimes several days' march away and divided into parts.

Napoleon's *Grand Quartier-Général* was unparalleled until the development of the Prussian General Staff in the years after 1806. Its sophistication enabled Napoleon to centralize authority to an astonishing degree and during the early, victorious years of the Empire this made it easier for him to coordinate all his resources, maintain secrecy and surprise his opponents. But he did encounter problems because of this centralization, especially in 1809–13 when he tried to control as many as half a million men

Waterloo: Napoleon at his command post.

deployed in several armies in a large theatre of war, while at the same time directing operations in the Peninsula at the opposite end of Europe by remote control.

Such difficulties were exacerbated by frequent mistakes and omissions in French staff work. The initial victorious campaigns of the Grand Army in 1805–7 bred over-confidence and shoddy habits, while Napoleon failed to encourage his subordinates to exercise initiative and habitually did everything on the spur of the moment, calculating that this agitated system kept his staff alert and obedient. Raymond de Montesquiou, the Duke de Fezensac, who served for several years as a staff officer, recalled:

> As for messages taken on horseback, I have already said that no person took the pains to inquire if we had a horse that could walk, even when it was necessary to go at a gallop; or if we knew the country, or had a map. The order must be executed without waiting for the means. ... This habit of attempting everything with the most feeble instruments, this wish to over-look impossibilities, this unbounded assurance of success, which at first helped to win us advantages, in the end became our destruction.

Flawed staff work was largely responsible for the French I Corps marching between the Battles of Quatre Bras and Ligny on 16 June 1815 without intervening in either, a fiasco that cost Napoleon his best chance of a decisive victory in the Waterloo campaign.

Napoleon rarely held councils of war. He did so after the Battles of Eylau (1807) and Smolensk (1812) and on the morning of Waterloo, but on these occasions he wanted to assess the mood of his army and invigorate his senior subordinates rather than genuinely to seek their advice. In fact, he had surprisingly few outstanding sub-ordinates. Even among his famous twenty-six marshals, only Davout, Massena, Soult and possibly Suchet could be entrusted with a major, independent command. During the 1813 campaign in particular, Napoleon found that the marshals he detached to command armies on secondary fronts were repeatedly defeated as he could not be everywhere to supervise them in person.

Except for his stepson, Eugène de Beauharnais, the Viceroy of the Kingdom of Italy, Napoleon did not systematically instruct his senior subordinates in the higher art of war. This was partly because he was jealous of potential rivals and wary of creating an overly powerful general who might challenge his position, in the way that many commanders during the Roman Empire used their armies to seize power. Napoleon was also conservative and, according to Caulaincourt: 'He did not like change. He held on to the men whom he employed and preferred the worst servant to the best, rather than change him.'

But he did allow his more capable corps commanders some scope for initiative. He would issue them with directives to explain his overall aim and the initial moves, so they could operate within that plan, with further guidance being issued as the campaign or battle developed. Thus, on 5 October 1806, Napoleon wrote to Marshal Soult, the commander of the IV Corps, at the start of his offensive against Prussia:

> At this moment, the chief of staff is writing your orders, which you will receive this day. My intention is that you will be at Bayreuth on the 8th. As soon as you reach Bayreuth, return the orderly officer, whom I am sending to you, to me with all the information on the place that you collect. . . . I believe you should know my plans, so that this knowledge can guide you in important moments.

Napoleon then described the situation of his army and explained that Soult formed the head of the right wing, with Ney's corps half a day's march behind him. His plan was to concentrate superior numbers against the Prussians wherever they made a stand:

> If, however, the enemy appears against you with fewer than 30,000 men, you may, in concert with Marshal Ney, concentrate your troops and attack him. But if he is in a position that he has occupied for a long time, he will have been careful to reconnoitre and fortify it and in this case, act with caution. . . .

He added that Soult was to correspond frequently with him and that, when he passed the town of Hof, he should either incline more towards his left or take up an advanced position, depending on the intelligence he had of the Prussians.

Other marshals were incapable of exercising such initiative and required Napoleon's personal supervision. For example, the slow-witted Marshal François Lefebvre understood tactics on a battlefield, but was out of his depth conducting the Siege of Danzig (1807) or manoeuvring on a detached mission in Spain a year later.

Napoleon's ability to control a battle depended on its size. Borodino (1812) was too big for him to be everywhere and partly for this reason he commanded for most of the day from the rear through his staff and senior subordinates, although he did in fact ride forward later in the day to assess the situation for himself and was so exposed to Russian musketry that he had to be begged to retire. The problem was greater when he had to divide his army into two wings to tackle two enemy forces simultaneously, for example in the 1815 campaign when he commanded at Ligny but could not simultaneously supervise the headstrong Marshal Ney six miles away at Quatre Bras.

Napoleon's standard practice was to reconnoitre personally before a battle began, often more than once and up to, or beyond, his outposts. For example, at Dresden on 26 August 1813, he reconnoitred outside the city, leaving almost all his retinue behind so as not to attract attention. A page was wounded while accompanying him on this reconnaissance. During an actual battle, Napoleon tended to spend most of his time at one or two command posts, from where he had a good view of the battlefield, could control the action as a whole and where his corps commanders knew they could find him. But he did sometimes move to different sectors of the field as the battle developed, as on the second day of the Battle of Dresden, when he rode over to his eastern wing in the afternoon to accelerate its offensive. At Austerlitz, he moved forward to a new command post on top of the Pratzen heights in order to keep pace with his advance and thus maintain control of the fighting.

Wellington

It is often pointed out that Wellington's headquarters were smaller than Napoleon's, but this reflected their contrasting roles and responsibilities and the different sizes of their armies. Larger headquarters were not necessarily more efficient and, indeed, there was some duplication of functions between Napoleon's personal *Maison* and the French army staff. Wellington's headquarters were not undersized compared with those of the Allied armies: it is impossible to establish exact numbers of personnel, but he had at least 400 men in October 1813, not including his Portuguese and Spanish staffs. Wellington used his headquarters to command his army effectively and provide him with reasonable comfort, rather than impress observers. He actually had more personal servants in October 1813 than Napoleon took with him on his Russian campaign the year before, but at the same time he did not keep a glittering crowd of ADCs waiting outside his room.[14] Commissary August Schaumann often visited Wellington's headquarters in the summer of 1811 and was surprised by the atmosphere:

> Everything was strikingly quiet and unostentatious. Had it not been known for a fact, no one would have suspected that he was quartered in the town. There was no throng of scented staff officers with plumed hats, orders and stars, no main guard, no crowd of contractors, actors, valets, cooks, mistresses, equipages, horses, dogs, forage and baggage wagons, as there is at French or Russian headquarters! Just a few aides-de-camp, who went about the streets alone and in their overcoats, a few guides, and a small staff guard; that was all!

Wellington's headquarters were in line with the British army's traditional organization. Most of the staff work was shared between the Quartermaster-General's and Adjutant-General's departments. A Senior Department existed at the Royal Military College to provide training in staff work, but few of the officers on the staff of Wellington's army were professionally trained, for most were detached from regimental duty. Other key figures in Wellington's headquarters included the Surgeon-General, Apothecary-General, Paymaster-General, Commissary-General, Judge Advocate-General and the commanders of the Royal Artillery and Royal Engineers. Wellington also had a Military Secretary to assist him with his correspondence and a personal staff of ADCs, who formed a 'family' of young, trusted and spirited officers with whom he could relax.

Wellington had no formal chief-of-staff, but came to rely more heavily on the Quartermaster-General's department, largely owing to his trust in Major-General Sir George Murray, its capable head. Like Napoleon, Wellington personally went into much detail and reserved sole authority to decide his army's moves, but he did discuss plans with Murray and listen to his recommendations.

Some of the heads of department in the headquarters were theoretically responsible directly to their superiors in London. For example, the Commissary-General had to report to the Treasury and the artillery or engineer commanders to the Master-General of Ordnance. Wellington was fully aware of the inefficiencies of the British army's system of administration, within which he had to operate, but had the common sense to realize that he could do little to change the regulations against the weight of tradition and vested interests. Instead, he made the existing system work to its full potential. He explained that he had a 'hand of iron' and that he immediately came down on any sign of neglect.

Wellington was an experienced and well-connected political operator and this was an essential element in his success as a military commander. It enabled him to work closely with the British government and avoid the unfortunate quarrels and misunderstandings that had dogged the career of one of his foremost contemporaries, the more mercurial and less politically adept Lieutenant-General Sir John Moore. The British government regularly consulted Wellington and did its best to support him with money, supplies and reinforcements, despite his outspoken and often unreasonable complaints and despite its other, worldwide, commitments, including economic crises, domestic unrest and a war against the United States in 1812–14. But political connections did not solve all Wellington's difficulties, for he had to work within the constraints of the British military system and had limited authority in non-operational matters, unlike Napoleon, who was also a head of state.

Wellington had mixed success in handling allies, especially when they were less subordinate to British interests than were Portugal or Indian subsidiary states. Relations with the Spaniards in particular were sometimes strained, partly because he could have an autocratic manner, but partly also because of Spanish pride and inefficiency. It is, in fact, doubtful if a more diplomatic and less forceful approach would have secured greater or more reliable cooperation, for Sir John Moore encountered similar problems in the Coruña campaign.

Wellington's military success was underpinned by his remarkable system of logistics, which used a combination of river transport, ox-carts and mules to move supplies from ports and depots to the front. Britain's maritime supremacy and economic strength made it possible to bring grain and other supplies from as far away as America or the north African coast. He was therefore able to maintain his relatively small army, and keep it disciplined and concentrated for longer than the French, despite the infertile and impoverished nature of much of the Iberian Peninsula. 'I know of no [point]', he stressed, 'more important than closely to attend to the comfort of the soldier: let him be well clothed, sheltered and fed. How should he fight poor fellow if he has, besides risking his life, to struggle with unnecessary hardships.'

Superior intelligence was another of Wellington's key advantages. He usually operated in friendly countries and did his utmost to preserve the goodwill of the local people by punishing those of his troops who looted. In contrast, the French had to live partly off the country and, particularly in the Peninsula, antagonized inhabitants by plundering and committing often-indiscriminate atrocities in fighting the guerrillas. As a result, Wellington regularly obtained intercepted French dispatches, often stained with their bearers' blood, and other useful information from guerrillas, local inhabitants and secret correspondents from occupied areas, such as Dr Patrick Curtis, the Rector of the Irish College at Salamanca. To supplement this, and the information gathered by his army's patrols and outposts, Wellington sent out observing officers, intelligent, well-mounted and daring young men, notably Major Colquhoun Grant and Lieutenant-Colonel John Waters, who often penetrated, in uniform, deep behind enemy lines. Wellington himself reconnoitred whenever possible and sometimes personally questioned prisoners or deserters. He actually operated as his own chief of intelligence and his insistence on seeing to as much as possible in person, rather than relying on summaries prepared by his staff, gave him a first-hand grasp of the situation.

If there was a secret to Wellington's success, it was that he always paid close, personal attention to detail, though without losing sight of the larger picture. His complaint in 1811 encapsulates his thinking in this respect:

> It is to be hoped that the general and other officers of the army will at last acquire that experience which will teach them that success can only be attained by attention to the most minute details; and by tracing every point of every operation from its origin to its conclusion, and ascertaining that the whole is understood by those who are to execute it.

On a typical day when not actually fighting, Wellington would rise at 6 a.m. and write for three hours before breakfast. He would then see each of the key members of his staff until 2 or 3 p.m., or sometimes later. Then he would relax by riding or hunting until 6 p.m. In quiet afternoons while in the Peninsula, he sometimes left his headquarters in the Portuguese town of Freneda and walked up and down the town square, in conversation with anyone to whom he wanted to talk, on subjects as varied as India and Ireland. After dinner, he would retire at 9 p.m. and write until midnight.

Wellington's written orders were clear and precise, even if he had to write them in the thick of a battle, like the one he sent to the garrison commander of Hougoumont in the afternoon of Waterloo:

> I see that the fire has communicated from the Hay Stack to the Roof of the Chateau.
>
> You must however still keep your Men in those parts to which the fire does not reach.
>
> Take care that no Men are lost by the falling in of the Roof, or floors: after they will have fallen in occupy the Ruined walls inside of the Garden;

particularly if it should be possible for the Enemy to pass through the Embers in the Inside of the House.

Wellington made doubly sure that the officers at Hougoumont understood this order. Major Andrew Hamilton, who carried the message, handed it to Lieutenant-Colonel Francis Home of the 3rd Regiment of Foot Guards and then emphasized verbally that the farm was to be held 'to the very last, and on no account give it up or abandon it'. Major Hamilton then rode off, but returned soon afterwards to check that Home fully understood, since Wellington 'holds the maintaining of this post to be essential to the success of the operations of the day. It must on no account be given up.'

Wellington used staff officers not simply as messengers but also as his extra eyes and ears to keep him continually updated on the wider situation. At the height of the Battle of Waterloo, he noticed some units in confusion and sent an Assistant Quartermaster-General, Lieutenant-Colonel Dawson Kelly, to 'see what's wrong there'. Kelly sorted out the situation and then assumed command of the 73rd (Highland) Regiment of Foot, which according to a couple of its sergeants had lost all its officers. Similarly, Napoleon used his personal ADCs to carry messages, explain the overall situation to recipients and even to take command at critical points, with his personal authority.

Wellington has been accused of preferring mediocre subordinates who could be trusted to obey orders, such as Marshal Beresford and Lieutenant-General Sir Stapleton Cotton, to more brilliant but erratic and independent men like Major-General Robert Craufurd. But, like Napoleon, he had few senior generals fit for the demanding role of an independent command and, unlike him, had limited say in their appointment. On 29 August 1810, he sarcastically complained:

> Really when I reflect upon the characters and attainments of some of the general officers of this army, and consider that these are the persons on whom I am to rely to lead columns against the French Generals, and who are to carry my instructions into execution, I tremble . . . __ and __ will be a very nice addition to this list! However, I pray God and the Horse Guards to deliver me from General __ and Colonel __.

He was fond of saying of some of these men: 'I only hope that when the enemy reads the list of their names he trembles as I do.'

Despite the paucity of reliable generals, Wellington did entrust some of them, notably Sir Rowland Hill and Sir Thomas Graham, with commands larger and more independent than that of a division. This gave them opportunities to exercise initiative and develop their abilities. To some extent, Wellington became obliged to give subordinates more scope for initiative, for his army at Vitoria (1813) was as large as 75,000 men, four times what it had been at Vimeiro (1808). Later that summer, he found himself operating in the Pyrenees on a front of 40 miles and in rugged terrain with limited lateral communications. Wellington's Judge Advocate-General, Francis Larpent, noticed some relaxation in his hitherto close supervision under these circumstances: 'Lord Wellington is not as easily roused from his bed as he used to be. This is the only change in him; and it is said he has been in part encouraged to this by having such confidence in General Murray [his Quartermaster-General].'

Similarly, he entrusted the siege of San Sebastian to Sir Thomas Graham and kept his headquarters 15 miles away at the village of Lesaca. Larpent noted that Wellington had been over once to San Sebastian, 'but seemed to wish to leave it to Graham, and not to interfere immediately'.

In these final stages of the Peninsular War, Wellington felt increased confidence in taking such an approach, as his army had become more experienced and professional and had firmly established a moral supremacy over its French opponents after five years of victories. He sometimes shared his views and intentions: before the Battle of the Nivelle (1813), he explained to senior officers of the Light Division how he planned to break through the fortified French position. But he had sound security reasons for not discussing his plans widely, not least as letters sent home by some of his officers were published by their families in newspapers.

Nor did Wellington leave any doubt as to his ultimate authority. He told one of his subordinates that:

> I did not know what the words 'second in command' meant, any more than third, fourth, or fifth in command; that I alone commanded the army ... that ... I would treat ... him ... with the most entire confidence, and would leave none of my views or intentions unexplained; but that I would have no *second in command* in the sense of anything like ... superintending control; and that, finally and above all, I would not only take but insist upon the whole and undivided responsibility of all that should happen while the army was under my command.

One of the advantages of this centralization was that Wellington kept a tight grip on his army. He explained to Müffling that in many of his defensive battles he waited for an opportunity to switch to the offensive and take advantage of a false move by the enemy. This meant that his subordinates had to be able to move as soon as they received orders, but they could not do so if they were engaged in their own enterprises, unknown to their commander. He once furiously rebuked his Inspector-General of Hospitals, Sir James McGrigor, for moving some stores to Salamanca, where many sick and wounded men were collected: 'I shall be glad to know who commands this army – I or you? I establish one route, one line of communication – you establish another by ordering up supplies by it. As long as you live, sir, never do that again. Never do *anything* without my orders.'

Wellington complained in the Pyrenees in 1813 that there was nothing he disliked so much as extended operations that he could not direct personally and, indeed, some of his operations towards the end of the Peninsular War justified his insistence on keeping tight control. At the Battle of Toulouse (1814), he had to operate on three sides of the city simultaneously and his plan quickly broke down as he could not be present everywhere and prevent his subordinates launching mistimed or misjudged attacks. One of his officers, Lieutenant-Colonel Sir John Colborne, claimed that 'it was the worst arranged battle that could be, nothing but mistakes'.

Despite his centralized command style, Wellington did not prevent his subordinates from exercising initiative within reasonable limits. He knew that he had to strike a balance between allowing them the freedom to take advantage of local opportunities and preventing them from becoming dangerously carried away as they were at

Toulouse. At Waterloo, his cavalry commander, Lord Uxbridge, felt that Wellington had given him carte blanche, a free hand, 'and I never bothered him with a single question respecting the movements it might be necessary to make'. Uxbridge for his part authorized his brigade commanders to act discretionally under certain limitations. By Uxbridge's own account, it was he, acting on his own initiative, who unleashed the decisive charge of the British heavy cavalry which smashed Napoleon's main attack on Wellington's eastern wing in the afternoon. Similarly, Sir Augustus Frazer, the commander of the Royal Horse Artillery, ably created and controlled a highly mobile reserve of horse artillery batteries and used it to reinforce the front line as the battle progressed. At the climax of the battle, Sir John Colborne anticipated orders and wheeled the 52nd Regiment forward out of the front line and assailed the flank of the Imperial Guard in a decisive counter-attack.

Blücher

Wellington and Napoleon's refusal to share responsibility in any meaningful sense contrasted sharply with Blücher's command methods. Although an inspirational leader, Blücher needed the active assistance and advice of a chief-of-staff to help direct his army. When he was first appointed as a commander-in-chief in the spring of 1813, he had no prior experience of army command and had not even seen action for seven years. His first chief-of-staff for the Army of Silesia was Gerhard von Scharnhorst, Prussia's leading military theorist and reformer who had already served with him during the retreat from Auerstädt. Following Scharnhorst's death from an infected wound received at the Battle of Lützen, the post was filled by Gneisenau, who had won a reputation by holding the fortress of Colberg in the spring of 1807 until after the conclusion of peace.

Blücher once joked that he was the only man who could kiss his own head and proved it by kissing Gneisenau. He explained how:

> Gneisenau, being my chief-of-staff and very reliable, reports to me on the manoeuvres that are to be executed and the marches that are to be performed. Once convinced that he is right I drive my troops through hell towards the goal and never stop until the desired end has been accomplished – yes, though the officers trained in the old school may pout and complain and all but mutiny!

Blücher's command methods reflected the emergence in Prussia of a permanent and professional General Staff. Since they lacked an outstanding general capable of defeating Napoleon, the Prussians developed the General Staff to provide a more systematic, robust and institutionalized method of command and thus compensate for the absence of a great captain. The officers of the General Staff were trained in a common doctrine and then attached to the army, corps and brigade commanders. They were partners rather than mere assistants and shared their commanders' responsibility for decisions. Blücher and his chief-of-staff provided a template in this system of dual command for the army as whole. The common training of the General Staff officers helped give coherence to the army's operations and the use of the General Staff was particularly suited to the scale of the 1813 campaign, for even Napoleon found it difficult to control large armies over such distances with a centralized and personal command system.

Blücher once summarized his partnership as 'Gneisenau directs and I go forward', but this was an oversimplification. Similarly, Müffling exaggerated when he claimed: 'It was no secret to Europe that old Prince Blücher ... understood nothing whatever of the conduct of a war; so little, indeed, that when a plan was submitted to him for approval, even relating to some unimportant operation, he could not form any clear idea of it, or judge whether it were good or bad.' Blücher was both intelligent and experienced and his letters to his wife and friends show that he had at least a basic understanding of his army's situation and the course of the war as a whole. He was never merely a figurehead who could be guided into any course of action, for he was a strong personality and a good judge of character. Captain Fritz __ wrote: 'Blücher again proved the great knowledge of men that he possessed to such an exceptional degree. With all his apparent joviality and mildness, the old man was in this respect a very cunning fox, who knew how to see through and judge everyone.' Blücher was loyal to staff officers who had earned his respect, but lost all confidence in those who expressed needless concerns and doubts about an operation that had already been agreed. After he approved plans he had the determination and moral courage to enforce them regardless of alarms or contrary advice.

His ultimate authority was never in doubt. Orders and proclamations were issued in his name and usually bore his signature; even when he did not personally write them, he discussed the general issues beforehand with members of his staff.

Gneisenau's role in the partnership has been overrated, for he was not, in fact, an ideal staff officer. He did not have the intellect or balanced outlook of his predecessor, the quieter and more scholarly Scharnhorst, and said that he felt like a pygmy compared to him. He was tempestuous and had fought several duels as a young officer. He also tended to be inconsistent, sometimes restraining Blücher when boldness was required and sometimes encouraging his wilder ideas, as Schwarzenberg complained when the Army of Silesia advanced headlong on Paris in 1814. He also lacked Blücher's astuteness and lightness of touch in dealing with allies and corps commanders. He was unpopular with the army and with the Russian contingent in particular. He was junior to many of the Prussian corps commanders and also socially inferior to them, having been born in Saxony as the son of an artillery officer, yet he too easily gave offence to such men through his passionate and demanding nature.

In theory, the General Staff system should have alleviated this problem, as Gneisenau could have influenced the corps commanders through their chiefs-of-staff. In practice, he often found himself in conflict with both the commanders and their staffs, bitterly so in the case of General Yorck. His notorious suspicions about Wellington's reliability in 1815 need to be seen against the wider, troubled background of his relations with allies and colleagues and his similar suspicions of Austrian and Russian motives in the 1814 campaign.

Gneisenau's reputation must also be qualified by the importance of other members of the headquarters, especially the Quartermaster-General. He himself admitted: 'I am not sufficiently inflated to believe that I can do without the help of brilliant men; I always welcome good advice. I honour myself in this confession.' He referred to the Quartermaster-General as his 'better half' and wrote to the Minister of War:

You know as well as I do, that I lack some important qualities of a Chief of the General Staff. I am not sufficiently equipped for this position either by disposition or by scholarly education. In my partnership with Blücher, I only have an effect, on him mainly through my character, and on events, through a resolute view of the war, which I have developed by some study of history and by attentively considering the events.

In deciding the Army of Silesia's movements, Gneisenau usually discussed the situation with Müffling, the Quartermaster-General, who would be responsible for drawing up the necessary orders. Once the decisions had been made, Müffling explained the planned moves to Blücher, in Gneisenau's presence and using a map with the positions marked on it by officers of the General Staff. These presentations were normally held every day. (In 1815, the Quartermaster-General was General Carl von Grolman, while Müffling became Wellington's Prussian liaison officer.)

Müffling was a vain man, who exaggerated his influence in his memoirs, but it is undeniable that he was capable and more sophisticated, balanced and educated than Gneisenau. Major von Brünneck, who served as an adjutant in Blücher's headquarters, wrote:

Each of these men contributed to success according to his position, education and strength of mind: Blücher through his unshakeable determination and indomitable, heroic courage; Gneisenau through his energetic personality, spirit of enterprise and wealth of ideas; Müffling through prudence, education, tenacity and efficiency. As a rule, Gneisenau produced the ideas and also the decisions. Blücher approved and interested himself in the most animated way for them to be put into effect. But it was Müffling, through his experience of business and war, who brought them into being.

It was unfortunate that Müffling's relations with Gneisenau broke down during the 1814 campaign. Indeed, the events of 1814 fully demonstrate the falseness of the view that Blücher was a mere figurehead, or that Gneisenau was always right when they did differ. Blücher's views usually coincided with Gneisenau's since both men tended, at least in 1813, to bold options. But Gneisenau then became more cautious and reluctant to risk heavy casualties. At the start of March 1814, the Army of Silesia was reinforced by a Prussian corps under General von Bülow, which had hitherto been operating in the secondary theatre of the Low Countries. Nostitz explained that Bülow's Chief-of-Staff, Hermann von Boyen, completely influenced Gneisenau and persuaded him not to take any more risks. Gneisenau became concerned that if the Army of Silesia suffered a defeat, Schwarzenberg and the Army of Bohemia would withdraw in alarm to the Rhine, effectively ending hopes of toppling Napoleon. Gneisenau was also anxious that Prussia should have an intact army at the end of the war to ensure that her interests were not neglected in the peace settlement. He was conscious that Prussia's current allies could subsequently become opponents.

It was against this background that Blücher fell ill during the Battle of Laon. On the night of 9–10 March, details arrived of a successful attack on Napoleon's detached right wing under Marshal Marmont. Müffling drew up a plan for exploiting the success with a bold outflanking move. After Gneisenau had been woken to obtain his approval, the plan was sent to the corps commanders. But next day, Gneisenau suddenly cancelled the plan and thus allowed Napoleon to disengage and withdraw.

According to Nostitz, if Gneisenau was woken in the night to receive a report or authorize an order, he would have it read aloud to him, but was often unable to remember the conversation the next day. This is what happened at Laon: Gneisenau apparently could not recall having authorized Müffling's plan during the night.

The cancellation of the outflanking move paralysed the Army of Silesia and caused much recrimination. General von Yorck, who was reluctant to take orders from the more junior Gneisenau, believed that Blücher was too incapacitated to exercise command and claimed incorrectly that his signature was being forged on orders. Friction between the Russian and Prussian elements of the Army of Silesia also emerged into the open. The Russians suspected that Gneisenau's motive in cancelling the outflanking move was to shield the Prussian troops from casualties.

Gneisenau's biographer defended his inaction by arguing that he could not risk a fast-moving, offensive action against Napoleon, since he could not count on instant obedience from the more senior corps commanders. But the real reason seems to have been excessive caution. Captain Fritz __, who was serving at Blücher's headquarters at the time, recalled:

> As soon as old Blücher failed to appear in person, disorder after disorder entered the Army of Silesia and everything went backwards. Even a simple subaltern officer, who had only partly open eyes in his head, could see this everywhere. General Gneisenau was the best Chief of the General Staff that Blücher could find and achieved the extraordinary in 1813–15, but was hardly fit to be an independent commander-in-chief. He did not possess enough vigour for this, nor did he understand how to keep his disobedient corps commanders compliant, be it by good humour, derision or rudeness.

Nostitz was convinced that Blücher would not have hesitated to risk the outflanking move at Laon if he had been well. He also thought that Gneisenau would have advised him to do so, but that he was unwilling to take the responsibility himself in case of a check. The incident fully demonstrated the weight that Blücher had in major decisions and how he had to use his judgement even in questions of strategy.

In fact, the General Staff as a whole was better at managing an army than leading it. After the defeat at Ligny, it capably rallied the Prussian army and ensured that it continued to function despite Blücher's temporary absence, but it could not have restored morale in the way that Blücher did through his personal leadership over the next two days. Nor is it certain if Gneisenau on his own would have had the self-confidence and trust in Wellington to march promptly to his support at Waterloo on 18 June. Nostitz felt unable to answer the question of what would have happened if Blücher had been killed or wounded at Ligny: 'But I doubt if there would have been such compliant support from all subordinates, such a general devotion in the will of the [replacement] commander, as that which made 18 June 1815 so rich in results.' No staff system, however professional, can compensate for flawed or absent leadership.

Blucher was informal and familiar with his young officers and convivial at dinner. He harangued those around him, hoping that this would create a robust, fighting spirit that would transmit itself through the army when his staff officers left to carry messages to subordinates. In particular, he wanted to counter the pessimists, the 'committee of safety' or *Trübsals-Spritzen* ('affliction-squirts') as he derisively called them, who undermined morale. By debating options openly, he and Gneisenau sought to foster teamwork among the headquarters staff. But this openness could cause problems, for if Blücher and Gneisenau publicly ruled out a retreat, they would have difficulty in reversing that decision without loss of face. There were advantages to Wellington's more aloof command style, as Müffling pointed out:

> It was not the custom in [Wellington's] army to criticize or control the Commander-in-Chief. Discipline was strictly enforced; every one knew his rights and his duties. The Duke, in matters of service, was very short and decided. He allowed questions, but dismissed all such as were unnecessary. His detractors have accused him of being inclined to encroach on the functions of others, – a charge which is at variance with my experience.

But the differences between the Prussian command system and Wellington's methods should not be exaggerated. Under a strong leader like Blücher, there was, in fact, a limited tolerance of dissent. For example, at the end of September 1813, he swiftly stamped out opposition to the planned move of the Army of Silesia around Napoleon's northern flank and across the Elbe river. There were objections that it was too risky and that it should be discussed by all the generals of the army, but Blücher curtly insisted: 'I do not hold councils of war.' He later wrote to Baron Karl von Knesebeck, the Prussian King's ADC: 'Gneisenau, Müffling and my Goltz are those with whom I agree in everything, but I have the devil of a job with the other, safety-first, superintendents. Once I have made my decision, I have to force my way through with my iron will alone.' Thus, the apparent openness at Blücher's headquarters was intended more to persuade subordinates than consult them and to gain approval for decisions rather than encourage disagreement or heed cautious objections.

The Prussian General Staff was still in its infancy at the time of Waterloo and did not truly come of age until the campaigns of General Helmuth von Moltke against Austria (1866) and France (1870–1). By then, the development of railways had contributed to the growth in the size of armies and theatres of war and had made a decentralized system of command and control unavoidable. But the full development of the Prussian system also enhanced its inherent problems. Moltke repeatedly found that after setting his army in motion, he had a looser grip and was unable to prevent headstrong corps commanders from launching bloody and fruitless frontal attacks, most notoriously at Gravelotte-St Privat (1870). The reduction of the commander-in-chief to a figurehead gave the General Staff too much power, which entailed the dangers of command by committee, institutional arrogance and an over-concentration on detail at the expense of the bold and imaginative direction of the operations as a whole. Thus, Wellington's methods of command and personal intervention are still important and even on the large and complex battlefields of today can be implemented using modern communications technology to project a commander's presence artificially.

Chapter 20

Strategy and Tactics

'The instantaneous flash of an idea'

Wellington was once asked the reason for his success and replied: 'I attribute it entirely to the application of good sense to the circumstances of the moment.' This common sense, combined with experience and self-confidence, gave him an intuitive grasp of what to do. He described this vividly:

> There is a curious thing that one feels sometimes; when you are considering a subject, suddenly a whole train of reasoning comes before you like a flash of light; you see it all (moving his hand as if something appeared before him, his eye with its brightest expression), yet it takes you perhaps two hours to put on paper all that has occurred to your mind in an instant. Every part of the subject, the bearing of all the parts upon each other, and all the consequences are there before you.

For Napoleon, the process was similar: 'A battle is a dramatic action which has its beginning, its middle and its conclusion. The result of a battle depends on the instantaneous flash of an idea.' Neither man was born with this intuition, but acquired it by years of experience and study. They also carefully considered all possible options in advance, as for example when Wellington issued confidential orders to his senior subordinates on 30 April 1815, six weeks before the start of the Waterloo campaign, outlining the possible invasion routes open to Napoleon and detailing what they should do in each case.

Napoleon and Wellington both had strongly analytical minds, partly because of their aptitude for mathematics. They planned carefully, using all the information they could find, and analysed it methodically to make decisions. As Napoleon explained: 'The art of war lies in calculating odds very closely to begin with, and then in adding exactly, almost mathematically, the factor of chance. Chance will always remain a sealed mystery for average minds.' Similarly, Wellington once told a friend: 'All the business of war, and indeed all the business of life, is to endeavour to find out what you don't know by what you do; that's what I called "guessing what was on the other side of the hill".' Napoleon explained how such careful consideration made possible his flashes of inspiration:

> If I appear to be always ready to reply to everything, it is because I have meditated for a long time before undertaking anything and I have foreseen what might happen. It is not a spirit that suddenly reveals to me what I have to say or do in a circumstance unexpected by others. It is reflection, meditation. ...
> There is no greater coward than I when I am drawing up a plan of

campaign. I magnify every danger, every disadvantage that can be conceived. My nervousness is painful; but I still show a cool face to those who are about me. I am like a woman in the throes of childbirth. When once my decision is made, however, I forget all, except what may carry it through to success.

Caulaincourt described how:

The Emperor went into the smallest details. He wanted to impose his genius on everything. ... Nothing escaped his concern. We can use this word to describe his foresight, for to him no detail seemed unworthy of attention. Everything that could contribute to the successes and well-being of his soldiers seemed to him worthy of fixing his attention each day. It can not be said that the Emperor ever went to sleep soundly, for, immediately after obtaining a success, regardless of its magnitude, he concerned himself with all the precautions that he would have taken if he had had a defeat.

Wellington stressed how indispensable it was thoroughly to master the military profession:

One must understand the mechanism and power of the individual soldier, then that of a company, a battalion, a brigade and so on, before one can venture to group divisions and move an army. I believe I owe most of my success to the attention I always paid to the inferior part of tactics as a regimental officer. There are few men in the Army who knew these details better than I did; it is the foundation of all military knowledge.

'Depend upon it,' he added, 'it requires time for a general to inspire confidence or to feel it; for you will never have confidence in yourself until others have confidence in you.'

Blücher, too, had acquired enough experience and self-confidence to take immediate action on a battlefield. As a cavalry officer in the early stages of his career, he had become accustomed to making snap decisions and seizing opportunities.

Napoleon had also mastered the details, especially in his chosen arm, the artillery: 'There is nothing in the military profession I cannot do for myself. If there is no one to make gunpowder, I know how to make it; gun carriages, I know how to construct them; if it is founding a cannon, I know that; or if the details of tactics must be taught, I can teach them.'

It is true that Napoleon had risen to high rank faster than either Wellington or Blücher. But the popular idea that this prevented him from mastering each level of command, or from becoming familiar with infantry tactics, is a myth. He had learnt the basic infantry drill at Brienne and the *Ecole militaire* and as part of his training to be an artillery officer he had to learn all the regulation manoeuvres of an infantry battalion, for he had to know how infantry operated, especially in battle, if he was to be effective as a gunner. He was second-in-command of a battalion of volunteers in Corsica and in 1793 he spent three months at Toulon working closely with infantry, including in the final assault. He personally led more infantry attacks at Lodi and Arcole in Italy (1796). He was confident enough to make changes to his infantry's tactical formations, such as the introduction of large, divisional squares during his Egyptian campaign (1798–9).

Six days before the Battle of Austerlitz (1805), he had instructions issued to his corps commanders on a new tactical deployment suited for use against the massed formations of the Russians, while in the autumn of 1813 he ordered the replacement of the three-deep line with one of two ranks.

In contrast, even Wellington, whose proficiency at handling infantry was never in doubt, relied on the British army's approved drills and made no true tactical innovations of his own. He merely introduced an unprecedented proportion of skirmishers (about one-fifth of each of his brigades in the Peninsula was composed of light infantry) and had his battalions form in lines two ranks deep, not the officially prescribed three. Even this was hardly an innovation, as two ranks had already been used by several other British commanders.

Napoleon

All three commanders were bold and aggressive and sought out opportunities. Napoleon rarely fought on the defensive, even when he was outnumbered, for he believed that it was essential to take the war to the enemy, find his weak points and concentrate superior forces against them. He sought a decisive battle to destroy the opposing army and thereby obtain a quick and victorious end to the war. He once remarked: 'There are in Europe many good generals, but they see too many things at once. I see only one thing, namely the enemy's main body. I try to crush it, confident that secondary matters will then settle themselves.' He usually seized the initiative at the outset and repeatedly surprised his opponents by the timing, speed and direction of his onslaughts. He informed his brother Joseph in 1806: 'The loss of time is irreparable in war. The excuses made are always bad, for operations come to nothing only through delays.'

Napoleon organized his army into permanent corps, self-reliant formations usually 15,000 to 30,000 men strong and containing infantry, cavalry and artillery, plus supporting services such as engineers and their own staff. The corps organization also increased the army's cohesion, flexibility and speed of reaction. In contrast, in the early years of the Empire other armies often lacked permanent formations larger than a division or even a brigade and had to group their units into temporary formations for a battle.

On campaign, Napoleon's army would usually start an offensive by marching dispersed and along parallel roads, in a formation known as the *bataillon carré*, because, like a well-commanded battalion, it was ready for anything. The dispersal eased congestion and made it possible for the army to march fast and live to a large extent off the country. At the same time, each corps was within a day or two's march of its neighbours, so the army could rapidly concentrate in any direction once contact was made with the enemy and quickly build up a local superiority of numbers. Napoleon explained the concept in his directive to Marshal Soult at the start of the 1806 campaign:

> You will realize that with such an immense and concentrated numerical superiority, I wish to leave nothing to chance but to attack the enemy wherever he decides to make a stand, with double his strength. . . .
> You will certainly think that it will be a fine thing to move around this

THE *BATAILLON CARRÉ:*
NAPOLEON'S 1806 CAMPAIGN AGAINST PRUSSIA

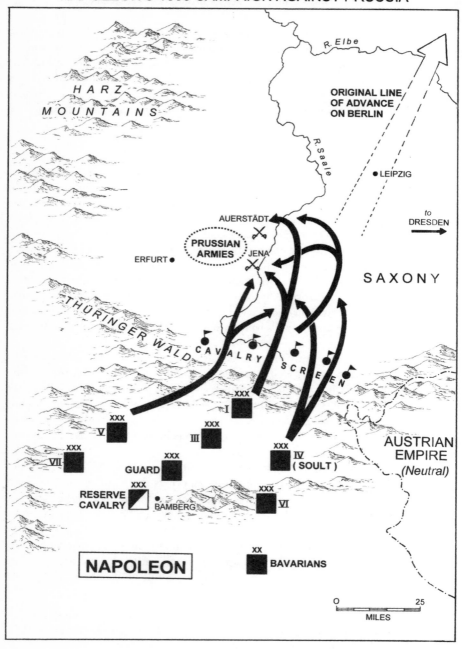

place [Dresden] in a *bataillon carré* of 200,000 men. But all this requires a bit of skill and some fighting.

In 1806, Napoleon used his *bataillon carré* to outflank the Prussian armies to the east, before swinging round and threatening their lines of communication to Berlin, thereby forcing them to fight decisive battles at Jena and Auerstädt instead of retreating beyond his reach. Napoleon repeatedly used this outflanking strategy, the *manoeuvre sur les derrières*, throughout his career, especially when he enjoyed numerical superiority, and he often combined it with feint attacks to distract his enemy's attention.

Wellington expected Napoleon to attempt an outflanking manoeuvre when he invaded the United Netherlands in 1815. Instead, Napoleon used a different and more direct strategy, that of the central position, which he tended to employ when he faced two enemy armies in the same campaign theatre and was numerically inferior to their combined strength. He would penetrate between them and then exploit this central position to defeat them piecemeal before they could concentrate and unite against him. His key advantage was being able to march in a direct line when he switched his attention between his two enemies. This meant he could quickly achieve a local superiority, whereas his opponents had to communicate and manoeuvre around him on longer, exterior lines. But this strategy was less likely to end in a truly decisive victory as Napoleon could not fully pursue one enemy until he had also defeated the other.

Napoleon's battles reflected his campaign strategy in their ruthless quest for a decisive outcome. He usually opened with a succession of attacks to pin down his opponent and draw in his reserves, sometimes by threatening a flank. When he judged the moment ripe, he would concentrate the fire of a massed artillery battery against a vulnerable point in the enemy's now beleaguered battle line and then break through it with his powerful reserve units, including, if necessary, the Imperial Guard.

Napoleon summarized the essential elements of his strategy when he wrote to General Jacques Lauriston in 1804: 'Always remember these three things: concentration of strength, activity and the firm resolve to die gloriously. These are the three great principles of the military art that have always made fortune favour me in all my operations. Death is nothing, but to live defeated and ingloriously, is to die every day.'

But the relentless energy and aggressiveness of Napoleon's strategy could backfire if a campaign failed to win a quick and decisive victory. Caulaincourt noted:

> He was always improvising and thus immediately wore out and disorganized in a few days, by the speed of his marches, everything that his genius had just created. If a thirty-day campaign did not produce the results of a year, most of his calculations turned out to be wrong, because of the losses he had suffered, for everything was so rapid and unexpected and his subordinates were so inexperienced and careless and, above all, had been so spoiled by the previous successes, that everything was disorganized, squandered and scattered.

Wellington

It was by exploiting this fatal flaw in French strategy that Wellington checked Marshal Massena's invasion of Portugal in 1810. He avoided a decisive battle against the odds and instead withdrew inside the Lines of Torres Vedras around Lisbon after devastating the countryside outside, eventually obliging the French to retreat by starving them out.

Despite popular belief, Wellington was not simply a master of the defensive. Indeed, regarding him as such was a mistake that many distinguished French commanders made in the Peninsula until they were taught otherwise by the harsh experience of defeat and the loss of their reputation. Wellington actually attacked at most of his battles. In this sense, Waterloo was not, in fact, a typical battle for him and one can appreciate his annoyance at historians who concentrated on it, thereby provoking his complaint that anyone would think that the British army had never fought a battle before.

He had become accustomed in India to seizing the initiative and making immediate and vigorous, but disciplined attacks, for that was the only way to defeat larger armies of native Indian troops and establish a moral supremacy over them. He retained this aggressiveness in the Peninsula and was even bolder than the results of some of his battles there suggest. At both Vitoria (1813) and Orthez (1814), he had hoped to trap and destroy the French army and although in each case he won a major victory, he was unable to complete it by moving fast enough to cut the French line of retreat.

Even when forced by numerical inferiority to fight a defensive battle, Wellington did so in an active and flexible way. He used his eye for the ground to select a naturally strong position. He garrisoned any farms or villages that could serve as strongpoints against frontal attack, but generally avoided using extensive earthworks or field for-tifications, which tended to immobilize troops, as indeed the French found when he himself attacked them at the Battle of the Nivelle (1813). Instead, he habitually kept his troops on the reverse slopes of a ridge, where they were hidden from observation and sheltered from much of the French artillery fire. He could then surprise the French assaults with sudden counter-attacks and overthrow them before they could deploy and establish themselves. He held that 'the great secret of battle is to have a reserve' and skilfully drew units from quiet sectors to achieve local superiority against each successive French attack, but fed in only the necessary minimum of reinforcements, without unbalancing his army or losing his grip on the battle as a whole.

In some battles, Wellington began on the defensive, but then switched to the offensive, most famously when he rolled up Marshal Marmont's army at Salamanca (1812), but also at Quatre Bras and Waterloo, where he drove the French from the field with a general advance at the end of the day after repelling all their attacks.

He usually lacked enough guns to imitate Napoleon and use them in mass as a decisive arm in their own right and, in any case, the terrain of the Peninsular battle-fields often made it difficult for artillery to play a major role. Instead, he usually deployed his batteries individually to support key points of his line. In later years, he occasionally found it possible to concentrate his artillery, especially at Vitoria, where he used seventy-five guns to pound the French centre, at Orthez and also at Waterloo, where he had a mobile reserve of horse artillery ready to reinforce threatened sections of his front line.

Similarly, he lacked a large cavalry force until the final years of the Peninsular War. A few notorious mishaps in which units charged too far undermined his confidence in his cavalry, although in fact it generally served him well both in battle and on reconnaissance and outpost duties.

Wellington could not afford heavy casualties, for most of the British army was needed to garrison colonies and naval bases around the world and defend the British Isles from the threat of both invasion and internal unrest. 'I could lick those fellows any day,' he observed of the French in 1810, 'but it would cost me 10,000 men, and, as this is the last army England has, we must take care of it.'

In fact, he rarely lost more than 5,000 to 6,000 men in a battle, with the notable exception of Waterloo, where he had 15,000 casualties. In contrast, Napoleon lost 30,000 at Wagram and Blücher 12,000 at Leipzig. Napoleon had unrivalled resources at his disposal and for the sheer numbers of troops needed to feed his military machine could rely on both conscription and contingents extracted from allies and satellite states. He was able to replace his army twice in a single year after it was destroyed in the 1812 and 1813 campaigns. Wellington once remarked that he could hardly imagine anything greater than Napoleon at the head of an army, especially a French army, but added that he had one great advantage:

> He had no responsibility – he could do whatever he pleased; and no one has lost more armies than he did. Now with me the loss of every man told. I could not risk so much; I knew that if I ever lost five hundred men without the clearest necessity, I should be brought upon my knees to the bar of the House of Commons.

Partly because of his constraints of manpower, Wellington sought to win battles as cheaply and decisively as possible, without the heavy casualties inherent in attritional actions like Talavera or, indeed, Waterloo. When he attacked, he outflanked his enemy whenever possible, or at least used outflanking moves after pinning down his opponent with frontal attacks, as at Roliça and Orthez. He was imaginative and flexible and repeatedly surprised the French by doing what they least expected. When attacking across the Bidasoa river in October 1813, he did so near the tidal estuary, which the French had believed to be impassable. A month later, when he attacked the French on the Nivelle river, he avoided the heavily defended coastal sector and this time made his main attacks further inland.

One of his most remarkable campaigns was his offensive in the spring of 1813, when he forced the French to retreat right across northern Spain by relentlessly outflanking them. He then veered round and fell on them at Vitoria on 21 June, pinning them down with a frontal attack from the west while the rest of his army converged in several columns against their northern flank. His ultimate aim was to try and cut their line of retreat to the east and, although he failed to do this entirely, he inflicted a major defeat. He had in fact replicated, intentionally or otherwise, Napoleon's famous *manoeuvre sur les derrières*. He even shifted his lines of transportation during his advance, so that instead of receiving supplies from his original bases, he began to do so by shorter supply lines based on ports in northern Spain.

Wellington planned carefully, but was opportunistic and swift to exploit opponents' mistakes. He suddenly decided to attack at Salamanca when he noticed that the French army had become overextended and vulnerable to a counter-attack. Similarly, he was pragmatic in the face of setbacks and explained that the French marshals 'planned their campaigns just as you might make a splendid piece of harness. It looks very well; and answers very well; until it gets broken; and then you are done for. Now I made my

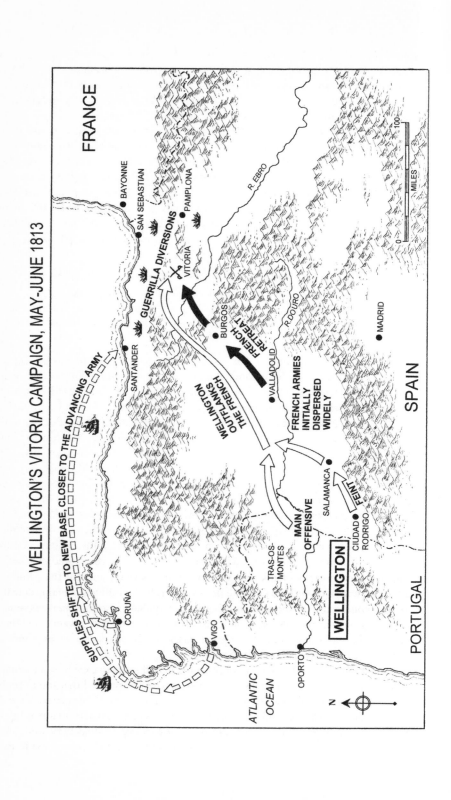

WELLINGTON'S VITORIA CAMPAIGN, MAY–JUNE 1813

campaigns of ropes. If anything went wrong, I tied a knot; and went on.' For example, at Orthez, his initial attacks were checked and he had to resume the offensive using a new plan involving nearly all his available forces. In fact, Orthez was similar, in small scale, to many of Napoleon's battles, with the enemy being pinned down and un-balanced by a combination of frontal and flank attacks and then broken by a general attack, which included the use of reserve troops from the crack Light Division.

Wellington's conduct of sieges had mixed success in the Peninsula. He could not afford heavy casualties and yet was handicapped by the British army's shortage of trained engineers and the need for speed before the French could concentrate superior numbers of troops for a relief attempt. It was only after the storming of Badajoz (1812) with heavy loss of life that the Royal Sappers and Miners were formed as a result of Wellington's recommendation.

It is sometimes claimed that Wellington was never defeated, unlike Napoleon and Blücher. It is true that he never lost a battle, but he did suffer a defeat in the minor action of Sultanpettah Tope in India (1799) and again when he tried to capture Burgos (1812). His Talavera campaign of 1809 was also a failure, for, despite his victory in the actual battle, he had to retreat back to Portugal without achieving his key objective, the liberation of Madrid.

Blücher

Unlike Napoleon and Wellington, Blücher was a fighting general who was as likely to have a sword in his hand as a telescope. In keeping with his nickname, 'Marshal Forwards', he preferred strategies that promised quick and decisive outcomes. He did not react well when presented with plans for a battle lasting a whole day and, as Müffling noted: 'The Field Marshal *never* made difficulties when the talk was of advancing and attacking. In retrograde movements, even when he had acknowledged their necessity, his vexation at this sometimes overpowered him; however, he soon recovered himself.'

Even when he lost, he always bounced back and in fact, few great generals have suffered so many defeats. But the dynamism and vigour shown by his army on cam-paign have to be balanced against its sometimes rash or hurried moves. Blücher was too impatient and his obsessive nature led to fixations with certain objectives, such as capturing Paris, which made him resolute but sometimes also blinkered and inflexible. As Wellington recalled, he was 'a very fine fellow, and whenever there was any question of fighting, always ready and eager – if anything too eager'.

Blücher had a limited education and a narrower experience of warfare in terms of variety, geographical scope and level of command. Whereas Napoleon and Wellington fought in a wide spectrum of climates, cultures and terrains, including the Middle East or India, Blücher spent his entire military career in a rectangular swathe of northern Europe between East Prussia and France. It is true that Blücher had become a soldier a decade before Napoleon and Wellington were born, but this was less significant than the length of time spent in an independent command. Until 1813, Blücher had little personal experience of the higher art of war, being confined mainly to command of a subordinate cavalry force. Moreover, his formative experiences as a soldier had been under Frederick the Great, when the Prussian cavalry was the best in Europe and a decisive, battle-winning arm in its own right. It was difficult for him to appreciate that this was no longer the case by the time of the Napoleonic Wars: much of his experience was outdated or the wrong type.

But Blücher compensated by keeping an open and active mind on many issues. Unlike officers who grew old and inflexible as a result of long periods in peacetime garrisons with slow promotion, Blücher remained young in spirit even in his seventies, largely because of his wild temperament as a hussar. In contrast with more conservative officers, he supported the reform efforts after Jena. It is notable how many of the Prussian military reformers came from the scientific arms, the artillery or engineers, or, like Blücher, the light cavalry or infantry, rather than the more senior and fashionable units. Moreover, the limited geographical extent of Blücher's campaign experience was in one sense an advantage, for he already knew the regions in which he fought in 1813: he had, for example, already been at Leipzig in 1761 during the Seven Years' War.

One key characteristic of Blücher's strategy when he worked with Scharnhorst and Gneisenau was the quest for a decisive battle. This contrasted with the more cautious and traditional strategy pursued by Schwarzenberg and many of the other Allied leaders, in which the occupation of important geographical points took precedence over seeking out and destroying the enemy army. This quest was a lesson that the Prussians had learned well from Napoleon. It also suited their temperaments and, for Gneisenau especially, reflected the belief that it was necessary to mobilize the whole Prussian nation and wage a people's war of liberation instead of the more limited warfare of the eighteenth century. In seeking to destroy Napoleon's army, Scharnhorst and Gneisenau realized that encircling it would be more decisive than merely attacking frontally. Napoleon's defeat at Leipzig was the result of the Allies' outflanking him and trying to cut him off from France, with the Army of Silesia opening the manoeuvre. It has even been claimed by Walter Görlitz in his history of the German General Staff that the origins of the Schlieffen Plan, the strategy for the invasion of France in 1914 by wheeling through Belgium and surrounding Paris, can be traced back to Gneisenau's preference for encircling moves in the campaigns of 1813–14. It is certainly true that the strategy of encirclement became prominent in the General Staff's thinking during the nineteenth century, especially after its use to win a crushing victory over the French at Sedan in 1870.

The importance of encirclement and decisive victory in Prussian strategic thought helps explain Blücher's apparent obsession with capturing the village of Plancenoit at Waterloo. He has been criticized for repeatedly attacking it instead of trying to seek a decision with fewer casualties in the open countryside to the north, but it was at Plancenoit, at the southern end of his line, that he had the best opportunity to cut Napoleon's line of retreat.

As part of the quest for a decisive battle, Blücher believed strongly in vigorous pursuits. Several of his subordinates disagreed with the degree to which he pressed his men in his drive for results. At the time of the Battle of the Katzbach (1813), Yorck interrupted Blücher and Gneisenau at dinner and angrily exclaimed: 'You are destroying the troops, you are marching them to no purpose!' Similarly, General von Bülow wrote in horror when he reinforced the Army of Silesia with his corps at the start of March 1814: 'The army is nearly starved, all discipline and order are dissolved, and I confess to our shame that it looks not unlike a band of robbers.'

When Blücher's army entered Paris at the end of that month, many of his men lacked shoes or socks and had their feet bound in rags. His Russian soldiers often wore items of uniform taken from dead Frenchmen, with the addition of white armbands to distinguish them as friends. As the troops marched through the city, King Frederick William III asked Yorck if he had seen his Prussian Guards. Yorck is said to have indicated Blücher's troops and to have answered proudly: 'Your Majesty, those are your Guards!'

Blücher's insistence on driving his army so hard was probably a reaction against the fatal slowness and indecision of the Prussian high command in 1806. Nor was it easy to mount a sustained and truly effective pursuit. Napoleon managed it only on rare occasions, such as after Rivoli (1797) and Jena (1806). Wellington was unable to exploit his two most famous victories in the Peninsula, Salamanca and Vitoria, partly as he refused to outrun his supplies and allow his army to become indisciplined. Owing to the small size of his army and the way it was recruited, he could not afford the wastage rate in sickness, straggling and desertion that would have resulted from a close pursuit. The contrast between his and Blücher's approach was most clearly demonstrated during their joint advance on Paris after Waterloo, when the Prussians advanced faster, but left behind a trail of devastation.

Despite making great demands on his army, Blücher lost neither its love nor its trust, largely as he led by example, drove himself as hard as his men and shared their dangers in battle. Nor did he believe in being hard unless it was necessary, for he disagreed with corporal punishment and had prohibited its use when he was a regimental officer.

Blücher's generalship on the battlefield has rarely been examined as critically as that of Wellington or Napoleon. Most historians have echoed the verdict that Wellington himself gave when asked if Gneisenau had been an excellent tactician:

> Not exactly a tactician, but he was very deep in strategy. By strategy, I mean a previous plan of campaign; by tactics, the movements on the field of battle. In tactics Gneisenau was not so much skilled. But Blücher was just the reverse – he knew nothing of plans of campaign, but well understood a field of battle.

In fact, this was too neat and oversimplified a view on several counts. Gneisenau, for example, had played a key role in producing the new tactical doctrine for the Prussian light infantry after 1806. The key issue is whether the Prussian system preserved unity of command. In some actions, Blücher remained at Gneisenau's side and worked with him as a team. We know that he did this for at least part of the time at Waterloo, for he conferred with Gneisenau when Colonel Baron Johann von Hiller, the commander of 16th Brigade, announced that he was ready to take the village of Plancenoit.

'What do you think, Gneisenau, should we let him go?' asked Blücher.

'I believe that the moment has come,' was the reply.

Blücher then noticed that the French were moving troops towards the village, but Hiller exclaimed that he would reach it first and that reinforcements could then be sent.

Blücher therefore gave permission to advance: 'Now, in God's name!'

But at other battles, Blücher failed to coordinate his actions with Gneisenau and insisted on intervening personally wherever he thought best. His personal leadership was invaluable in encouraging his troops. One of his subordinates, General de Langeron, noted that his 'overall eye for a situation was outstanding and his heroic courage swept the troops along with him'. But his absences from Gneisenau and the General Staff during these interventions made it difficult to impose a regular and cohesive control on the battle, particularly as he sometimes found himself alone apart from a few adjutants.

The Battle of Ligny is a case in point. Blücher's headquarters were initially located at the central point of the mill of Bussy, with a view of most of the battlefield. But Gneisenau and the General Staff later rode forward to the village of Ligny and, according to Lieutenant Ludwig von Gerlach, who was serving with the headquarters, seemed to focus exclusively on the fighting there, simply because of its proximity. Blücher, meanwhile, rode off elsewhere. Gerlach thought that Gneisenau concentrated more on whether the Prussians would win the battle, rather than how they should do so, and that he moved about more than he actually took action. Nor was it sensible for Gneisenau to remain so near Ligny, for it was a particularly exposed location, as was shown when a cannonball killed his horse. Gneisenau then returned to Bussy mill, where he rejoined Blücher.

According to Nostitz, Blücher had been in the thick of the action during this time: 'The Prince was always seen where the fighting was heaviest. His presence stimulated and intensified the efforts of the troops. He attached himself to them, without paying the slightest heed to the great danger.'

In the evening, the firing noticeably slackened. Lieutenant von Gerlach wrote that a general apathy suddenly seemed to settle on the headquarters, for it looked as if the battle was over, at least for the day. The headquarters personnel even dismounted, sheltered behind the buildings at Bussy mill and discussed the day's events.[15] But it was only a lull before Napoleon sent in his Imperial Guard and the Prussians failed to use this time to reorganize their now disordered army. Nor did they replace the units that they had fed into the contested villages by promptly moving brigades westwards from the largely unengaged III Corps in the eastern sector of the battlefield.

The Prussian commanders had used up their reserves too quickly, partly because they sought to compensate for the inexperience of many units by using weight of numbers, but partly also because Blücher made such frequent counter-attacks throughout the afternoon. Often, these counter-attacks were over-hasty and therefore weak and piecemeal. They also undermined command and control as brigades and even regiments were split up and their component units sent to different sectors of the battlefield. The order of battle was so scrambled that the corps commanders had to be allocated all troops, from whichever formation, in a particular sector of the battlefield: General von Ziethen on the western wing and General von Pirch I at Ligny in the centre. The overall battle control suffered as a result of these haphazard arrangements. At the moment when Napoleon's Imperial Guard attacked the village of Ligny, the last infantry reserve standing behind it was ordered by an adjutant to move off towards Sombreffe, which was not in fact under threat.

Despite his years of experience, Blücher was not even particularly adept at cavalry charges, as he had repeatedly shown throughout his career. 'Blücher is no Seydlitz,'

Marshal Davout at Auerstädt, 1806.

commented Yorck, in reference to Frederick the Great's famous cavalry commander of the Seven Years' War. Blücher made the same mistakes in his charge at the end of the Battle of Ligny as he had made at Auerstädt nine years before: impatience, inadequate preparation, over-hasty and piecemeal attacks with whatever squadrons were available and personally leading the charge instead of coordinating the action as a whole.

Blücher's insistence on intervening in person and on the spur of the moment also undermined his subordinates. Colonel Carl von Clausewitz wrote to his wife after the Battle of Lützen: 'That old Blücher was also very brave you can well imagine. What is left for the other leaders to do, that the commander-in-chief has not done?' According to Lieutenant-Colonel von Reiche, his corps commander, General von Ziethen, remained 'nearly totally passive' after Blücher's arrival on the eve of the Battle of Ligny, at least until the start of the fighting, as he did not want to anticipate his decisions.

Blücher's habit of personally indulging in the fighting also set a bad example for others. One persistent failing of the General Staff officers was regularly to give in to the temptation of joining the action. 'I would give my life to command for a single day,' wrote Scharnhorst in May 1813. He was mortally wounded at Lützen after spending the day in the thick of the fight, waving his sword, encouraging the men with shouts of 'Long live the King!' and leading several charges. This was hardly sensible, especially as Blücher later wrote that he would rather lose a battle than Scharnhorst.

Similarly, it was frustrating for Gneisenau to have no opportunity of distinguishing himself again, in the way that he had won fame for his defence of Colberg in 1807. During the 1813–14 campaigns, some Prussian corps commanders won victories in their own right, as for example General von Bülow did at Dennewitz (6 September 1813) while serving with the Army of the North. When Gneisenau came under fire from skirmishers at the Battle of Leipzig (16 October 1813) and was advised to withdraw, he replied: 'I would not hold it against you if you rode away, for if you remain [dead] on the battlefield, nobody will speak of you any more on the day after tomorrow. But a general who falls in battle belongs to history!'

Gneisenau was bitterly disappointed in 1815 not to have an independent command and even claimed that Blücher was ungrateful to him. 'Probably no one knows the whole extent of my self-sacrifice,' he complained, 'if I must remain only a henchman all my life.' The Prussian Chancellor, Prince Karl von Hardenberg, wrote on 1 April to commiserate with him:

> Once more you are not in a very agreeable position. The credit for what you accomplish will be claimed by another. But how can it be helped? The King adheres to the system of advancement by seniority; otherwise it is you who would command the army. At present you actually do command; but old Blücher gives his name. Few will be deceived about that matter.

Under these circumstances, it is hardly surprising that Gneisenau personally led the pursuit of Napoleon in the evening of Waterloo, or that he later described it as the finest night of his life. But it was also neglect of duty and he deserved censure, not praise. As Chief of the General Staff, he should have been doing his duty: reorganizing the Prussian army after the battle and preparing it for the advance on Paris. He had no business leading the advanced guard, a job that could have been done by any energetic and determined troop commander.

Conclusion

It would be difficult to find three men with greater confidence, yet they all occasionally lost their self-belief. Napoleon tried to poison himself after abdicating in 1814 and later, while travelling through southern France to exile on the island of Elba became openly terrified of being lynched by mobs. Blücher had nervous breakdowns as a result of alcohol and exhaustion, notably at the Battle of Laon (1814), when he lost all interest in the campaign, complained about his ailments and was openly afraid of dying. Wellington in India lost his nerve during the failed night attack on Sultanpettah Tope in India (1799) and was observed with an ashen face and slack jaw when he thought that his attempt to storm the fortress of Badajoz had failed in 1812.

But more often, their problem was over-confidence. Napoleon's invasion of Russia remains the supreme example of over-ambitious folly. Wellington seriously under-estimated his opponents at Assaye (1803), the likelihood of liberating Madrid in conjunction with his Spanish allies in the Talavera campaign (1809) and the difficulties in capturing Burgos (1812). Blücher lost 16,000 men and was nearly captured when he boldly advanced on Paris in February 1814 and allowed his army to become strung out and exposed to Napoleon's sudden counter-attack into his southern flank.

Some historians believe that Napoleon declined in energy, skill and clear-sightedness and that he was not at his best at Waterloo, but the reality is that he made mistakes throughout his career. He was nearly defeated at Marengo (1800) as a result of his miscalculations and suffered disastrous checks after invading Syria (1799), Spain (1808) and Russia (1812). His later campaigns were unsuccessful not so much because of any decline in his own powers, but because he faced more comprehensive and solid coalitions; armies that had been reorganized and trained in new tactics; and capable and determined generals, like Wellington and Blücher, who had developed effective strategies for countering his art of war. At the same time, the quality of Napoleon's own troops declined as thousands of veterans became casualties in his relentless wars and were replaced with young and inexperienced conscripts, especially in 1813–14. He became increasingly dependent in battle on massed formations and great batteries to achieve a breakthrough. In addition, the Russian disaster of 1812 left him particularly short of cavalry, which crippled his ability throughout 1813 to gather intelligence, deliver a knock-out blow in battle or pursue after a victory.

Napoleon also encountered problems in exercising effective command and control over the massive armies that he commanded in 1812–13. On his battlefields in Italy in 1796–7, he could exercise a highly personal command style, for he usually had only 20–30,000 men. Similarly, in his battles of the 1814 campaign, he generally commanded 30–50,000 men. But it was impossible to command in the same way, or to maintain such a tight grip, in the battles of 1809–13, when he often had to control armies of 100–200,000 men. In contrast, Wellington never commanded more than 88,000 men in battle (at the Nivelle in 1813) and usually had a battlefield strength of

40–50,000. Blücher as an independent army commander generally had 60–100,000 men in his battles of 1813–15, though occasionally fewer.

Moreover, in his later campaigns, Napoleon often operated in countries like Poland, Spain and Russia, which were more infertile, lacked the road network of Germany and northern Italy and could not support a concentrated army for long. This made it difficult for him to move his army quickly by reducing its logistical tail and supporting it to a large extent off the land and from captured enemy supply depots.

Napoleon himself exaggerated the ease of some of his early victories, including Austerlitz (1805), his most famous and decisive victory, which despite its brilliant concept and execution was actually a hard-fought battle and cost him nearly 9,000 men in killed and wounded, or 12 per cent of his army. Another 16,000 died from disease in the months that followed. Nor had the battle gone entirely to plan, for stout resistance by the Allied right wing under General Bagration had prevented him from wheeling his entire army round to the south to cut the Allied line of retreat.

In fact, Napoleon exercised some of his most brilliant generalship in the later years, such as when he escaped across the Beresina river during the retreat from Moscow (1812) in the face of three Russian armies, or when he defeated Schwarzenberg's army at Dresden (1813), or, most spectacularly, when he manoeuvred between the two Allied armies in February 1814 and won a string of victories. Wellington himself considered Napoleon's 1814 campaign as his finest. It was, he remarked:

> Excellent – quite excellent. The study of it has given me a greater idea of his genius than any other. Had he continued that system [of manoeuvring] a little while longer, it is my opinion that he would have saved Paris. But he wanted patience – he did not see the necessity of adhering to defensive warfare ... and he threw himself imprudently on the rear of the Allies.

Napoleon's failure was less as a general than as a statesman, for he failed to recognize the need for an accommodation with the other powers to achieve a stable international order. He did not recognize the limits to what his military genius could realistically attempt or set himself clear political goals. He reached Moscow in 1812 without knowing how to bring the war with Russia to an end and he refused seriously to negotiate for peace in 1813–14. As a Minister of the Empire observed, 'it is strange that though Napoleon's common sense amounted to genius, he never could see where the possible left off.'

The over-confidence that undid Napoleon in 1815 had been present throughout his career and, indeed, had often been responsible for winning battles that other commanders would not have dared to fight. But never before had Napoleon faced a combination of two such formidable opponents as Wellington and Blücher in the same campaign. Despite their individual mistakes, especially in the opening stages, they complemented each other's strengths and at Waterloo were able to inflict Napoleon's final and most famous defeat.

Blücher was not a great captain, one of the select few commanders of history to excel at every level of the art of war and combine nearly all the qualities desired in a commander. As a result, Wellington has traditionally been seen as the senior of the two Allied commanders in 1815, with Blücher in the secondary and supporting role of loyal ally. Yet it was Blücher who bore the brunt of the first two days of the campaign when

Napoleon lost his best chances of a decisive victory. It was Blücher who gave battle at Ligny and thereby won time for the Allies to concentrate their armies from cantonments. It was Blücher who insisted on taking the bold and risky decision to march to Wellington's support on 18 June and it was Blücher who thus united the two Allied armies on a battlefield and enabled them to defeat Napoleon by their combined numerical superiority. Although the least brilliant of the three commanders-in-chief in 1815, he was the only one who fought the campaign from the start without labouring under serious illusions. Wellington wrongly believed right until the morning of 18 June that Napoleon would seek to turn his western flank. Napoleon initially expected the Allies to fall back rather than fight a major battle south of Brussels before they had united. Blücher, in contrast, had one clear aim: to fight and defeat Napoleon. Blücher repeatedly decided the outcome of the campaigns in which he fought as an army commander by initiative, moral courage and sheer force of personality. 'If I proposed something to him,' remarked Gneisenau, 'he always chose the boldest.' The full extent and importance of Blücher's role in 1815 has been overshadowed by Wellington's defensive fight at Waterloo in the spotlight of history.

Wellington, despite his usual confidence when faced with the French marshals in the Peninsula, veered between under- and overestimating Napoleon in 1815. Initially, he believed that Napoleon was unlikely to reach Paris and regain power. He then came to think that Napoleon would not invade the United Netherlands and, when he did, he fought the campaign under the persistent misapprehension that Napoleon would try to outflank him, both during the opening stages of the invasion and at the Battle of Waterloo itself. Wellington had a healthy respect for Napoleon's abilities as a general, but was perhaps too cautious as a result. He had never before faced Napoleon, unlike Blücher who had already commanded against him at Brienne, La Rothière, Vauchamps, Craonne, Laon and Ligny. Of these, Blücher lost four and won two and, as part of an allied force, he also helped beat Napoleon at Leipzig and Waterloo. No other general had such a record against Napoleon.

Wellington was fortunate that he never had to face Napoleon's Grand Army in its heyday, 1805–7, as for example Blücher had to do as part of the Prussian army in 1806. In the Peninsula, Wellington encountered French troops who were mostly of inferior quality or else demoralized by repeated defeats. The rugged terrain of many Peninsular battlefields made it difficult for the French to coordinate their attacks or to support their infantry closely with powerful artillery batteries and massed cavalry, as Napoleon often did with devastating effect in central Europe. It was only at Waterloo that Wellington had to contend with powerful French cavalry and artillery and, ironically, the French on that occasion attacked for most of the day with unsupported cavalry or with infantry alone.

Blücher was the only commander in Europe who was not overawed by Napoleon. He admitted in private to a grudging admiration for his opponent: 'if you had brought Napoleon to me I could not have received him but with the greatest respect, in spite of the fact that he has often called me a drunken hussar. He is still a tremendously brave man.' But in public, Blücher referred scathingly to 'that fellow', 'Mr Napoleon', or 'the swaggerer Napoleon'. He was never in awe of him and remarked after Bautzen (1813) that he was 'really nothing but a stupid fellow'. In February 1814, he claimed: 'I fear the Emperor Napoleon no more than I fear his marshals.'

The clash between Wellington and Napoleon is usually seen as one of the great duels of history, like those between Churchill and Hitler, Montgomery and Rommel, Grant and Lee, Richard III and Saladin. Yet this perception is inaccurate, for they met each other in battle only once, at the end of their active military careers, and hitherto Napoleon's main opponents had been the commanders of the large Allied forces in central Europe, men like Archduke Charles, who had commanded the Austrians against him in 1797 and 1809; or Tsar Alexander I, who was present at Austerlitz in 1805 and accompanied the Allied armies in the field in 1813–14, or Kutusov, the Russian commander at both Austerlitz (1805) and Borodino (1812); or Schwarzenberg; or indeed Blücher. Even in Britain, Wellington was just one of the famous political and military figures who led the fight against Napoleon, including William Pitt the younger, Vice-Admiral Horatio Nelson and Lieutenant-General Sir John Moore.

Waterloo was the last battle for all three commanders. Since it was also their most famous action, it has overshadowed their earlier careers and thus distorted and over-simplified the way in which we see them. Yet few battles and few commanders are more rewarding to study and by continually reassessing them in the light of ongoing research, we can gain a fuller and more balanced understanding of the art of war as a whole.

Notes

1. C. Duffy, *Frederick the Great: A Military Life* (London, 1985), p. 228.
2. To be 'pregnant with an elephant' was Berlin slang, meaning to be full of anger, but Blücher may well have come to believe it literally.
3. Blücher's leading units were about 50 miles east of Paris.
4. At the time, 'staff' included the generals who held commands in the army and did not refer just to staff officers in the modern sense.
5. His surname is unrecorded.
6. D. Boulger, *The Belgians at Waterloo* (London, 1901), p. 45.
7. J. Sweetman, *Raglan* (London, 1993), p. 63.
8. H. Maxwell, *The Life of Wellington* (London, 1907), vol. 2, p. 78.
9. A. Roberts, *Napoleon and Wellington* (London, 2001).
10. J. David Markham, *Imperial Glory: The Bulletins of Napoleon's Grande Armée 1805–1814* (London, 2003), p. 147.
11. See note 5.
12. Different accounts of the speech exist: not surprisingly, the Colonel of the 4th Regiment recorded a less critical version.
13. W. Fraser, *Words on Wellington* (London, n.d.), pp. 1, 2; G. Jones, *Battle of Waterloo* (London, 1852), p. 174.
14. A. D. Harvey, *Collision of Empires: Britain in Three World Wars, 1793–1945* (London, 1992), p. 140.
15. H. Schoeps, *Aus den Jahren preussischer Not und Erneuerung: Tagebücher und Briefe der Gebrüder Gerlach und ihres Kreises, 1805–1820* (Berlin, 1963), pp. 148–9.

Further Reading

General

Brett-James, Antony, *The Hundred Days: Napoleon's Last Campaign from Eye-witness Accounts* (London, 1964).

Chalfont, Lord, ed., *Waterloo: Battle of Three Armies* (London, 1979).

Chandler, David, *Waterloo: The Hundred Days* (London, 1980).

Ellis, Geoffrey, *The Napoleonic Empire* (Basingstoke, 2003).

Esposito, Vincent and Elting, John, *A Military History and Atlas of the Napoleonic Wars* (1965; reissued London, 1999).

Glover, Gareth, ed., *Letters from the Battle of Waterloo: Unpublished Correspondence by Allied Officers from the Siborne Papers* (London, 2004).

Haythornthwaite, Philip, *The Napoleonic Source Book* (London, 1990).

Haythornthwaite, Philip, *Who was Who in the Napoleonic Wars* (London, 1998).

Hofschröer, Peter, *1815: The Waterloo Campaign. Wellington, his German Allies and the Battles of Ligny and Quatre Bras* (London, 1998).

Hofschröer, Peter, *1815: The Waterloo Campaign. The German Victory* (London, 1999).

Houssaye, Henry, *Waterloo 1815* (Evreux, 1987).

Hussey, John, 'At what time on 15 June 1815 did Wellington learn of Napoleon's attack on the Prussians?' in *War in History* 6 (1), 1999 and 7 (4), 2000.

Keegan, John, *The Face of Battle: A Study of Agincourt, Waterloo and the Somme* (1976; reissued Harmondsworth, 1987).

Keegan, John, *The Mask of Command: A Study of Generalship* (London, 1987).

Roberts, Andrew, *Napoleon and Wellington* (London, 2001).

Siborne, H. T., ed., *The Waterloo Letters* (1891; reissued London, 1983).

Smith, Digby, *The Greenhill Napoleonic Wars Data Book* (London, 1998).

Uffindell, Andrew, *Great Generals of the Napoleonic Wars and their Battles, 1805–1815* (Staplehurst, 2003).

Uffindell, Andrew and Corum, Michael, *On the Fields of Glory: The Battlefields of the 1815 Campaign* (London, 1996).

Napoleon

Barnett, Correlli, *Bonaparte* (New York, 1973).

Boycott-Brown, Martin, *The Road to Rivoli: Napoleon's First Campaign* (London, 2001).

Chandler, David, *The Campaigns of Napoleon* (London, 1966).

Chandler, David, ed., *Napoleon's Marshals* (London, 1987).

Coignet, Jean-Roch, *The Notebooks of Captain Coignet: Soldier of the Empire, 1799–1816* (reissued London, 1986).

Colin, J., *L'Éducation militaire de Napoléon* (Paris, 1900).

Connelly, Owen, *Blundering to Glory: Napoleon's Military Campaigns* (Wilmington, 1987).

Cronin, Vincent, *Napoleon* (London, 1971).

Elting, John, *Swords around a Throne: Napoleon's Grande Armée* (London, 1988).

Englund, Steven, *Napoleon: A Political Life* (Cambridge, Mass., 2004).

Gachot, Edouard, *Histoire militaire de Massena: la première campagne d'Italie (1795–1798)* (Paris, 1901).

Geyl, Pieter, *Napoleon: For and Against* (London, 1948; reissued 1987).

Haythornthwaite, Philip, *Napoleon's Military Machine* (reissued London, 1988).

Horricks, Raymond, *Marshal Ney: The Romance and the Real* (Tunbridge Wells, 1982).

Lawford, James, *Napoleon: the Last Campaigns, 1813–15* (Maidenhead, 1977).

Markham, J. David, *Imperial Glory: The Bulletins of Napoleon's Grande Armée 1805–1814* (London, 2003).

Marshall-Cornwall, Sir James, *Napoleon as Military Commander* (London, 1967).

Rogers, H. C. B., *Napoleon's Army* (London, 1974).

Schur, Nathan, *Napoleon in the Holy Land* (Greenhill Books, London, 1999).

Thompson, J. M., *Napoleon Bonaparte* (1952; reissued Oxford, 1990).

Thompson, J. M., ed., *Napoleon's Letters* (reissued London, 1998).

Vachée, Jean Baptiste, *Napoleon at Work*, trans. G. Frederic Lees (London, 1914).

Wellington

Brett-James, Antony, *Wellington at War 1794–1815* (London, 1961).

Crossard, Jean-Baptiste de, *Mémoires militaires et historiques pour servir à l'histoire de la guerre depuis 1792 jusqu'en 1815 inclusivement*, 6 vols (Paris, 1829).

Ellesmere, Earl of, *Personal Reminiscences of the Duke of Wellington* (London, 1903).

Fletcher, Ian, *Galloping at Everything: The British Cavalry in the Peninsular War and at Waterloo, 1808–15* (Staplehurst, 1999).

Glover, Michael, *Wellington as Military Commander* (London, 1968).

Griffith, Paddy, ed., *Wellington Commander* (1985).

Guedalla, Philip, *The Duke* (London, 1931).

Gurwood, J., ed., *The General Orders of Field Marshal the Duke of Wellington, K.G.* (London, 1832).

Gurwood, J., ed., *The Dispatches of Field Marshal the Duke of Wellington during his Various Campaigns in India, Denmark, Portugal, Spain, the Low Countries, and France, from 1799 to 1818*, 13 vols (1834–8).

Guy, Alan, ed., *The Road to Waterloo: The British Army and the Struggle against Revolutionary and Napoleonic France, 1793–1815* (London, 1990).

Haythornthwaite, Philip, *The Armies of Wellington* (London, 1994).

Holmes, Richard, *Wellington: The Iron Duke* (London, 2002).

Kincaid, John, *Adventures in the Rifle Brigade, in the Peninsula, France, and the Netherlands, from 1809 to 1815* (1830).

Liddell Hart, Basil, ed., *The Letters of Private Wheeler 1809–1828* (London, 1951).

Longford, Elizabeth, *Wellington: The Years of the Sword* (London, 1969), reissued with its sequel (*Wellington: Pillar of State*) in 1992 as an abridged one-volume edition.

Muir, Rory, *Britain and the Defeat of Napoleon 1807–1815* (London, 1996).

Muir, Rory, *Salamanca 1812* (London, 2001).

Oman, Sir Charles, *Wellington's Army, 1809–1814* (1913; reissued London, 1993).

Robertson, Ian, *Wellington at War in the Peninsula 1808–1814: An Overview and Guide* (Barnsley, 2000).

Schaumann, August, *On the Road with Wellington: The Diary of a War Commissary* (1924; reissued London, 1999).

Sherer, Joseph Moyle, *Recollections of the Peninsula* (London, 1827).

Stanhope, Fifth Earl, *Notes of Conversations with the Duke of Wellington 1831–1851* (London, 1938).

Stepney, S. Cowell, *Leaves from the Diary of an Officer of the Guards* (London, 1854).

Thomas, Robin, 'Wellington in the Low Countries, 1794–1795,' in *The International History Review*, 11 (1989).

Uffindell, Andrew, *The National Army Museum Book of Wellington's Armies* (London, 2003).

Ward, Stephen G. P., *Wellington's Headquarters: A Study of the Administrative Problems in the Peninsula, 1809–14* (London, 1957).

Ward, Stephen G. P., *Wellington* (1963).

Weller, Jac, *Wellington in India* (London, 1972; reissued 1993).

Weller, Jac, *Wellington in the Peninsula* (London, 1962; reissued 1992).

Weller, Jac, *Wellington at Waterloo* (London, 1967; reissued 1998).

Weller, Jac, *On Wellington: The Duke and his Art of War* (London, 1998).

Wellington, second Duke of, ed., *Supplementary Dispatches, Correspondence, and Memoranda of Field Marshal Arthur Duke of Wellington, K.G.*, 15 vols (1858–72).

Blücher

Brett-James, Antony, *Europe against Napoleon* (London, 1970).

Crepon, Tom, *Leberecht von Blücher: Leben und Kämpfe* (Berlin, 1988).

Görlitz, Walter, *The German General Staff: Its History and Structure*, trans. Brian Battershaw (London, 1953).

Henderson, Ernest, *Blücher and the Uprising of Prussia against Napoleon 1806–1815* (London, 1911).

Lettow-Vorbeck, Oskar von, *Der Krieg von 1806 und 1807*, 4 vols (Berlin, 1891).

Marston, James Edward, ed., *The Life and Campaigns of Field-Marshal Prince Blücher of Wahlstadt ... translated in part from the German of General Count Gneisenau ... with considerable additions, by J. E. Marston, Esq.* (1815; reissued London, 1996).

Nostitz, August von, 'Das Tagebuch des Generals der Kavallerie Grafen v. Nostitz', in *Kriegsgeschichtliche Einzelnschriften*, vol. 1, parts 5 and 6 (1885).

Otto, Hans, *Gneisenau: Preußens unbequemer Patriot* (Bonn, 1979).

Parkinson, Roger, *Hussar General: The Life of Blücher, Man of Waterloo* (London, 1975).

Pertz, Georg and Delbrück, Hans, *Das Leben des Feldmarschalls Grafen Neithardt von Gneisenau*, 5 vols (Berlin, 1864–94).

Reiche, Ludwig von, *Memoiren des königlich preußischen Generals der Infanterie Ludwig von Reiche*, 2 vols (Leipzig, 1857).

Schoeps, Hans Joachim, *Aus den Jahren preussischer Not und Erneuerung: Tagebücher und Briefe der Gebrüder Gerlach und ihres Kreises, 1805–1820* (Berlin, 1963).

Schwartz, *Leben des Generals Carl von Clausewitz und der Frau Marie von Clausewitz*, 2 vols (Berlin, 1878).

Steffens, Henry, *Adventures on the Road to Paris, during the Campaigns of 1813–14* (London, 1848).

Uffindell, Andrew, *The Eagle's Last Triumph: Napoleon's Victory at Ligny, June 1815* (London, 1994).

Unger, Wolfgang von, *Blücher*, 2 vols (Berlin, 1907).

Unger, Wolfgang von, *Blüchers Briefe* (Stuttgart and Berlin, 1913).

White, Charles, *The Enlightened Soldier: Scharnhorst and the Militärische Gesellschaft in Berlin, 1801–1805* (New York, 1989).

Wolzogen, Ludwig von, *Memoiren des königlich preußischen Generals der Infanterie Ludwig Freiherrn von Wolzogen* (Leipzig, 1851).

General Index

Armies commanded by Napoleon, Wellington or Blücher, and formations within those armies, are listed in the Index of Armies and Formations. Other units are listed within the main index, either as an Army, e.g. 'Army of Bohemia', or under a country, e.g. 'Sweden'.

Abensberg, Battle of, 30
Abercromby, Major-General Ralph, 53, 55, 60
Aboukir Bay, 16
Aboukir, Battle of, 18
Acre, see St-Jean-d'Acre
Adda river, 13
Adige river, 14
Ahmednuggur, 61
Aisne river, 44, 108
Ajaccio, 3, 5, 6–7
Alberti, Jäger Wilhelm, 102
Albuera, Battle of, 74
Alessandria, 20
Alexander I, Tsar of Russia, 200
  in 1805–7, 24, 28, 76, 159
  in 1812, 32, 36,
  in 1813, 38, 100, 104, 105
  in 1814, 107, 111
  in 1815, 84,
Alexander the Great, 5, 16
Alexandria, 15
Alle river, 27
Almeida, 72, 74
Alpone river, 14
Alten, Lieutenant-General Sir Charles, 82, 133
Alvintzy von Berberek, General Baron Joseph, 14
Ambleteuse, 22
American War of Independence (1775–83), 58
Amiens, Peace of, 20, 22
Angers, 51
Antwerp, 20, 53, 115
Apsley House, 147
Arcis-sur-Aube, Battle of, 45, 110, 160
Arcole, Battle of, 14, 160, 184

Argaum, Battle of, 62
Army of Bohemia (1813–14), 39, 40, 41–2, 103, 106, 107, 180
Army of Poland (1813), 104
Army of the North (1813–14), 39, 41, 42, 103, 108, 195
Ascension island, 145
Aspern-Essling, Battle of, 30–1, 163
Assaye, Battle of, 61–2, 197
Auerstädt, Battle of, 26, 94, 96, 178, 187, 195
Augereau, Marshal Pierre, 11, 14
Austerlitz, Battle of, x, 25, 28, 30, 34, 35, 64, 94, 159, 173, 185, 198, 200
Austria
  before the French Revolution, 88, 90
  in French Revolutionary wars, 11, 14, 18, 19, 20, 52, 53, 55, 91, 200
  in 1805, 23, 25, 64, 94
  in 1806, 26
  in 1809, 29, 30–1, 32, 71, 72, 99, 163, 200
  in 1812, 34
  in 1813, 38, 39, 41, 79, 102
  in 1814, 46, 83, 106
  after the Napoleonic wars, 145, 182
Austrian Netherlands, 52, 91, 93
Autun, 4
Auxonne, 5, 6, 8
Auzouy, Captain, 152
Avignon, 7

Bacler d'Albe, General Louis, 170
Badajoz, 74–5, 76–7, 197
Baden, 22
Bagration, General Prince Peter, 34, 198
Baird, Major-General David, 59, 60
Bajee Rao II, 60

Barclay de Tolly, Prince Mikhail, 34
Barras, Paul, 9, 14
Bassano, Battle of, 14
Bassein, Treaty of, 60
Batavia, 60
Bautzen, Battle of, 39, 102, 103, 152, 199
Bavaria, 23, 30, 42
Bayonne, 42, 82, 83, 84
Bayreuth, 172
Beauharnais, Eugène de, 172
Beauharnais, Josephine de, *see* Josephine,
  Empress
Beaulieu, Generals Baron Johann, 11, 13
Belgium, 14, 42, 52–3, 106, 108, 116, 117,
  146, 192; *see also* Austrian Netherlands
  and United Netherlands
Bellerophon, HMS, 144
Belling, Colonel Wilhelm Sebastian von, 89,
  90, 169
Bengal, 56, 60
Bennigsen, General Levin von, 27, 28, 98,
  104
Berar, *Rajah* of, *see* Bhonsla, *Rajah* of
  Nagpur
Beresford, Lieutenant-General William Carr,
  71, 74, 134, 176
Beresina river, 37, 198
Berlin, 26, 41, 46, 94, 99, 100, 122, 126, 145,
  187, 201
Bernadotte, Marshal Jean-Baptiste (later
  Crown Prince of Sweden), 39, 102, 103,
  104, 105, 168
Berthier, Marshal Louis, 170
Bhonsla, *Rajah* of Nagpur (alias *Rajah* of
  Berar), 60, 61, 62
Bidasoa river, 80–1, 189
Bieske, Dr Carl, 126, 156–7, 167
Billon, Chasseur François, 27
Blaze, Captain Elzéar, 158–9
Blücher, Berthold, 89
Blücher, Burchard, 89
Blücher, Captain Christian Friedrich von, 87
Blücher, Franz (Blücher's son), 145
Blücher, FM Prince Gebhard Leberecht
  von,
  childhood, 87–8
  as an outsider, 87
  education, 87, 89
  mentors and patrons of, 88, 89
  begins military career in Swedish army, 88

captured by Prussians (1760), 88
resigns from army (1773), 90
reinstated in army (1787), 90
and French Revolutionary Wars, 91–3
marries, 90
remarries, 93
and 1806 campaign, 26, 94–8
meets Napoleon, 98
appointed Governor-General of
  Pomerania, 99
supports reforms of Prussian army, 99,
  192
and 1813 campaign, 39, 40, 41, 42, 101–6
makes his reputation as an army
  commander, 100
violates armistice, 103, 157
appointed Field Marshal, 105
and 1814 campaign, 42, 43, 44, 45,
  106–10
at Battle of Laon, 180–1
made Prince of Wahlstadt, 110
meets Wellington (1814), 110
visits Britain (1814), 111
and 1815 campaign, 47, 111, 115–26, 130,
  133–4, 136, 138, 139
marches to support Wellington at
  Waterloo, 130, 133
importance of intervention at Waterloo,
  134, 136
meets Wellington in evening of Waterloo,
  138
advances on Paris faster than Wellington,
  143, 193
after Waterloo, 144–5
known as 'Father of the Fatherland', 148
popular view of, x
appearance, 144, 156
personality, 156–7
shrewdness, 87, 167, 169
languages, 90, 138
loyalty, 99, 157
wildness, 89–90, 91, 92
too impatient, 123, 134
dislikes retreats, 101–2, 103, 191
health, 104, 107, 110
alcoholism and nervous breakdowns, 91,
  99, 109–10, 180–1
believes self to be pregnant with an
  elephant, 201
wounded, 88, 101

nearly captured, 107, 108, 124, 126
methods of command and control, 178–82
man-management skills, 87, 110
handles subordinates, 168, 179, 181, 195
relations with allies, 168, 179
openness at headquarters, 181–2
limited tolerance of dissent, 182
leadership style, 166–9
eloquence, 168
proclamations, 169, 179
effect on morale of troops, 125, 133, 156, 167, 194
nicknamed 'Papa Blücher', 166
nicknamed 'Marshal Forwards', 105, 167
over-confidence and impatience, 91, 92, 96, 102, 106, 156–7, 197
discounts value of spies, 157
tired of bloodshed, 143–4, 157
role in partnership with Gneisenau, 179–82, 193–6
strategy and tactics, 184, 191–6
record of battles fought and won against Napoleon, 199
size of armies, 198
quest for decisive battle, 192–3
vigorous pursuits, 192–3
tactics, 107
personally involved in fighting as an army commander, 101, 102, 108, 157, 194, 195
not adept at cavalry charges, 194–5
narrower experience of war than Napoleon or Wellington, 191–2
opinions on Napoleon, 102, 103, 106, 143, 144, 199
opinions on Wellington, 79, 100, 110, 133, 139
role in partnership with Wellington (1815), 198–200
Blücher, Gustav, 89
Blücher, Margarete, 88
Blücher, Siegfried, 88
Bois-le-Duc, 53
Bombay, 56, 61
Bonaparte, *see* Buonaparte
Bordeaux, 83
Borisov, 37
Borodino, Battle of, 34–5, 130, 172–3, 200
Bourcet, General Pierre de, 5

Bourmont, General Louis, Count de Ghaisne, 157
Bowles, Captain George, 125
Boxtel, Battle of, 53
Boyen, Hermann von, 99, 180
Brenta river, 14
Breslau, 39, 100, 145
Brest, 20
Brienne-le-Château, 4, 5, 51, 184
    Battle of, 43, 106–7, 157, 163, 199
brinjarries, 63
Britain, *passim*
    Royal Marines, 18
    Royal Military College, 173
    Royal Navy, 16, 18, 19, 28, 29, 65, 144
British army, 147; *see also* Wellington's armies, at end of index
    recruits for, 161
    Grenadier Guards, 147
    Rifle Brigade, 147
Brünn, 24
Brünneck, Major von, 180
Brunswick, Karl Wilhelm Ferdinand, Duke of, 91, 94, 96
Brussels, 51, 115, 116, 117, 120, 121, 126, 133, 134, 136, 139, 155, 199
Brye, 124
Bullum, *Rajah* of, 60
Bülow, General Friedrich von, 125, 133, 134, 180, 192, 195
Buonaparte,
    Carlo-Maria, 3, 4, 5
    Caroline, 3
    Elisa, 3
    Jérôme, 3, 41
    Joseph, 3, 4, 6, 20, 28–9, 44, 45, 170, 185
    Louis, 3, 164
    Lucien (Napoleon's brother), 3, 19
    Lucien (Napoleon's great uncle), 5
    Maria-Letizia, 3
    Napoleon, *see* Napoleon I, Emperor of the French
    Pauline, 3
Burghersh, Lady, 107, 110
Burgos, 78, 79, 152, 161, 191, 197
Burrard, Lieutenant-General Sir Harry, 67, 70
Bursche, Major von, 124
Busaco, Battle of, 72–3, 127, 132, 164, 165
Bussy mill, 194

Byng, Major-General Sir John, 139
Byron, Lord, 154

Caesar, Julius, 5, 55
Caia river, 75
Cairo, 16, 18
Calcutta, 56, 61
Campbell, Lieutenant Colin, 61
Campo Formio, Treaty of, 14
Campo Maior, action of, 165
Cannes, 46
Cantillon, André, 146
Cape of Good Hope, 55
Cape St Vincent, Battle of, 56
Carlos IV, King of Spain, 28
Caroline of Brunswick, Queen, 146
Carteaux, General Jean-François, 8
Carthage, 15
Catholic Emancipation Act (1829), 146
Casal Nova, 73
Castaños, General Francisco, 28
Castiglione, Battle of, 13
Castlereagh, Robert Stewart, Viscount, 84
Cathcart, Lieutenant-General Lord, 64, 65
Caulaincourt, General Armand de, 46, 152,
    163–4, 172, 184, 187
Cawnpore, 61
Ceylon, 60
Châlons-sur-Marne, 43, 106
Champaubert, Battle of, 43, 108
Charlemagne, 28, 154
Charleroi, 116, 117
Charles XII, King of Sweden, 34
Charles, Archduke, 14, 30–1, 163, 200
Charles, Captain Hippolyte, 10
Château-Thierry, Battle of, 43, 108
Chaumont, Treaty of, 44
Chelsea, 51
Chemin des Dames, 44, 108
Cherasco, Armistice of, 13
Cherbourg, 20
Chichagov, Admiral Paul, 37
Churchill, Winston S., 200
Cintra, Convention of, 67
Ciudad Rodrigo, 72, 74, 75, 76, 77
Clausel, General Bertrand, 77
Clausewitz, Colonel Carl von, 195
Close, Lieutenant-Colonel Barry, 59, 61
Coa river, 75, 166

Coblenz, 106
Coignet, Captain Jean-Roch, 151, 160
Colberg, 100, 178, 195
Colborne, Lieutenant-Colonel Sir John, 82,
    136, 138, 177, 178
Colli, Baron Michael von, 11, 13
Collingwood, Vice-Admiral Cuthbert, 162
Colomb, Katharina Amalia von, 93
Conaghull, Battle of, 59–60, 161
Concordat (1801), 20
Confederation of the Rhine, 25, 30, 94
Congress of Vienna, *see* Vienna, Congress of
Constantinople, 9
Constant-Rebecque, Baron Jean-Victor de,
    117
Continental System, 28, 32
Cooke, Major-General George, 133, 139
Copenhagen, 28, 65
Cork, 52, 65, 67
Cornwallis, Lord, 58
Corsica, 3–7, 9, 52, 184
Coruña,
    Campaign of, 174
    Battle of, 29, 70, 71
Cossacks, *see under* Russia
Costello, Private Edward, 76, 77
Cotton, Lieutenant-General Sir Stapleton,
    176
Council of the Five Hundred, 19
Cowell, Captain John Stepney, 59, 156
Craonne, Battle of, 108–9, 199
Craufurd, Brigadier-General Robert, 166,
    176
Crawley, Tom, 76
Creevey, Thomas, 139
Crimean War (1854–6), 144, 147
Croker, John Wilson, 65
Crossard, Baron Jean-Baptiste de, 154–5,
    163
Cruttwell, Mr, 148
Cuesta, Don Gregorio Garcia de la, 71
Curtis, Dr Patrick, 175

Dalrymple, Lieutenant-General Sir Hew, 67,
    70
Damascus, 16, 18
Danube river, 23, 24, 30–1
Danzig, 27, 88, 172
Daru, Pierre, 170

David, Jacques-Louis, 154
Davout, Marshal Louis, 26, 27, 42, 94, 96, 172, 195
Deccan, 61, 62
Dego, Battle of, 9, 13
Delaborde, General Henri, 67
Delhi, 61, 62
Denmark, 28, 65, 87, 89, 98
Dennewitz, Battle of, 41, 195
Desaix, General Louis, 16, 20, 152, 158
Dhoondiah Wao ('King of the Two Worlds'), 59–60
Directory, 13, 14, 15, 18, 19
Djezzar, Ahmed, 16, 18
Dnieper river, 34
Dommartin, Major, 8
Don river, 167
Donauwörth, 30
Douro river, 71, 79,84, 164
Dover, 111
Dresden, 101, 103, 187
  Battle of, 40–1, 173, 198
Drouet, General Jean-Baptiste, Count d'Erlon, 120, 121, 123
Dublin, 51, 52, 65
Ducor, Henri, 36–7
Dugommier, General Jacques, 8
Dumouriez, General Charles, 55
Dungannon, see Hill, Arthur, Viscount Dungannon,
Dupont de l'Etang, General Count Pierre, 28–9

East India Company, 56, 58, 59, 62
Eblé, General Baron Jean-Baptiste, 37
Ebro river, 29
Ecole militaire, see under Paris
Eggmühl, Battle of, 30
Egypt, 14–18, 19, 58, 60, 160, 161, 184
El Bodon, Action of, 164
El Arish, 16
Elba, 45, 46, 84, 144, 197
Elbe river, 40, 41, 98, 100, 102, 104, 182
Elers, Captain George, 154
Elizabeth, Tsarina, 44
Elster river, 42
Elvas, 74, 75
émigrés, 6, 20
Enghien, Duke d', 22, 23

Erfurt, 38
Erlon, Count d', see Drouet, General Jean-Baptiste, Count d'Erlon
Essling, see Aspern-Essling
Eton, 51
Eugène, Prince of Savoy, 5
Eylau, Battle of, 27, 152, 160, 171

Farruckabad, Battle of, 62
Ferdinand IV, King of Naples, 13
Ferdinand VII, King of Spain, 28, 84
Ferdinand, Archduke, 9
Fezensac, Duke de, see Montesquiou, Raymond de, Duke de Fezensac
Finkenstein, Château of, 98
Flahaut de la Billarderie, General Count, 121
Fleurus, 53, 116, 123
Fontainebleau, Treaty of, 45, 46
Foy, General Maximilien, 77, 121
Foz d'Arouce, action of, 73
France, *passim*
  Ancien Régime army
    Regiment of Artillery of La Fère, 5, 6
    Swiss Guards, 7
  French Revolutionary armies; see also under Napoleon's armies, at end of index
    Army of the Interior, 9
    Army of the Moselle, 91
    Army of the Rhine, 20
    Army of the West, 9
  National Guard, 38, 45
  navy, 15
  Second Empire, 145
  Senate, 22, 37, 45
Francis I, Emperor of Austria, 24, 29, 30, 32, 46, 99, 105, 154, 159
Frazer, Sir Augustus, 178
Frederick II, King of Prussia ('the Great'), 26, 88, 89
  and Napoleon, 5, 6, 44
  and Wellington, 55, 77, 154
  and Blücher, 90, 99, 191, 195
Frederick Augustus I, King of Saxony, 40
Frederick William II, King of Prussia, 90
Frederick William III, King of Prussia, 100, 145,
  in 1806–7, 25, 26, 94, 96, 98, 99,

in 1813–14, 38, 105, 107, 110, 111, 157, 193
Freneda, 175
Friedland, Battle of, x, 27–8, 35, 116
Frioul, 14
Frischermont, 127
Fritz __, Captain, 124–5, 156, 167, 168, 179, 181
Fuenterrabía, 81
Fuentes de Oñoro, Battle of, 74, 127

Garda, Lake, 14
Gawilghur, 62
Gaza, 16
General Staff, *see under* Prussia
Genoa, 20
George III, King, 65, 94
George IV, King (previously Prince Regent), 124, 144, 146, 164
Georges, Mademoiselle, *see Weimar, Josephine*
Gerlach, Lieutenant Ludwig von, 194
Gibraltar, 67
Gleig, Reverend George, 83
Gneisenau, August von, 99, 103, 104, 107, 111, 126, 130
    as Blücher's chief-of-staff, 178–82, 193–4
    and Blücher's proclamations, 169
    opinions on Blücher, 196, 199
    suspicions of Wellington, 130, 179, 181
    quest for decisive battle, 192
    preference for encircling moves, 192
    drives troops too hard, 192
    as tactician, 193
    frustration at not having a command, 195–6
    unable to recall discussions held after being woken at night, 181
    cautious, 109, 130, 180, 181
    reckless, 106
Golymin, Battle of, 26
Gordon, Lieutenant-Colonel the Hon Sir Alexander, 139
Görlitz, Walter, 192
Goubert, Louis, 51
Graham, Lieutenant-General Sir Thomas, 80, 176, 177
Grammont, 117
Grant, Major Colquhoun, 175

Grant, Ulysses S., 200
Grassini, Josephina, 10
Grattan, William, 166
Gravelotte-St Privat, Battle of, 182
Great Britain, *see* Britain
Great Exhibition (1851), 148
Grenoble, 46
Grey, Lord, 147
Grolman, General Carl von, 126, 180
Gronow, Ensign Rees, 132, 144, 153
Gross Raddow, 90
Grossbeeren, Battle of, 41
Gross-Renzow, 87
Grouchy, Marshal Emmanuel de, 126, 130, 143, 145
Guadarrama mountains, 29
guerrilla warfare, ii, 29, 70, 74, 90, 175
Guibert, General Count Jacques de, 5
Gustavus Adolphus, 5

Halkett, Major-General Sir Colin, 133
Hamburg, 42
Hamilton, Major Andrew, 176
Hamilton, Lieutenant Archibald, 135
Hanau, Battle of, 42
Hannibal, 5, 154
Hanover, 23, 25
Hardenberg, Prince Karl von, 196
Hare, Dr, 166
Harris, Air Marshal Sir Arthur, 134
Harris, Lieutenant-General George, 58, 59
Hassenhausen, 94, 96
Hastings, 64
Hastings, Warren, 63
Haynau, Battle of, 102, 104
Heilsberg, Battle of, 27
Henry V, King of England, 155
Hesse-Cassel, 87
Hill, Anne, 51
Hill, Arthur, Viscount Dungannon, 51
Hill, Lieutenant-General Sir Rowland, 77, 82, 127, 130, 132, 133, 138, 176
Hiller, Colonel Baron Johann von, 193
Hindustan, 61, 62
hircarrahs, 63
Hitler, Adolf, 200
Hoche, General Lazare, 91
Hof, 26, 172
Hohenlinden, Battle of, 20

Hohenlohe-Ingelfingen, General Prince
    Friedrich von, 96, 98
Holkar, Jeswunt Rao, 60, 61, 62
Holland, 42, 53, 60, 90, 91, 93, 146, 164; *see
    also* United Netherlands
Holy Roman Empire, 25
Home, Lieutenant-Colonel Francis, 176
Hood, Vice-Admiral Lord, 8
Hope, Lieutenant James, 125–6
Hope, Lieutenant-General Sir John, 83
Hougoumont, 127, 130, 131, 135, 162, 163,
    175–6
Hume, Dr John, 139
Hyderabad, 56, 58, 59, 61

India, x, 15, 16, 55–63, 64, 154, 161, 174,
    175, 188, 191, 197
India Act (1784), 58
Ireland, 51, 52, 65, 146, 175
Isar river, 30
Italy, Kingdom of, 23, 172

Jackson, Lieutenant Basil, 138
Jacobins, 6, 8, 9, 19
Jaffa, 16
Jena,
    Battle of, x, 26, 28, 94, 98, 160, 187, 192,
        193
    Pont de, *see under* Paris
Jolyet, Major Jean-Baptiste, 121
Josephine, Empress, 9–10, 23, 26, 27, 145,
    151
    divorce of, 32
Junot, General Andoche, 28, 29, 67
Jurdão, Captain Joachim Telles, 164

Kaiserslautern, Battle of, 91–2
Kalisch, Convention of, 100
Katzbach river, Battle of the, 41, 103–4,
    110, 169, 192
Kaub, 106
Kavelpass, 88
Keegan, John, 162
Kellermann, General François, 20
Kelly, Lieutenant-Colonel Dawson, 176
Kempt, Major-General Sir James, 82
Kincaid, Lieutenant John, 137–8, 155

Kiøge, Battle of, 65
Kléber, General Jean-Baptiste, 19
Knesebeck, Baron Karl von, 182
Knights of St John, 15
Kolin, Battle of, 89
Königsberg, 28
Kosboth, General von, 91
Krackwitz, Captain von, 88
Krasnoë, Battle of, 36–7
Kray von Krajova, General Baron Paul, 19,
    20
Krieblowitz, 111, 145
Kulm, Battle of, 41
Kunersdorf, Battle of, 89
Kutusov, General Mikhail, 24, 34, 35–6, 37,
    38, 101, 200

La Belle Alliance, 131, 138
La Haie Sainte, 127, 135, 136
La Haye, 127, 138
La Maddalena, 7
La Rothière, Battle of, 43, 107, 157, 199
La Vendée, *see* Vendée
Laffrey defile, 46
Lake, General Gerard, 61, 62
Landshut, 30
Langeron, General Count Louis de, 110,
    168, 194
Laon, Battle of, 45, 109, 168, 180–1, 197,
    199
Larpent, Francis, 154, 155, 176
Lauriston, General Jacques, 187
Lauter river, 91, 92
Lavallette, Count Antoine Marie, 46–7
Le Caillou, 130
Leach, Jonathan, 81
Lee, General Robert E., 200
Lefebvre, Marshal François, 172
Leghorn, 13
Legion of Honour, 158
Leipzig, 38, 89, 103
    Battle of, 41–2, 101, 104–5, 107, 189, 192,
        195, 199
Lemonnier-Delafosse, Major, 131
Leoben, Convention of, 14
Lesaca, 177
Levavasseur, Colonel Octave, 136
Lieber, Franz, 122–3
Liebstadt, 98

Ligny, 116, 117, 118, 152
  Battle of, 120, 121, 122–5, 126, 134, 157, 171, 173, 181, 194, 195, 199
Lisbon, 29, 67, 70, 71, 72, 73, 100, 156, 187
Lithuania, 34
Livorno, *see* Leghorn
Lloyd, Major-General, 55
Lodi, Battle of, 13, 160, 184
Loire river, 144
Lombardy, 14
Lonato, Battle of, 13
London, 51, 58, 64, 124, 146, 147, 148, 174
  St Paul's Cathedral, 148
Longford, third Baron, 52
Longwood, 145
Louis Ferdinand of Prussia, Prince, 26
Louis Napoleon, *see* Napoleon III
Louis XVI, King of France, 3, 4, 6, 7, 52
Louis XVII, King of France (uncrowned), 8
Louis XVIII, King of France, 46, 144
Louise, Queen of Prussia, 25
Louisiana Purchase, 21–2
Lowe, Lieutenant-General Sir Hudson, 145
Löwenberg, 167
Lübeck, 88, 98, 157
Lunéville, Peace of, 20
Lützen, Battle of, 38–9, 101–2, 103, 123, 157, 160, 168, 178, 195
Lützow, Major von, 103, 123, 124
Lyons, 5, 42

Maas river, 91
Macdonald, Marshal Jacques, 41, 103, 104, 107
Maceira river, 67
Mack von Leiberich, General Baron Karl, 23
Macready, Ensign Edward, 118, 120
Maddan, Reverend Spencer, 155
Madras, 56, 58
Madrid, 28, 29, 46, 70, 71, 77, 84, 191, 197
Mahon, Lord, 148
Mainz, 42
Maitland, Captain, 144
Maitland, Major-General Peregrine, 139, 162
Malet, General Claude François de, 37
Malmaison, Château of, 143
Malojaroslavets, 36, 163
Malta, 15

Mameluke Ali, 123
Mamelukes, 15–16
Manila, 56
Mannheim, 106
Mantua, 13, 14
Maratha War, Second (1803–5), 60, 61–2
Maratha War, Third (1817–19), 62
Marathas, 56, 58, 59, 60–2
Marbeuf, Count Louis de, 3, 4
March, Captain the Earl of, 166
Marengo, Battle of, x, 20, 27, 28, 116, 152, 160, 197
Marie-Louise, Empress, 32, 45, 46, 145
Marienwerder, 98
Marlborough, John Churchill, first Duke of, 77
Marmont, Marshal Auguste, 45, 74, 76, 77, 109, 180, 188
Marne river, 44
Marseilles, 8
Massena, Marshal André, 8, 11, 72–4, 121, 132, 151, 172, 187
Mauritius, 58, 60
Mayer, Pierre Louis, 153
McGrigor, Dr James, 78, 177
Meaux, 157
Mecklenburg-Schwerin, Duchy of, 87, 89
Mehling, Karolina von, 90
Melas, General Baron Michael von, 20
Milan, 13, 20, 151
Mills, Lieutenant James, 80
Mincio river, 20
Mississippi river, 22
Möllendorf, Field Marshal Richard von, 92
Moltke, General Helmuth von, 182
Mondego Bay, 67
Mondovi, Battle of, 13
Mons, 117
Monson, Colonel William, 62
Mont St Jean, 126, 127
Montenotte, Battle of, 13
Montereau, Battle of, 1, 43, 151
Montesquiou, Raymond de, Duke de Fezensac, 24, 171
Montgomery of Alamein, Field Marshal the Viscount, 200
Montmirail, Battle of, 43, 108
Moore, Lieutenant-General Sir John, 29, 70, 71, 174, 200
Moreau, General Jean-Victor, 20, 22

Mornington, *see* Wesley, Garret, first Earl of Mornington *and* Wellesley, Richard, second Earl of Mornington
Mortier, Marshal, 45
Moscow, 34, 35–6, 38, 46, 100, 161, 167, 198
Mount Tabor, Battle of, 18
Müffling, General Baron Carl von, 130, 157, 177, 179, 180, 181, 182, 191
Münster, 93
Murat, Marshal Joachim, King of Naples, 36, 43
Murray, Major-General Sir George, 82, 174, 176
Mysore, 58, 59, 60, 61
Tipoo Sultan of ('Tiger of Mysore'), 56, 58, 59
Mysore War, Fourth (1799), 58–9

Namur, 116, 143
Nancy, 106
Nangis, 43
Napier, General Sir George, 166
Naples, Kingdom of, 8, 13, 23, *see also* Murat, Marshal Joachim, King of Naples
Napoleon I, Emperor of the French, childhood, 3–4
education, 4–6
spelling mistakes, 87
languages, 98
self-identification with Corsica, 3, 6, 7
trains as a gunner, 5
takes lead in family affairs, 56
tried to advance self in Corsica, 6–7
supports Jacobins, 6, 9
sees action for first time, 7
arrested after fall of Robespierre, 9
crushes insurrection with a 'whiff of grapeshot', 9
marriage to Josephine, 9–10, 32
mistresses, 10
writes *Le Souper de Beaucaire*, 8
at siege of Toulon, 8, 51
and Italian campaign (1796–7), 11–14
expedition to Egypt (1798–9), 14–18, 19, 58, 60
seizure and consolidation of power, 19–22
and campaign in northern Italy (1800), 19
civil achievements of, 20–2

plans to invade Britain, 15, 22
Emperor of the French (1804), 64
loss of fleet at Trafalgar, 64
and Austerlitz campaign, 23–5, 94
and 1806 campaign, 25–6, 98
and 1806–7 campaign in East Prussia and Poland, 26–8, 98
and Treaty of Tilsit, 65, 98, 99
and Continental System, 28, 32
and Peninsular war, 28–30, 32, 65, 70, 73, 79, 80
and 1809 campaign, 30–1, 99
marriage to Marie-Louise, 32
over-extension of empire, 32
and invasion of Russia, 32–8, 76, 79, 100
failed coup by General Malet, 37
and 1813 campaign, 38–42, 79, 83, 100, 101, 102, 103, 104, 105, 106
and 1814 campaign, 42–5, 83, 106, 107, 108, 109, 110
abdicates (1814), 45, 84, 110
causes of downfall, 84
exiled to Elba, 45–6, 84, 111
returns from Elba, 46–7
and 1815 campaign, 91, 115–39
abdicates (1815), 143
at St Helena, 144, 145
appearance of, 131, 152–3, 154
popular view of, x
as an outsider, 87
personality, 151–3
belief in his destiny, 151, 156
self-confidence, 197, 198
boldness, 185
not a self-made man, 151
benefits from family influence, 4, 8, 88
mentors and patrons of, 5, 6, 8, 9, 14, 19, 89, 151
health, 136
wounded or bruised, 8, 30
assassination attempts against, 22
over-ambitious, 55, 62
lack of conscience, 90
failure as a statesman, 198
methods of command and control, 170–3, 197
command system at Waterloo, 134–6
Grand Quartier-Général, 170–1, 173, 176
and poor French staff work, 120–1, 171

insistence on centralisation of command, 13

rarely holds councils of war, 171–2

shortage of outstanding subordinates, 39–40, 172

allows some initiative to capable subordinates, 172

strategy and tactics, 183–7

size of armies, 197

corps organisation, 185

supposed decline as a commander, 197–8

plan at Waterloo, 130

improvisation by, 187

master of manoeuvre, 132

bataillon carré formation, 185–7

logistics, 24, 34, 39

limited personal interventions in fighting, 160

familiar with infantry tactics, 184–5

nicknamed 'le Tondu', 151

leadership style, 158–61

favouritism, 163–4

fails to secure genuine loyalty to his regime, 37

dictates letters, 87

distorts the truth, 18, 20

use of propaganda, 152

proclamations, 11, 15–16, 34, 35, 46, 116, 159

opinions on Wellington, 73, 130, 145, 146

Wellington not his main opponent in the Napoleonic wars, 200

opinions on Blücher, 110, 145

meets Blücher, 98

Napoleon II, *see* Rome, King of

Napoleon III, Emperor of the French, 145

Naveau mill, 123, 134

Neipperg, General Count Adam von, 145

Neisse river, 103, 169

Nelson, Vice-Admiral Horatio, 16, 22, 64, 162, 200

Netherlands, *see* Holland *and* United Netherlands

New Orleans, 21

Ney, Marshal Michel
  in 1806, 172
  in 1812, 36, 38
  in 1813, 39, 41, 102
  at Quatre Bras, 117, 118, 120, 121, 122, 123, 126, 136, 173

at Waterloo, 134, 135, 136, 145

executed, 144

Nice, 8, 9, 11

Niemen river, 28, 34, 38

Nile, Battle of the, 16

Nive, Battle of the, 82–3

Nivelle, Battle of the, 81–2, 177, 188, 189, 197

Nivelles, 117

Northumberland, HMS, 144

Nostitz, Captain August von, 104, 108, 109, 110, 116–17, 123, 124, 125, 126, 133–4, 148, 180, 181, 194

Odeleben, Major Ernst von, 38

Oder river, 110

Oldenburg, Grand Duchy of, 32

Olmütz, 24

Ompteda, Colonel Christian von, 133

Oneglia, 9

Oporto, 71, 164

Orange, Prince William of, 115, 118, 127, 132, 133, 135, 138, 164

Orthez, Battle of, 83, 134, 163, 166, 188, 189, 191

Osten-Sacken, *see* Sacken, General Fabian von der Osten-

Ostend, 53

O'Toole, Lieutenant-Colonel, 164

Ottoman Empire, 9, 15, 16, 18, 34, 89

Oudh, *Nawab* of, 60

Oudinot, Marshal Nicolas, 41

Pajol, General Count Claude, 43

Pakenham, Kitty, 52, 65, 147

Pamplona, 80, 117

Paoli, Pasquale, 3, 4, 6, 7

Papal States, 32

Papelotte, 127, 138

Paris, 37, 38, 70, 73, 101
  before Napoleon became Emperor, 6, 8, 9, 11, 14, 19, 22
  in 1814, 42, 43, 45, 84, 106, 108, 110, 157, 161, 179, 191, 192, 193, 197, 198
  in 1815, 46, 126, 143–4, 145, 146, 156, 165, 168, 193, 196, 199
  Treaty of, (1815), 144
  construction projects in, 20

Church of St Roch, 9
Ecole militaire, 4, 5, 6, 18, 184
Invalides, 145
Louvre, 20
Pont de Jena, 144
Tuileries palace, 7, 9, 22, 46
Parma, Duchy of, 13
Passarge river, 98
Peel, Robert, 146, 147
Penang, 56
Peninsular War, ii, x, 28–30, 32, 38, 59, 65–84, 100, 104, 115, 121, 127, 130, 154, 155, 171, 174–5, 177, 185, 188, 193, 199
significance of, 84
Perponcher, Henri-Georges de, 117
Perron, General Pierre, 61
Pétiet, Colonel Auguste, 131
Phélipeaux, Colonel Louis Edmond de Picard de, 18
Philippines, 56
Piacenza, 13
Piave river, 14
Picton, Lieutenant-General Sir Thomas, 127, 131, 135, 138
Piedmont, *see* Sardinia
Pirch I, General von, 194
Pisa, 4
Pitt, William, the younger, 64, 200
Pius VI, Pope, 13
Pius VII, Pope, 20, 22, 32
Plancenoit, 134, 135, 136, 192, 193
Pleischwitz, Armistice of, 39, 102
Po river, 13, 20
Poland, 25, 26–7, 34, 89, 90, 92, 98, 198; *see also* Warsaw, Grand Duchy of
Pombal, 73
Pomerania, *see under* Prussia
Ponte Nuovo, 3
Poona, 61
Pope, *see* Pius VI *and* Pius VII
Poppel, 94
Portland, Duke of, 65
Portsmouth, 64
Portugal, 28, 29, 67–75, 77, 78, 79, 100, 156, 174, 175, 187, 191
Powell, Captain Harry Weyland, 136
Pradt, Abbé de, 151
Prague, 39
Prenzlau, 98
Pressburg, Peace of, 25

Preussich-Eylau, *see* Eylau
Prince Regent, *see* George IV
Prussia, *passim*
Military Re-organisation Commission, 99
Pomerania, 90, 99
Silesia, 100, 111, 145, 169
Blücher Hussars, 92
General Staff, 116, 170, 178–82, 192, 194, 195
Guards, 115, 193
Pultusk, Battle of, 26
Putigny, Captain, 122
Pyramids, Battle of the, 16, 18
Pyrenees, 32, 80, 81, 82, 117, 176
Battle of the, 80, 164, 177

Quatre Bras, 117, 126
Battle of, 118–22, 136, 163, 171, 173, 188

Ramolino, Maria-Letizia, *see* Buonaparte, Maria-Letizia
Ratisbon, 30, 160
Redinha, 73
Reiche, Lieutenant-Colonel Ludwig von, 92, 102, 117–18, 195
Reichstadt, Duke of, *see* Rome, King of
Rey, General Louis, 78
Rheims, 45
Rhine river, 14, 22, 23, 26, 34, 42, 83, 91, 93, 94, 105, 106, 168, 180
Rhine, Confederation of the, *see* Confederation of the Rhine
Rhodes, 16, 18
Richard III, King, 200
Richmond, Duchess of, 117, 155
Rivoli, Battle of, 14, 193
Robertson, Sergeant Duncan, 165
Robespierre, Augustin, 8
Robespierre, Maximilien, 8, 9
Robinaux, Lieutenant Pierre, 38–9
Rochefort, 143, 144
Rocca, Colonel Colonna Cesari, 7
Röder, General, 123
Roermond, 91
Roliça, Battle of, 67, 189
Rome, Ancient, 15, 172
Rome, King of (Napoleon's son), 32, 37, 46, 145

Rommel, Erwin, 200
Rostock, 87, 88, 89, 169
Royal Navy, *see under* Britain
Rügen, 88, 98
Russia, 18, 19, 23, 24, 25, 26, 27, 28, 29, 39,
    44, 45, 64, 72, 83, 84, 87, 88, 90, 94, 98,
    100, 101, 103, 106, 108, 109, 145, 167,
    169, 179, 181, 185, 193
    Napoleon's invasion of (1812), 32, 34–8,
        76, 100, 130, 161, 173, 197, 198
    Army of the Danube, 37
    Cossacks, 36, 41, 45, 88, 163, 167
    Imperial Guard, 28, 159

Saalfeld, 26
Saar river, 91
Saarbrücken, 92
Sabugal, Action of, 73
Sacken, General Fabian von der Osten-, 168
Sahagun, Battle of, 70
St Amand, 122
St Bernard pass, 154
Saint-Cloud, Palace of, 19
Saint-Dizier, 45
Saint-Georges, Battle of, 158
Saint-Germain, Count Claude-Louis de, 4
St Helena, 144, 145
St-Jean-d'Acre, 16, 18, 31
St Petersburg, 36, 37, 159
St Pierre, Battle of, 82
St Raphäel, 19
Saladin, 200
Salamanca, 79, 175, 177
    Battle of, 77, 79, 163, 165, 188, 189, 193
Saliceti, Antonio Cristoforo, 8
Salisbury, Lady, 155
Sambach, 91, 92
Sambre river, 116
San Sebastian, 80, 117, 177
Santarém, 73
Saorgio, 9
Sardinia, Kingdom of (included Piedmont),
    7, 8, 9, 11, 13
Saxe, Marshal de, 55
Saxony, 26, 38, 40, 42, 101, 103, 115, 179
Scharnhorst, Gerhard von, 99, 100, 178,
    179, 192, 195
Schaumann, Commissary August, 154, 161,
    165, 173

Schill, Major Ferdinand von, 99
Schlieffen Plan, 192
Schönbrunn, Peace of, 31, 72
Schwarzenberg, Prince Karl von, 192, 200
    in 1813, 39, 40, 41, 42, 103, 104, 198,
    in 1814, 42, 43, 44, 45, 106, 107, 108, 110,
        179, 180,
Scindia, Dowlut Rao, 60, 61, 62
Sedan, Battle of, 192
Seine river, 20, 43
Selim III, Sultan, 16
Semmering Pass, 14
Seringapatam, 58–9, 60
Seven Years' War (1756–63), x, 15, 44, 56,
    88, 89, 192, 195
Seydlitz, Friedrich Wilhelm von, 194
Shakespeare, William, 155
Shelley, Lady, 143, 162
Sherer, Lieutenant Joseph Moyle, 72, 73
Shore, Sir John, 56
Sieyès, Emmanuel, 19
Silesia, *see under* Prussia
Simmons, Lieutenant George, 73
Smith, Captain Harry, 79, 80, 81–2
Smith, Captain Sir Sidney, 18
Smohain, 127
Smolensk, 36
    Battle of, 34, 35, 171
Soissons, 45
Sombreffe, 124, 194
Sorauren, Battles of, 80, 163
Soult, Marshal Jean-de-Dieu, 27, 29, 70,
    117, 172, 185
    opposed to Wellington in the Peninsular
        War, 71, 74, 75, 80, 81, 82, 83, 84
Spain, 8, 28–30, 56, 65, 70, 71, 72, 74,
    76–81, 84, 120, 152, 155, 172, 174, 189,
    197, 198
    guerrillas, *see* guerrilla warfare
Spree river, 102
Steffens, Henrik, 168
Stein, Baron Heinrich von, 93
Stevenson, Colonel James, 61, 62
Stewart, Major-General the Hon Charles,
    156
Stralsund, 88, 98, 99
Studianka, 37
Suchet, Marshal Louis, 76, 172
Sultanpettah Tope, 59, 191, 197

Sweden, 26, 28, 34, 38, 39, 87, 88, 89, 90, 98, 102
  Crown Prince of, *see* Bernadotte, Marshal
  Swedish Hussar Regiment (later Mörner Hussar Regiment), 88, 89, 98
Swedish Pomerania, 88, 98
Syria, 16, 18, 197

Talavera, Battle of, 71, 72, 161, 163, 189, 191, 197
Talleyrand-Périgord, Charles-Maurice de, 19, 144
Tarutino, 36
Tauroggen, Convention of, 100
Teil, General Baron Jean-Pierre du, 5
Teil, General Jean du, 8
Tende Pass, 9
Thames river, 51
Thielemann, General Johann von, 143
Tilsit, Peace of, 28, 32, 34, 65, 98, 99
Tipoo Sultan, *see* Mysore, Tipoo Sultan of
Torres Vedras, Lines of, 72, 73, 187
Toulon, 7–8, 9, 15, 51, 158, 160, 184
Toulouse, Battle of, 83–4, 134–5, 177, 178
Tourcoing, Battle of, 53
Trachenburg conference, 39
Trafalgar, Battle of, 22, 64, 162
Trento, 13
Treskow, General von, 123
Trim (County Meath), 51, 52
Trincomalee, 60
Troyes, 43
Tula, 36
Turenne, Henri de la Tour d'Auvergne, Viscount de, 5

Ulm, 23
United Kingdom, *see* Britain
United Netherlands, 46, 115, 187, 199
United States of America, 21–2, 58, 144, 174
Uxbridge, Lord, 127, 135, 138, 162–3, 178

Valence, 5
Valencia, 76
Valladolid, 152
Vandamme, General Dominique, 41

Vauchamps, Battle of, 43, 108, 157, 199
Vendée, 9
Venice, 14
Verner, Captain William, 138
Verona, 14
Versailles, 143
Viasma, 36
Victor Amadeus III, King of Piedmont (Sardinia), 7, 13
Victor, Marshal Claude-Victor Perrin, known as, 71
Victoria, Queen, 147
Vienna, 11, 14, 20, 24, 25, 30, 46
  Congress of, 84, 111, 155
Vilna, 34
Vimeiro, Battle of, 67, 176
Vitebsk, 35
Vitoria, Battle of, 79–80, 176, 188, 189, 193

Waal river, 53
Wagram, Battle of, 31, 72, 99, 152, 189
Wahlstadt, 110
Walmer Castle, 148
Warsaw, 26, 98
  Grand Duchy of, 28, 32
Wartenburg, 104
Waterloo, 126, 127, 138
  Battle of, x, 51, 63, 87, 91, 115, 127–39, 143, 145, 153, 155, 156, 162–3, 164, 165, 168, 171, 175–6, 181, 188, 189, 193, 196, 197, 198, 199, 200
  Campaign of, 115–44, 171, 183, 198–9
Waterloo Medal, 166
Waters, Lieutenant-Colonel John, 175
Wavre, 125, 126, 130, 134, 143
Weimar, Josephine ('Mademoiselle Georges'), 10
Weisseritz river, 41
Wellesley, Henry, 56
Wellesley, Richard, second Earl of Mornington, 51–2, 56, 58, 60, 62, 63, 65, 100
Wellesley-Pole, William, 67, 139, 163
Wellington, FM Arthur Wellesley, Duke of, childhood, 51–2
  as an outsider, 87
  ambition subordinated to duty, 62
  benefits from family influence, 52, 88
  relations with brother Richard, 51–2, 100

mentors and patrons of, 52, 56, 58, 60, 89,
174
education, 51, 55, 89
begins military and political career, 52, 88
and Kitty Pakenham, 52, 65, 147
in Low Countries (1794–5), 52–4, 93
first sees action, 53
in India, x, 55–63
meets Nelson, 64
and expedition to northern Germany
(1805), 64
and expedition to Copenhagen (1807), 65
in Peninsular War, 29, 32, 42, 65–84
becomes Viscount Wellington, 72
appointed Field Marshal, 79
becomes Duke of Wellington, 72, 84
as British ambassador in Paris, 84
represents Britain at Congress of Vienna,
84
and 1815 campaign, 47, 91, 115–22,
125–39
slow to react to Napoleon's offensive, 117
controversy over promises to support
Blücher at Ligny, 118
position at Waterloo, 127
meets Blücher in evening of Waterloo,
138
escapes death or injury at Waterloo,
138–9, 163
appalled by carnage of Waterloo, 139, 143
opinion on Waterloo, x
advances on Paris more slowly than
Blücher, 143, 193
after Waterloo, 144, 145–8
as a national institution, 148
health, 51, 60
wounded, 83, 163
assassination attempts against, 146
popular view of, x
appearance, 72, 73, 83, 117–18, 125–6
personality, 153–6
mistresses, 10, 155
self-confident, 78, 155–6, 161, 197
leadership style, 161–6
calmness under fire, 121, 155
effect on morale of troops, 155, 161, 162
enjoys confidence of troops, 72, 73, 74, 78,
80–1, 83, 133
praises troops, 138, 139, 163–6
discourages cheering, 137, 153

refers to 'an infamous army', 115
refers to troops as 'scum of the earth', 161
discipline, 166
methods of command and control, 173–8,
182
command system at Waterloo, 127, 130,
132–3
command style, 134–5
headquarters, 115, 153, 173–7
shortage of reliable subordinates, 176
supportive of subordinates, 166
not always an aloof commander, 82, 163,
166, 177
tolerant of an initial failure by others, 59
allows some initiative to capable
subordinates, 176–8
sweeping criticisms by, 78, 165
strategy and tactics, 183–5, 187–91
undefeated, 161
not simply a master of the defensive,
188–9
master of manoeuvre, 132
attains moral ascendancy over French, 77
never had to face Grand Army in its
heyday, 199
size of armies, 197–8
unable to afford heavy casualties, 189
and sieges, 191
and pursuits, 193
opinion on his cavalry, 188
personal interventions in action, 131–2,
135, 136, 161–3
military intelligence, 63, 175
logistics, 53, 58, 59, 61, 63, 73, 78, 79, 82,
174–5, 193
as a political operator, 174
ability to handle allies, 174
opinions on Napoleon, 116, 132, 143, 144,
145–6, 160, 189, 198, 199
opinions on Blücher, 139, 191
role in partnership with Blücher, 198–200
Weser river, 53
Wesley, Garret, first Earl of Mornington, 51
West Indies, 55
Westphalia, 28, 41, 42, 115
Wheeler, Sergeant William, 161
'White Terror', 144
Winchilsea, Lord, 146
Winzingerode, General Ferdinand von, 100

Wittgenstein, General Ludwig von, 37, 38, 101, 102
Wolzogen, Colonel Baron Ludwig, 101–2
Wrede, General Count Karl von, 42
Wurmser, General Count Sigismond von, 13, 14
Württemberg,
    Crown Prince of, 43
    Kingdom of, 42

Yonne river, 43
Yorck, General Hans von, 100, 109–10, 168, 179, 181, 192, 193
York, Duke of, 52, 53, 146, 164

Zama, Battle of, 15
Ziethen, General Hans von, 116, 194, 195
Zülow, Dorothea Marie von, 87

Index of Armies and Formations

Napoleon's armies
Army of Italy (1796–7), 9, 11, 12–14, 158, 159
Army of the Reserve (1800), 20
Grand Army (1805–14), 23, 26, 34, 46, 94, 171, 199
Army of Portugal (1810–12), 72–4, 75, 77
Army of the North (1811), 74, 75
Army of the South (1811), 74
Army of Aragon (1812), 76
Army of the Bober (1813), 103
Army of the North (1815), 116
  senior officers, 116, 130
  quality of, 116

Formations
Imperial Guard, 27, 35, 36, 41, 46, 108, 115, 123, 124, 134, 136–7, 151, 158, 160, 163, 178, 187, 194
  Old Guard, 37, 43, 45, 136
  Young Guard, 45, 135
  artillery, 42
  cavalry, 43, 45, 170
  Grenadiers à pied, 153
  Grenadiers à cheval, 152
  Chasseurs à cheval, 152, 153
Reserve Cavalry (1807, 1815), 27, 123

I Corps (1815), 120, 123, 131, 171
III Corps (1807), 27
IV Corps (1806), 172
VI Corps (1815), 132, 134, 135
III Cavalry Corps (1815), 135

4th Demi-brigade, 158
18th Demi-brigade, 158
32nd Demi-brigade, 158
39th Demi-brigade, 159
85th Demi-brigade, 159

1st Regiment of Light Infantry, 121
1st Regiment of Line Infantry, 121
3rd Regiment of Light Infantry, 121
4th Regiment of Line Infantry, 159–60, 201

5th Regiment of Line Infantry, 46
33rd Regiment of Line Infantry, 122
35th Regiment of Line Infantry, 153
139th Regiment of Line Infantry, 38

Wellington's armies
Peninsular army (1808–14), 104
  medical arrangements, 79
  discipline and quality of, 71, 76–7, 78, 79–80, 83, 143, 193
  creation of divisions, 71
  engineers, 76, 78
  siege train, 76, 78
  Portuguese troops, 71, 72, 73, 79, 164
  Spanish troops, 79, 84
Army of the Low Countries (1815), 115
  organisation of cavalry, 135
  quality of, 115
  senior officers, 115
  Brunswick contingent, 115
  Dutch-Belgian contingent, 115, 118, 136
  Nassau contingent, 115, 162
  Hanoverian contingent, 115
Army of Occupation (1815–18), 146

Formations
Light Division (Peninsula), 72, 79, 80, 177, 191
2nd Division (Peninsula), 72
3rd Division (Peninsula), 77
1st Division (1815), 133, 139
3rd Division (1815), 133
2nd Dutch-Belgian Division (1815), 117
3rd Dutch-Belgian Division (1815), 130

2nd (or Royal North British) Regiment of Dragoons (Scots Greys), 135
7th (or The Queen's Own) Regiment of Light Dragoons (Hussars), 138
13th Regiment of (Light) Dragoons, 165
1st Hussars, King's German Legion, 165
1st Regiment of Foot Guards, 118, 132, 136, 153

Coldstream Regiment of Foot Guards, 59, 125, 156
3rd Regiment of Foot Guards, 176
29th (or the Worcestershire) Regiment of Foot, 74
30th (or the Cambridgeshire) Regiment, 118
33rd (or the 1st Yorkshire West Riding) Regiment of Foot (later The Duke of Wellington's Regiment), 52, 53, 54, 55, 56, 58, 64, 93
34th (or the Cumberland) Regiment of Foot, 72
40th (or the 2nd Somersetshire) Regiment of Foot, 80
43rd Regiment of Foot, 165
44th Regiment of Foot, 120
45th (or the Nottinghamshire) Regiment of Foot, 165
51st (or the 2nd Yorkshire West Riding) Regiment of Foot (Light Infantry), 161
52nd (or the Oxfordshire) Regiment of Foot (Light Infantry), 82, 137, 138, 165, 178
69th (or the South Lincolnshire) Regiment of Foot, 121
73rd (Highland) Regiment of Foot, 52, 176
79th Regiment of Foot, 132
85th (or the Bucks Volunteers) Regiment of Foot (Light Infantry), 83
88th (or the Connaught Rangers) Regiment of Foot, 165, 166
92nd (Highland) Regiment of Foot, 120, 121, 122, 125, 165
95th Regiment of Foot (Riflemen), 73, 76, 81, 137, 155, 165

Royal Artillery, 165, 174
Royal Horse Artillery, 178, 188

Royal Engineers, 174
Royal Sappers and Miners, 191
Royal Staff Corps, 138
Staff Corps of Cavalry, 79

Blücher's armies
Army of Silesia (1813–14), x, 39, 41, 42, 43, 44, 79, 101–10, 156, 169, 178, 179, 180, 181, 182, 192, 193
friction within, 109, 167, 168, 179, 180–1, 182
senior officers, 168
quality of, 104, 166
Army of the Lower Rhine (1815), 111, 115
cavalry, 115
engineers, 144
indiscipline of, 143
Landwehr, 115, 133
quality of, 115, 166
senior officers, 116

Formations
I Corps (1815), 116, 117, 123, 137
III Corps (1815), 143, 194
IV Corps (1815), 125, 130, 133

16th Brigade (1815), 193

6th Uhlans, 124
East Prussian Cuirassier Regiment, 102
1st Westphalian Landwehr Cavalry, 124
Elbe Landwehr Cavalry, 124
Lützow's Freicorps, 103
9th (Colberg) Infantry Regiment, 122